MW00659361

Living in

HUNGARY

JEAN-LUC SOULÉ PHOTOGRAPHS BY ALAIN FLEISCHER

Flammarion

CONTENTS

IN PRAISE OF BEAUTY

The beauty of the Magyar land is expressed in a great variety of ways. Many aspects of the Hungarian art of living are as yet little known, and are a source of constant fascination to visitors: the ancient bathing tradition, the fascinating, decorative architecture (left), the urban lifestyle in which the café plays a vital role – a wonderful example is the famous Gerbeaud Café in Budapest (facing page).

The book you are holding is eloquent, dear reader, and will fulfill your every expectation. Its subject is a country that many travelers already know and love; and those who have yet to make its acquaintance will not be disappointed.

Writer Jean-Luc Soulé is a connoisseur of our country; Alain Fleischer is a photographer of Hungarian origin with an international reputation. Together they have painted a vivid picture of Hungary that will instantly endear it to the reader; moreover, their portrayal is a particularly accurate one.

Their work is all the more remarkable as it deals not only with the deservedly famous sights of the country, but also highlights the kind of little detail that is essential to penetrate the mystery of the Hungarian soul. Page by page, we rediscover the regions we already love, and enjoy exploring those we do not yet know.

This book stands in praise both of Hungary and (I make the claim without bias) of beauty. Every phrase and image betray the authors' enthusiasm and affection for the country, and awaken the reader to beauty, sensitivity, emotion and curiosity.

This book also takes its readers on a journey. From the comfort of an armchair, we begin to dream of traveling through the glorious landscapes whose descriptions are so enticing. The route we follow is an enchanting one, rich in unforgettable experiences; we are left spellbound.

Our curiosity is aroused from the outset, with an introduction to Budapest and its incomparable lifestyle. We then explore the mysterious area around Lake Balaton, before making our way through Transdanubia. We linger by the riverbanks, lie down to rest on the great plains (*pusztas*) and, when our imaginary journey has tired us, we take a break in the cool shade of the hillsides whose vineyards produce such remarkable wines.

The dual perspective of writer and photographer reveals not only what is visibly attractive, but also what is imperceptible to the naked eye. The result is a pageant of Hungarian lifestyle, age-old customs and history.

As I turn the pages, I am reminded of the words of our great poet Miklós Radnóti: This is my home. And if a plant should lean towards me, its name and its flowers are familar to me; familiar too are those who pass along the way, and I know their destination…

I find it extraordinarily moving that the authors of this magnificent book should view Hungary with as much respect as its native sons; such affection is a gift to all Hungarians. We are grateful to them for their bright and knowledgable perception of our country; their work helps light the way for the travelers of today.

Dr. Péter Medgyessy
Prime Minister of Hungary

HUNGUEST HOTELS

Anyone who loves unspoiled nature will appreciate the wide-open landscapes of the Great Plain in southeastern Hungary, or the fabulous scenery in the north, such as Lillafüred in the Bükk mountains (left). Following the course of the Danube and its great tributary, the Tisza, is like traveling back in time to the golden age of the Danubian civilization, reflected in the Baroque charm of the towns and villages in the west of the country, such as the little artists' town of Szentendre (above).

BUDAPEST: THE PEARL OF CENTRAL EUROPE

May is without doubt the best month to see Budapest for the first time. In the words of the great Hungarian poet Bálint Balassi, ("Song for Wine Drinkers"):

Pentecost is the blessed season,
Healthy climate and serene skies and exquisite weather
And such a gentle wind for those seeking adventure.

The visitor to this, the most beautiful city in Central Europe, will be enchanted by the many faces of the capital: the changing light on the Danube, the majestic river that runs through the city; the fragrance of the large flowering paulownia trees in the public gardens; the delicious pleasure of slipping out to enjoy a morning dip in one of Budapest's many outdoor thermal pools.

You won't ever see Budapest in the same light twice, depending on what season of the year you visit it. It enjoys nearly 2,500 hours of sunshine a year, a similar amount to that of more southerly countries. Winter may offer the unusual sight of the Danube frozen over—something that happens every three years or so—when ponds in the city and nearby suburbs are transformed into skating rinks frequented by young winter-sports aficionados. Spring is the season of music festivals and folkloric events, when the entire city is in full celebration. It's a perfect time to discover the narrow Baroque streets around Empress Maria Theresa's former palace on the hills of Buda or to admire the urban planning and virtuosity of nineteenth-century architectural styles in the Pest neighborhood, on the left bank of the river, built over a large plain that marks the start of the Carpathian Basin.

The history of this capital city (in reality three cities joined in one) is linked to its geographical site. It's an ancient settlement; Roman legions guarding the *limes* (the frontier of the Roman empire) set up a fortified camp here in the early first century C.E., which was later expanded by the Emperor Hadrian. There are well-preserved remains of the Roman city in Óbuda, the northern part of the modern city. The city has suffered a turbulent history since then. The Mongols conquered it in the thirteenth century. Buda enjoyed a brilliant renaissance during the reign of King Matthias Corvinus (Mátyás) in the second half of the fifteenth century. The Ottoman Turks occupied the city from 1526 to 1686, and in 1698 Prince Eugene of Savoy, at the head the imperial army, incorporated it into the Austrian Habsburg empire.

Buda, with neighboring Pest and Óbuda, flourished under the Habsburgs. The urban, economic, and cultural developments that took place during the nineteenth century were some of the most remarkable on the entire European continent. However, it was not until 1873 that the three cities of Buda, Pest, and Óbuda came together as Budapest. The Hungarian capital thus created was a dynamic

From the Citadel (facing page) the whole of Budapest is visible: you can observe the subtle interplay between the historic city of Buda, dotted with modern buildings, the lazy majestic river, and the hills surrounding it to the north and west. The sight of Maria Theresa's palace, the glazed tile rooftops of Matthias Church, and the fanciful towers of the Fisherman's Bastion (left) will certainly entice you to explore further.
The industrial city of Pest, extending along the left bank, often surprises with its examples of inventive urban planning.

Some of the medieval houses in the streets of old Buda have kept their old shop signs. Strolling along, you glimpse the neo-Gothic Parliament building through the archways of the Fisherman's Bastion, adorned with statues of historic figures. The evening sun bathes turrets and cupolas in a pink light reflected in the river below. The water throws back a shimmering, shifting mirror image of the architecture along the riverbank.

counterbalance to the proud city of Vienna during the Austro-Hungarian Dual Monarchy, established in 1867 by Emperor Francis Joseph. The Parliament building constructed on the Pest side of the river between 1884 and 1904 became the symbol of a determined urban and national ambition, combining as it did a neo-Gothic façade that imitated London's Houses of Parliament with an interior decorative plan designed to glorify Hungarian history and traditions.

Budapest has retained a dual outlook derived from its composite heritage and contrasting geography. Long regarded as the last Western bulwark against the Ottoman Empire, the city is easier to comprehend when it is also seen as the gateway to the distant Middle East.

This confrontation between Western and Eastern traditions, and the city's central location in the heart of Europe, have created a unique lifestyle, a blend of hedonism and determination, abandonment and rigor, in which everyone finds something to identify with. Visitors from all over the world succumb to the powerful charm of this city that has contrived to absorb and assimilate into a single melting pot the elements of various waves of conquest.

Exceptional urbanism and architecture, exemplars of a sophisticated lifestyle

The best way to get an overall sense of the urban development of the last three centuries is from the Citadel on top of Gellért Hill (Gellért hegy). From here, the view stretches out across buildings and bridges to the majestic landscape fashioned by the curve of the river.

In the foreground rises Castle Hill (Vár hegy), where Maria Theresa, Empress of Austria and Queen of Hungary, built Buda Palace (Budavári Palota) in the eighteenth century; it has been remodeled many times since and was largely rebuilt after the devastating bombing during the siege of Budapest during the winter of 1944–45. Hungarians often visit the castle, as it houses the vast collection of the Hungarian National Gallery, several other museums, and the National Széchényi Library. Slightly farther away on the same hill is the Matthias (Mátyás) Church, transformed many times during its proud one-thousand-year history and in its present form representing the dynamic architectural syncretism of late-nineteenth-century Budapest. Its glazed-tile roofs and other features borrowed from diverse stylistic traditions were integrated into the building at the request of Emperor Francis Joseph and Empress Elizabeth—the famous Sissi, beloved by all Hungarians—during the restoration of 1873. Around the church, the façades of medieval and Baroque houses offer a human backdrop to a neighborhood otherwise dominated by church and royal architecture. They shelter behind ramparts and bastions built during the Turkish occupation, as well as turn-of-the-century revival buildings, like the Fisherman's Bastion, an astonishing contemporary neo-Romanesque reconstruction of the Matthias Church.

In the distance, still on the right bank of the river, you can see the hills of Buda. The slopes are initially fairly clear of vegetation, but the trees grow

denser toward the top. This lovely stretch of greenery is a select neighborhood for the city's wealthiest residents. The many villas, mostly built between 1850 and 1930 (or in the 1990s as part of a recent surge in real estate and home construction), reflect the quality of life in this section of Budapest. Breezes disperse the clouds of pollution that hang over the lower town and cool the air during the often blisteringly hot summers. Large homes with rough-cast façades in shades ranging from ocher and pistachio to brick red are representative of the colors to be found all over Central Europe. A few writers and intellectuals also have homes here, although they tend to be more modest. Among them is a remarkable couple who have created an outstanding private collection of traditional art, housed in a lovely apartment in the Hill of Roses *(Rózsa domb)*. It contains masterpieces of Hungarian, Romanian, Austrian, Serbian, and Croatian art.

Buda's charms extend farther than its intellectual and moneyed neighborhoods. Just a few steps from the art collection on the Hill of Roses is an octagonal mausoleum constructed four centuries ago by a Muslim holy man as his final resting place; the view of the river from here is spectacular. The Tomb of Gül Baba remains a pilgrimage and religious site for Muslims. Thanks to Saudi funding, it has undergone a recent but excessive restoration.

After this initial excursion into Buda, let's cross the river, taking one of the five bridges visible from the promontory of the Citadel. The most famous is the Chain Bridge (Széchenyi lánchíd), a favorite landmark among Budapest residents, as it was the first stone bridge to span the 1,310 feet (400 meters) across the Danube prior to the Revolution of 1848. It was built on the initiative of Count István Széchenyi, a major urban planner of the Hungarian national revival. It was destroyed during World World II, but rebuilt in its exact original form.

To fully appreciate the architectural wealth of the city, stroll through the central districts. You'll see elements borrowed from every period and place transformed into styles that express the Hungarian spirit: Magyar Baroque, Classicism, Romanticism, Eclecticism, Secession Art (the Central European version of turn-of-the-century Art Nouveau), Art Deco, and finally, Organic Art since the 1960s.

The talent for pastiche is best exemplified at Vajdahunyad Castle in City Park (Városliget). This fantasy was built in 1900 to commemorate the settlement of the Magyar peoples and the millennium of the coronation of King Stephen (István), the founder of Hungary, in about 1000. In a surprising blend of styles, a Romanesque chapel stands alongside a medieval residence with a Gothic tower—the influence of the Transylvanian castles of Bram Stoker and Count Dracula is visible here—and a Baroque palace housing an agricultural and hunting museum. The architect Ignác Alpár gave free rein to his imagination and integrated Romanesque statuary and Gothic ornamentation. Today, young Hungarian couples love to have themselves photographed here, in memory of a glorious past and as a promise of a radiant future.

If you're looking for a culinary break, the Gundel restaurant is the place to stop. Opened over one hundred years ago, this national monument to Hungary's gastronomic tradition is worth a visit, if only to enjoy the unique décor: the bar, dining room, small private rooms, and the terrace (where the sound of the big cats from the nearby zoo can be heard during summer months) are all worth a look. The wine cellar deserves mention, as George Lang, the restaurant's owner and author of a classic book on Hungarian cooking, is also a wine connoisseur who will share his knowledge with you, along with a certain number of specially selected vintages.

The nearly one-and-a-half-mile-long thoroughfare of Andrássy Avenue, with its banks, luxury boutiques, trendy restaurants, traditional cafés, influential cultural institutions, and Bohemian-chic apartments, perfectly symbolizes this section of the city. It was designed in the 1870s by the major Hungarian architect Miklós Ybl to link Erzsébet Square near the river to Heroes Square, and is a model of urban street design,

The Fisherman's Bastion (facing page and left) overlooking the Danube is built on the site of a former fishing village in a pastiche style that combines neo-Romanesque features with a more exuberant sense of design.
With this building, completed in 1873, the architect Frigyes Schulek gave the newly unified city of Budapest a visible symbol: old Buda seeming to contemplate the new, rapidly developing neighborhoods of Pest with gentle melancholy from its ramparts. Light streams through the Bastion's large, cloister-like arches. Just visible through the trees is the Matthias Church, embodying the pride of the Habsburgs, who undertook a major renovation of the building in the late nineteenth century. The rather fanciful statue of Saint George slaying the dragon reminds visitors of the need to oppose evil.

The city's full complexity can be appreciated from the hills of Buda and the Castle district. In the background, Hungary's immense Parliament Building, completed in 1902, rises above the old houses. The first Hungarian Parliament met in 1896 to mark the millennium of the country's founding. Before World War I, Hungary was three times its present size, and the country required a Parliament Building worthy of its stature. The view toward the west looks out across Buda's rich tapestry of rooftops (above).

featuring well-designed intermediary squares and side lanes. Hungarians love to stroll along its tree-lined sidewalks. Inside some of the numerous distinguished private mansions and elegant old-fashioned bourgeois apartments of Andrássy Avenue you may catch glimpses of staircases decorated with frescoes (unfortunately often in bad condition, but restoration work has picked up considerably in recent years), and inner courtyards. Many have balconies enclosed with finely worked wrought-iron railings. These are an important feature of apartment life in Pest. There is scarcely a novel or short story by such assiduous observers of the capital's intimate life as Gyula Krúdy, Dezsu Kosztolányi and György Konrád that does not describe these open-air theaters of the human comedy, where emotional crises and passions are acted out in public view.

As you stroll up Andrássy Avenue from Heroes Square along one of the old riding paths beside the lovely, although somewhat dilapidated, Italianate villas, do not fail to notice circular Kodály köröند, one of the most beautiful squares in Pest, surrounded by four large residences that reflect the neighborhood's aristocratic tradition. Past Oktogon, a major intersection of Andrássy Avenue and the Great Boulevard, you'll enter the heart of the capital's artistic life, symbolized by the Academy of Fine Arts, a neo-Renaissance building built in 1875. An Oriental-style gallery runs around a pale-yellow atrium on the upper floor, accessed by a beautiful stone staircase and marble balustrade. Enclosing it is an ornate wrought-iron grille topped by a pulpit, a rather unexpected element. Geometric stained-glass windows provide a subdued light that plunges the bronze busts into mysterious shadow. These busts stand out against the colored marble, the domed ceiling decorated with allegorical figures, and the medallion portraits of women in the gallery.

A stroll through Pest

This initial tour of Pest was meant to pique the enterprising stroller's curiosity. Now it is time for a longer journey on foot though the melancholic neighborhoods around City Park (Városliget). As you wander along these calm streets, with such promising names as Hermina út, Ajtósi Dürer sor and Stefánia út, you can enjoy the springtime scents from the nearby City Park and the subtle fragrances of the large flowering paulownias.

Interlaced floral designs scroll across the façade of a high school, while right next door is a school for the blind, designed by Sándor Baumgarten, which is in ornate Portuguese Manueline style with flamboyant lines. Baumgarten was a talented student of the remarkable Ödön Lechner. A prolific and talented representative of the Eclectic style, Lechner left a distinctive mark on Budapest, with designs for the Museum of Applied Arts, the Post Office Savings Bank and the Geology Institute, as well as the National Association for the Blind, a masterpiece of elegance and innovation.

A stroll through these few streets illustrates the entire history of the city, complete with its pride and prejudices, its conquests and failures. Several residences in the neighborhood were saved from demolition or, more prosaically, from the ravages of time, when they became diplomatic headquarters. They offer an insight into one of the realities of the history of this city, which was never so authentic as when it was playing the expensive courtesan flirting with foreign cupidity. Enchanted conquerors were instantly converted to the charms of the lovely captive. The copper plates on a number of buildings in this neighborhood proclaim a diversity of architectural alliances: the Jesuit style of an Italian Embassy with unusual garlands; the simple classicism of an Islamic Iranian building; the solemn appearance of a Swiss residence; and the unexpected combination of a truly magnificent ceramic relief by Lechner with an Oriental-style smoked-glass watchtower housing a department of the Libyan government.

There's no better way to appreciate the full flavor of Buda than by taking a walk through its streets, many lined with magnificent Baroque houses and even a few medieval buildings. Sparkling Italianate fountains are a reminder of the Dual Monarchy's links with Italy, but it was King Matthias Corvinus who hired the first Italian craftsmen to work in the city as early as the fifteenth century. The Románs live in a charming home; they own an extraordinary collection of folk art and are seen here among some of the pieces they have acquired over the years.

During the city's golden age, from 1860 to 1920, a number of magnificent villas were built on the Buda hills. Many have been restored in recent years. One such is located at the top of Mount Svábhegy, in a quiet street near the picturesque funicular that ascends to this residential neighborhood. There are spectacular views from the villa's windows, and light floods in from the garden to fill the spacious rooms, which have been tastefully decorated with a decided penchant for comfort. The sauna and swimming pool in the basement make no concessions to the past, but the furniture and décor elsewhere represent different periods and traditions. Architectural details such as the stained-glass windows in the library (facing page, bottom) date this home to the bewitching Art Nouveau period. The owners have successfully recreated its former charm.

The dark woodwork, the elegant Belle Epoque portraits, and the gypsy musicians with their unending repertory of tunes all contribute to the charm of the Gundel restaurant (left and page 21, top, right). The lingering flavor of a long-lost European past is also perceptible in the elegantly decorated apartments along Andrássy Avenue (above).

SZÉCHENYI

The Chain Bridge, one of the city's proud symbols, was completed in 1849 by the Scottish engineer Adam Clark. The elegant metal design was intended to glorify a nation that prided itself on its style and technical prowess. Queen Elizabeth of Hungary, the lovely Sissi of tragic destiny, liked to cross the bridge from the Royal Buda Palace to promenade along the elegant avenues of Pest. A bronze bust with a melancholy smile represents the queen during a happier period of her life.

The National Opera is open for visits at specific times. It's definitely worth seeing, as every detail of the remarkable building designed by Hungarian architect Miklós Ybl is noteworthy. The graceful figures of ephebes (young men) facing the lobby seem to have only just stepped out of their dressing rooms, while portraits of famous operatic performers decorate the greenroom.

If you're tired after wandering around for so long, you might want to take the subway from Heroes Square that runs under Andrássy Avenue. This was the first subway line to be constructed in continental Europe (after London, but before Paris), and it's extremely clean and well maintained. Get off at the Opera stop and walk to the nearby Paulay Ede Street, parallel to Andrássy, to see one of the city's most beautiful Art Nouveau buildings, the New Theater (Új Szinház), with a white façade and a blue interior designed by Béla Lajta in 1909. Despite additional construction work in 1915 and a renovation in the early 1990s, the purity of the architectural lines of this building has remained intact; it offers an impressive program of concerts.

Returning to Andrássy Avenue, you'll be swept along toward the entrance of the State Opera (Állami Operaház) building, a neo-Renaissance structure designed by Miklós Ybl. The interior alone is worth a visit. The Opera has been a symbol of national pride since it opened in 1884. It has been restored regularly and maintained diligently, and so retains its authentic style. After a time, the 1,250-seat theater became too small, so a second theater, three times larger, was constructed in the 1960s in another part of the city. The façade facing Andrássy Avenue features a projecting porch and statues of composers looking out over the lively avenue from the upper floors. The large entrance gives an immediate impression of majesty. The pink marble lobby under the main staircase is lined from floor to ceiling with colorful, grotesquely ornamented mosaics bordered by four pillars of gray granite. In between are large bronze vases. The large staircase that leads to a more intimate area—if such a thing exists in such a sumptuous space—is an exceptionally theatrical element. You expect to see any number of the famous people who have frequented this theater since its construction walking down the steps: Emperor Francis Joseph and the beautiful Sissi, the composer Gustav Mahler and his wife Alma, conductors Otto Klemperer and Ferenc Fricsay, choreographers and prima ballerinas, and the "divas of the Empire."

It is worth attending a performance. If you are lucky you may hear a magnificent work such as *Hunyadi László* (1848) or *Bánk Bán* (1860), both composed by Ferenc Erkel, the father of the Hungarian National Opera (he also wrote the music for the national anthem). In any case, you will be able to study the splendid interior. The ceiling appears to be supported by a procession of cherubs in medallions contemplating the muses painted just above. The large box for the Emperor on the first balcony and the Empress's loge are ornate and exuberantly decorated, reminding us of the importance of opera to the Hungarian nation during the Dual Monarchy era. Before leaving this emblematic place, be sure to take some time to explore the lobby, covered with frescoes painted by the most famous and talented artists of the day, along with the white and black marble royal staircase topped with porphyry columns and bronze busts of illustrious composers.

After visiting this grandiose building by Miklós Ybl, you may want to seek out works by Ödön Lechner, a master of fantasy and illusion, whose buildings offer a counterpoint to Ybl's brilliant but solemn architecture.

The colored marble on the main staircase and the gilding in the main lobby prepare the operagoer for the magnificent columns inside the auditorium itself. Music lovers should not leave Budapest without attending one of the theater's almost daily opera performances. Although productions may vary in quality, the singers are usually superb.

The Új, located behind the Academy of Dance on Andrássy Avenue, is one of the most remarkable theaters in Pest; its programs reflect the richness of the Hungarian dramatic repertory. Foreigners should be able to follow the plays with relative ease because the performances are usually full of expression. One of the great nineteenth-century Hungarian works performed here is the poetic epic *Csongor and Tünde* by Mihály Vörösmarty, spokesperson for a romantic generation awakened to a national conscience by the revolution of 1848–49. During the intermission, walk through the theater lobbies to admire the stunning Art Nouveau interiors. Recent restoration work has returned the theater to its past glory; the royal blue velvet chairs in the auditorium echo the friezes in the main lobby, while the light dances over the metal railings, bracket lamps, and wall decorations.

Budapest was fertile ground for the innovative experiments of Art Nouveau architects such as Ödön Lechner and Emil Victor. Lechner, who designed the Museum of Applied Arts (above) and the Post Office Savings Bank (right), was able to call upon apparently endless resources of invention. Victor left his mark throughout the city with designs for industrial buildings, residential apartments, and private mansions such as the Bedo Palace (facing page); the staircase and stained-glass windows are characteristic of his architectural style.

You won't have to go far: the building of the Post Office Savings Bank (Posta Takarékpénztár) is next to the Opera. It was completed in 1900 and immediately acclaimed by the public. The radical innovation of this structure lies in the way it reconciles the serious purpose of the building (a savings bank) with an interesting design intended to enrapture the bank's clients. The architect used every possible element to amaze and astonish, including a generous use of colored tiles on the façades and roofs; symbolic floral motifs (tulips and lotuses) and animal motifs (bulls' heads, bees, serpents, and chimera); and light flooding into the building through a number of differently shaped windows. The Savings Bank represents one of the most progressive architectural designs from the turn of the century.

A nearby building, the Bedö Palace on Honvéd Street, was constructed in 1903 by architect Emil Vidor for the president of the Budapest Stock Exchange. The president's son was a well-known patron of the arts with an impressive collection of contemporary art. The Art Nouveau style is closely followed in this building, with references borrowed from the French School of Nancy (the influential turn-of-the-century design group founded by Emile Gallé and the Daum brothers). The minute attention to detail, however, was directly influenced by Lechner.

This unbridled architectural style is a perfect vehicle to illustrate the ability of the Magyar spirit to synthesize an underlying respect for nature with a concern for the people who would use the building. This capacity for reconciling various elements, a fortunate blend of intellectual abstraction and everyday common sense, resulted in a singular style that can only be fully grasped by a walk through the city streets.

City of cafés

If these long wanderings through the streets of the capital have worn you out, you may want to stop off in one of the famous coffeehouses, legacies of the literary cafés that flourished in Budapest during the Belle Époque. Coffee is the city's trademark. It was introduced into Hungary during the Ottoman conquest (together with heated baths). Coffee and the public rituals surrounding its consumption wrote themselves so firmly into Budapest life that the coffeehouse now essentially characterizes the Hungarian lifestyle. However, café life is obviously no longer as effervescent as it was in the late nineteenth century and even between the two World Wars, when intellectuals and artists, office workers and their bosses, the petit and the grand bourgeoisie, regularly met in particular establishments, according to the unchanging rites of their tribe.

A recently published book anthologizes extracts by Hungarian authors from 1908 to 1974 in praise of the literary cafés of Budapest. Many of the establishments they mention have gone out of business, but fortunately some still remain and have been restored to their former splendor. For nostalgic gourmets or anyone merely curious to see what remains—or has been restored—of this marvelous tradition, here's a short itinerary starting in Buda and ending in Pest.

As you leave the Matthias Church on Castle Hill and before entering the great museums in this neighborhood, stop in at one of the city's oldest gourmet institutions, the Ruszwurm, a tiny Biedermeier-style establishment with just a few tables that fill up almost instantaneously during the busiest part of the tourist season (Biedermeier is the cozy decorative style of nineteenth-century Central Europe).

It's best to stop by in the morning when the delicious *almás, meggyes,* and *túrós rétes* (flaky pastry filled with apples, cherries, or curd cheese) and various *krémes* (the *francia krémes*—pastries with a thick layer of custard, are considered to be the best) are still warm from the oven.

Once you've come down the hill to the river and Batthyány Square, you'll see a former eighteenth-century convent that runs along an entire side of the square. Be sure to take a look at the lovely

The buildings along Andrássy Avenue and other elegant streets lining City Park date from the second half of the nineteenth century. They are in many different styles, reflecting the great diversity and energy of the age: neo-Gothic, Eclectic, historicist, or Art Nouveau. Try to take a look at the interior of some of the courtyards, with their staircases decorated with frescoes (often under restoration). Note the traditional outside passageways protected by magnificent wrought-iron railings—the inhabitants of Pest used to conduct the daily dramas of their lives on these open stages. The Postal Museum offers a good example of this characteristic style of architecture (facing page, bottom).

HONFOGLALÁSKORI MAGYAR HIRVIVŐ
LOVÁSZ ÖS ELETI VISELETBE

Baroque interior of the Saint Anne's (Szent Anna) Church on the way. The tables set out on the terrace in warm weather mark the location of the Angelika Café; the interior has recently been restored with taste and features 1930s furniture arranged on light-colored marble slabs. There's plenty of space and you rarely feel hemmed in by customers at nearby tables. The café was one of the favorite haunts of author and essayist György Konrád, a major participant in the political changes in Hungary that took place in 1989–90. He came here regularly until fairly recently, and would write in peace or meet friends over a drink or a cup of coffee.

And finally, you can't leave Buda without stopping at the café of the Institut Français of Budapest, a luminous and architecturally audacious building constructed a decade or so ago according to the designs of Frenchman Georges Maurios. Order a flaky croissant and a good hot café au lait and sit down in front of the large glass window to enjoy the scene of Budapest residents going about their daily business. The café faces a building with a traditional crescent-shaped courtyard and the usual galleries leading to each apartment. The most distinguished figures of the capital meet at the Institut either before or after one of the many seminars, conferences, or artistic events scheduled by the cultural institution.

To reach the culinary stops of Pest, we recommend crossing from Buda on foot via the Chain Bridge, leaving behind the amazing Baroque world of Maria Theresa's Buda Palace. The stone and metal bridge crosses the Danube, leading to the Art Nouveau section of Pest. The Gresham Palace is perfectly aligned between the piers, designed in the form of triumphal arches, supporting the suspension cables.

There's no need to spend much time around the large hotels along the Danube on the Pest side—although the luxurious Café Viennois in the Intercontinental has an excellent selection of pastries for a mid-afternoon break and a spectacular view of the river. Walk up Andrássy Avenue and stop at the Muvész, near the Opera. It's a surprising spot, offering a haven of unexpected calm in the midst of this busy thoroughfare. It seems to be popular, and the clientele appreciates the discreet classical style of the rooms lined with old mirrors and furnished with comfortably well-worn Biedermeier-style chairs.

During the golden prewar age, Andrássy Avenue boasted several of Budapest's most famous cafés, including the Dreschler, housed in the ground-floor arcades of what is now the Dance Academy, a building designed by Ödön Lechner and one of his students. It was later converted into an international hotel. Only two cafés remain from this period, the Muvész and the Lukács, although the latter has lost much of its charm following a recent restoration.

The tradition of the literary café, however, seems be to thriving, and the Goethe Institute recently opened the Eckermann Cafe in its building on Andrássy Avenue, formerly the site of the Café of the Three Crows (Három Holló). The coffee is excellent, although the selection of pastries

The café is a long-standing Budapest institution, and the Gerbeaud café in Pest is one of the city's most popular—with its rich wall hangings, large windows, and elegant pedestal tables, it should satisfy even the most esthetically demanding of customers (following pages). Gourmets should also make a stop at the Angelika café (top), the café in the Budapest Nemzeti Hotel in Pest (facing page), or the Ruszwurm (right) in Buda to sample freshly made pastries such as fruit and poppy-seed strudels, Angelika torte (a type of chocolate and vanilla sponge cake), or the *almás pite*, stuffed with puréed apple and spices.

Nichtraucher Salon

could certainly be expanded. The atmosphere is rather studious; both professors and students of the Institute read the German-language news papers assiduously. Follow the boulevards back to the river, where you'll reach the temple of literary cafés, the New York. It should soon reopen after a major overhaul of the hotel, and will once again be a landmark on any gourmet tour. The Rococo decor is unique in Budapest. Immense coiled columns covered in gold leaf greet customers as they ascend from the café on the ground floor to the restaurant on the mezzanine. Corridors lead to small private rooms and reception rooms where the most famous literary figures of turn-of-the-century Budapest, contributors to the illustrious *Nyugat* (*West*) review, used to hold open house. In 1913, Dezsu Kosztolányi, for example, started his beautiful poem, "At the New York Café," with this stanza:

People of all ages enjoy the delicacies on sale at the Auguszt pastry shop (above) and the Muvész (facing page). You'll see elderly women leisurely enjoying their favorite cakes alongside businessmen stopping to indulge a sudden craving for a pastry. A trendy young clientele remains true to Budapest's old café traditions, and established or budding writers and intellectuals are able to sit and work undisturbed for hours at a table.

New York, you, the café where I have so often been,
May I come in and sit a moment?
Sit, like a bum resting on a bench
And see what remains around and within me.
While others sit late around a table during the summer,
Alone, I would like to have an evening coffee.
And like a good Christian, I will say my prayers.
Where is youth, the passions of yesteryear?

The literary review *2000* met here every week, until the temporary closure of the institution forced the staff to emigrate to the Central Café (Centrál Kávéház) and the Internet appeared as a simpler way to distribute the articles selected by the editor in chief.

Head back to the Danube along the large avenue named for the famous prince of Transylvania, Rákóczi, which then turns into another street named for the romantic and political hero Lajos Kossuth. You'll find two great places to stop, located almost across the street from each other: the coffee-house in the Astoria Hotel and the Auguszt Cukrászda pastry shop. The claim to fame of the first is that the Council Republic, the first democratic government of Hungary, was proclaimed here on March 21, 1919, in a room that is open to the public.

If this rather formal style is not to your liking, try the Auguszt Cukrászda, a friendly family-run establishment founded in 1870, whose walls are decorated with scenes of the business. You may have trouble locating it at the back of the courtyard that it shares with a number of other businesses, but the few tables placed in the somewhat old-fashioned and charming setting are rarely full, despite its loyal clientele. It's worth taking your time to explore the unrivaled specialties produced here: the rice cake (*rizs torta*), the cherry and poppy-seed cake (*meggyes-mákkos torta*) and the improbably named "E 80," a delicious coffee, chocolate, and marzipan dessert.

If you're not able to explore the New York Café, still under reconstruction as this book was going to press, you might choose to take a small detour in front of the Franciscan Church

DUNHILL
MŰVÉSZ KÁVÉHÁZ
DUNHILL
PERLE
Fodrász Stúdió
MŰVÉSZ
KÁVÉHÁZ
SAJÁT
KÉSZÍTÉSŰ
SPECIÁLIS
SÜTEMÉNYEK

(Ferences Templom) and the majestic University Library (Egyetemi Könyvtár), to reach the Central Café, once one of the centers of Budapest's intellectual scene. Frigyes Karinthy, a talented humorist and author of a tragi-comic autobiographical tale, *A Voyage Round My Skull*, adopted this place as his home, meeting up with his friends from *Nyugat*, poets Endre Ady, Dezsu Kosztolányi, and Mihály Babits. Other literary reviews such as *Új hold (New Moon)* and *A hét (The Week)*, also held their regular meetings here.

This short tour of Budapest's coffeehouses and pastry shops would not be complete without a trip to the Gerbeaud Café in the pretty Vörösmarty pedestrian square. Prepare to be sidetracked on the way. Music lovers may want to call in at the large record store located in the dark gray concrete building to choose works by Haydn, Liszt, or Bartók put out by the Hungaroton label. Or after admiring the elegant Secession façade with immense metal-framed windows on the building housing the Luxus department store, you may decide to step inside for a look at the decoration of the interior staircase. If you take advantage of this detour to do some clothes shopping, be warned: prices are similar to those in other major European capital cities. A beautiful Carrara marble statue of the romantic poet Mihály Vörösmarty adorns the middle of the square. If you're curious about this author, pick up *Csongor and Tünde*, his touching medieval fairy tale that combines elements of Hungarian traditions with references to Shakespeare's *Midsummer Night's Dream* and Goethe's *Faust*.

Having explored the area, it's finally time to enter the Gerbeaud. Built by the shop's founder, the Swiss confectioner Émile Gerbeaud, in 1884, its Art Nouveau façade has just been returned to its original splendor. A high-society meeting place in the early twentieth century, this enchantingly old-fashioned coffeehouse is an institution in Budapest. It's a must for tourists, who treat it as a national monument. The interior has been refurbished to match the style of the place perfectly. You'll find yourself transported by the charming setting, complete with crystal chandeliers, wood paneling, red and green wall hangings, turn-of-the-century furnishings, and colored marble floor and tables. The spirit of this establishment is characterized by a delightful painting of two mischievous-looking altar boys downing the holy chalice after mass.

The Secession-style Palace Hotel on Rákóczi Avenue in Pest has just been renovated and enlarged. Renamed the Novotel Budapest Centrum, it is a full-service luxury hotel in the heart of the city. The decoration in the main dining room is an elegant combination of stucco and gilding.

If you're looking for calm, breakfast is the best time to visit. And if you're a determined gourmet intent on experiencing the ultimate in desserts, find your table, then walk over to the magnificent counter overflowing with different pastries. Among the huge selection of freshly made cakes and sweets on offer, the eternally classic Gerbeaud, a cake of walnut paste and apricot jam covered with a thick black chocolate icing; the subtle *flódni*, which combines apples, walnuts, poppy seeds, and cherry jam; the *Diós csemege* fondant, a delicate blend of walnut and chocolate on a bed of almond paste; and the *Gesztenye szuz*, a soothing mixture of chestnut purée, buttercream, and chocolate, are all highly recommmended. A shop adjoining the coffee shop has a few tables and is often less crowded than the main store. You might want to buy some chocolate candy to take home as a souvenir of this bastion of Hungarian culinary tradition.

The Robinson restaurant on the lake in City Park is an excellent place to stop after a visit to the nearby Academy of Fine Arts (left). The neoclassical dining room in the Budapest Nemzeti Hotel in the center of Pest is a successful pastiche of styles. These hotels, like the venerable Astoria (top), offer a sophisticated alternative to the traditional cafés when you're in need of a restorative snack.

Music lovers will never tire of the Ferenc Liszt Academy of Music. Not only are the concerts outstanding, but the architectural details of the performance areas and the public spaces are wonderfully elegant. Music-playing putti on the façade entice passersby to come and see for themselves.

Musical venues

Music is an essential element of Hungary's cultural scene. Impressive musical productions and compositions, both old and new, demonstrate the popularity and diversity of this art. Composers, interpreters, and amateur musicians have all contributed to the revival of musical tradition. Numerous performance venues, extensive musical education, and a variety of musical styles have helped to create a diverse musical scene across the country.

Traditional music is still very popular among Hungarians, who have absorbed the rhythms of its well-loved songs and dances since childhood. "Dance houses" (*táncház*) are often set up out of doors. In the last thirty years, they have been responsible for teaching generations of enthusiastic performers the traditional folk music of Hungary, revitalized in the eighteenth century. If you want to attend one of these events, which bring together young dancers trained in traditional music and dance techniques with amateurs who perform just for the joy of it, head for the open-air theater on Margaret Island (Margit-sziget). It is located at the base of a large water tower built in 1911 and is an ideal venue for any number of summer performances.

Other theaters also program excellent shows throughout the year—these events lay to rest the clichés of Central European folklore. The ornate Pesti Vigadó hall, near the hotels along the river, is one such venue. It is a good example of the Hungarian romantic architectural style; the façade is lined with columns and decorated with a profusion of sculptures. In addition, the Bábszínház puppet theater company on Andrássy Avenue, near the Academy of Fine Arts, regularly schedules original shows. One of the most interesting and authentic venues is the cultural center (Almássy téri Szabadidu) on Almássy Square (Almássy tér), which offers a wide variety of popular and gypsy musical performances.

A wave of patriotic songs, such as the *Rakoczi March,* appeared after the victory over the Turks in the eighteenth century. At this time, recruiting officers working for the Habsburg monarchy and large aristocratic families hired gypsies to play "recruiting dances" or *verbunkos*—popular melodies jazzed up with a gypsy beat. The aim was to draw young men into military service without them asking too many questions. This mixture of musical styles—which influenced the *czardas* (country dances)—later became an essential component of the repertory played by gypsy groups, blurring the boundaries between traditional Hungarian and gypsy music. The public who listen today to gypsy musicians in tourist spots cannot tell the difference between traditional gypsy songs and Hungarian folklore tunes played on instruments such as the cimbalom (a dulcimer, or small stringed percussion instrument) and the *tárogató,* a strange cross of a clarinet and a violin. The tradition is dying and

The main staircase of the Liszt Academy is a marvelous example of Art Nouveau design carried out with a sumptuous use of materials. The colored marble (from Hungary's Northern Uplands) blends with the large, deep blue orbs of Zsolnay majolica, and details on the wrought-iron handrail are highlighted with gilding. The spirit of the Nabi school of artists can be seen in the lovely fresco on the upper floor: ***Art, A Source of Life.*** Indeed, this theme could be the leitmotif for the entire building—an inspired masterpiece uniting the talents of a fertile generation of artists and craftsmen.

No need to be a musician to enjoy a stroll around the Liszt museum (below). This is the first place that the famous composer taught when he returned here in the twilight years of his long and eventful life. His beloved pianos, his personal archives, and an organ that doubled as a desk, create a touchingly intimate atmosphere.

A sculpture of composer Béla Bartók stands like a sentinel over the house he lived in for a period of his life. The small garden on the hills of Buda is an oasis of calm away from the hubbub of the city. The collection of memorabilia and personal belongings, formed after Bartók's death in America, speaks eloquently of the man. Evening concerts are held at the house—the string quartets often feature well-known musicians—drawing an enthusiastic public that comes to hear the music born out of Hungary's past and soul.

many groups can only stay together by playing for foreign audiences. Indeed, many restaurants have in-house gypsy bands. One that deserves mention is Étteren, in City Park, one of the capital's best places to eat. Other eating places with gypsy bands include Kárpátia, where Transylvanian specialties are served in a Byzantine decor, and the Régi Sipos Halászkert, a friendly place located in the Óbuda neighborhood that serves excellent fish soup.

The orchestras and musicians of the capital's theaters are exponents of the classical style. Hungarian musical education is based largely on the method developed by the composer and teacher Zoltán Kodály and spread by his students. Kodály and the composer Béla Bartók—both prime figures in the early twentieth-century revival of classical Hungarian music—were friends, and in the years before World War I the two traveled throughout the countryside of Hungary (much larger then, before the losses of territory imposed by the Treaty of Versailles in 1919) recording traditional songs and melodies that were part of a fast-disappearing oral tradition. Kodály transcribed many of these works and elevated the traditional musical heritage of his country to an eminent position. Today, foreigners are often surprised to see a young, knowledgeable audience at classical music concerts, but ticket prices are usually highly affordable. During the season, the programming is so varied that music aficionados often have a choice of between four or even five European orchestras, excellent chamber music, and highly reputed soloists. The Hungarian violin school may not have the reputation of earlier years, but Hungarian pianists continue to travel around the world, and the annual International Liszt Piano Competition awards prizes to the most talented virtuosos.

The Ferenc Liszt Academy of Music, which schedules concerts almost every evening, is one of the most remarkable venues in Europe in terms of its architecture and acoustics. The building was entirely restored for Hungary's millennium celebrations. The composer and piano virtuoso Ferenc (Franz) Liszt was born in Hungary and returned there frequently, in between visits to Rome and Germany, during the last seventeen years of his life until his death in 1886. Liszt wanted to create a place devoted to the teaching of music and to concert-level performance. A first building was constructed in 1873 on Andrássy Avenue in a style inspired by the Italian Renaissance. The three rooms in which the composer lived now house the Liszt Memorial Museum (Liszt Ferenc Emlékmúzeum). Personal objects and Liszt's pianos create an enchanting and intimate atmosphere; nearby is a small concert hall where he often played.

Later, another building, the current Academy of Music, arose, between 1904 and 1907, on the same square, and was named for the great musician. The façade is a magnificent example of Art Nouveau architecture and features large bay windows between columns and a large bronze sculpture of Liszt crowned with a laurel wreath. Powerful atlantes (male figures) support the skylight above the public entrance, which is framed with marble friezes depicting cupids playing instruments. When you walk into the lobby, you are struck by the beauty of the architectural and decorative details: marble friezes and mosaics of the Graces, framed by crimson curtains covering the entrances to the theater; majolica ceramics from the famous Zsolnay factory; red marble; stained-glass partition doors; spectacular blue banisters and banister knobs. All these elements set the stage for the intense musical experience to follow. Once inside the large 1,200-seat theater, the first thing you see is the large gilded bronze organ case at the back of

The Martonvásár castle, not far from Budapest, is a great place for an outing on a summer's day. Beethoven liked to come here to play his music with a circle of friends; he also composed several pieces here. A visit to the small neo-Gothic castle is instructive, but the real appeal of this place is the well-designed gardens, where concerts are sometimes held.

the stage. The vaulted ceiling swarms with crowned cupids and musicians, tragiemasks, female busts, and edgy-looking serpents. Another smaller concert hall is accessible from the large upper-floor lobby. It is decorated with a fresco, all in blue tones, representing the fountain of life. The decoration is simpler than in the large theater, and the stained-glass windows create an effect of soft, gentle light, which is perfect for more intimate chamber music performances. The majesty of the Academy reflects that of the Opera on Andrássy Avenue, which we explored early on in this itinerary.

Other more intimate venues also illustrate the strong links between Hungarians and their music. The house in which Béla Bartók lived from 1932 to 1940, before he emigrated to the United States, is a good example. Situated in a residential neighborhood of Buda, this museum-home nestles amid lilacs. The view from the composer's restored apartment over the hills of Buda is lovely. Inside, pretty painted or carved pieces of furniture, plates, and earthenware jars from Transylvania—a region he often visited—are placed alongside embroidered textiles. Near the desk is a photograph of Bartók in his youth, as well as a patched old armchair and a Bösendörfer piano, all of which contribute to the cozy atmosphere.

The memories of other great musicians are kept alive within certain Hungarian homes today: for example, Joseph Haydn at the Esterházy Palace in Fertöd, or Beethoven, who sometimes stayed with the Brunswick family at the Martonvásár Castle near Budapest, on the road to Lake Balaton. Reconstructed in 1980, this neo-Gothic residence has a collection of paintings, etchings, and musical scores evoking Beethoven's visits here. The serene gardens and arboretum may certainly have contributed to Beethoven's enjoyment of his visits here, far from the turbulence and concerns of his life in Vienna. During the summer, the island in the middle of the lake is a venue for concerts.

City Park borders the large Heroes Square—the venue for military parades and public events during the Monarchy and Republic. The park is a vast open area used for different leisure activities on weekends. Greeting the visitor in the center of the park is Vajdahunyad Castle (left). This spectacular structure is an elaborate pastiche of the different architectural styles of Greater Hungary in the years before the Treaty of Versailles. The Romanesque chapel (top) comes from the western region of Transdanubia. Nearby is a Gothic tower with a fine balcony (bottom) and pointed roof. Beside it is a Baroque castle housing an agricultural and hunting museum. The only presence that disturbs this idyllic setting is the masked and disturbing gaze of Anonymous, "the nameless chronicler," whose sculpture greets the visitor entering this strange castle.

FROM THE DANUBE TO THE TISZA

The history and geography of Hungary have been profoundly influenced by two great rivers, the Danube and the Tisza. The Danube is the second longest river in Europe after the Volga. It enters Hungary in the northwest, runs along the border with Slovakia, then changes direction above Budapest and flows south for 150 miles (250 km) before reaching Croatia. The Tisza is a magnificent meandering river, which has its source in the eastern Carpathian Mountains, in Ukraine. It snakes across the Great Hungarian Plain for nearly 220 miles (350 km) before joining the Danube in Serbia, near Belgrade. The vast expanse of water that arrives from the west comes up against the Börszöny mountain range, then abruptly changes direction and heads south.

The Danube has long been a source of inspiration to poets, writers, and musicians. Who can forget the lilting *Blue Danube* waltz? One of the earliest of these was the Roman historian Tacitus, who mentioned the Danube in *Germania*, his description of the tribes living in the region in the first century CE. Among recent writers to celebrate it is the contemporary Italian writer Claudio Magris in his masterpiece *Danube* (1986), recently translated into English. The river provides a background to several novels by Jules Verne, including *Mathias Sandorf, The Secret of Wilhelm Storitz,* and *The Danube Pilot*. But it is Victor Hugo who best describes the splendor and majesty of the vast river in his poem "The Angry Danube":

For I am the vast Danube …
Devouring one hundred stone bridges,
Crossing eight Bavarias,
Greeting sixty rivers
To devour them in my course;
Swelling like a sea,
And like a serpent uncoiling,
From occident to orient,
Flowing over the globe.

Both rivers have shaped Hungary's geographical makeup. The country is divided into three main regions: all the lands west of the Danube are known as Transdanubia (Dunántúl), the region between the Danube and the Tisza and east of the Tisza to the Romanian border is called the Great Plain (Alföld) and the area of mountain and forest massifs in the northeast constitutes the Northern Uplands. Although the Danube has an average depth of only 10 to 13 feet (3 to 4 meters), it is generally 550 to 650 yards (500 to 600 meters) wide. In the past there were few crossings: the city of

The Danube valley in all its natural splendor at its narrowest stretch, north of Budapest near the Slovak border (preceding pages). Beyond Budapest the river is calmer and is frequented by many barges (facing page). The hospitality of local wine growers in their traditional costumes (left) is an invitation to discover the multiple facets of this little-known area, rich in vineyards.

The great river Tisza is well loved by Hungarians and has played an important role in the country's history. Its waters abound in fish, and the many boats moored to its banks are so many signs of the continuing importance of fishing, an activity which has long contributed to enriching the life of the nearby villages.

The watery landscapes of the Danube and the Tisza are full of bewitching charm; sailing through the marshes of Lake Tisza or cycling along the towpath makes for an unforgettable experience.

Budapest, which was divided into three separate towns before 1873, did not have a stone bridge until 1848. The river is perfectly navigable however, and has been a much-frequented communication route since the Middle Ages.

Floods are common, and so are mists, at times making it difficult to see where land and river meet. In his *Mémoires*, French composer Hector Berlioz gives a humorous account of an episode that must have caused him some trepidation at the time: a terrifying ride from Vienna to Budapest with an inebriated stagecoach driver who, unable to distinguish the towpath from the bank, threatened to topple vehicle and passengers into the river on several occasions. Even today the Danube can suddenly overflow its banks with disastrous consequences—the great floods of the summer of 2002 are still fresh in people's memories. Major hydrographic work over the last fifty years has managed to regulate the flow of the Tisza, but it, too, can be unpredictable, as described by Hungarian poet Endre Ady:

The storm can rage, the brushwood rustle,
The Tisza pour over the Hungarian plain...

Hungarian literature abounds with references to catastrophic floods. For example, in *The New Squire*, the great nineteenth-century romantic novelist Mór Jókai recounts a battle against floodwaters that unites two characters from very different backgrounds: a young lord, rewarded with land for his loyalty to the Habsburg Monarchy during the 1848 Revolution, and a young Hungarian woman landowner, hostile to this despoliation. Nowadays, the Danube and the Tisza flow through a wonderful natural landscape dotted with some of the loveliest scenery in Hungary; to follow their

Margaret Island is a paradise for swimmers of all ages, with a variety of facilities such as childrens' pools or therapeutic baths; the baths at the Thermal Hotel (above) have recently been renovated by the Danubius chain.

separate courses is to discover the multiple facets of Hungarian life and culture. The rivers have contributed to the development of a characteristic lifestyle in the countryside and towns along their banks; they are also part of the enchanting, mysterious landscape of the Great Hungarian Plain with its age-old traditions, shimmering mirages, and the exceptional flora and fauna which thrive in this natural setting, whose tranquility is a welcome antidote to the hustle and bustle of the city.

Excursion along the Danube to the islands of Budapest and the old town of Szentendre

The Danube dominates the capital city, which grew up as two separate towns on either side of its banks, and the islands of the river are among Budapest's great attractions. Margaret Island (Margit-sziget), upstream of the city, is accessible either by car across the Árpád Bridge (Árpád híd), or by tramway and bus across the magnificent Margaret Bridge (Margit hid). Cross this at night for a magical panorama of the river and the monuments lining both banks. The bridge's architect, Ernest Gouin, trained in Gustave Eiffel's workshop; the French engineer gave the city its West Station, the elegant metallic structure of which has recently been renovated.

Margaret Island was once a hunting ground belonging to the Arpadian dynasty of Hungary founded by King Stephen, and later became church property. The ruins of several medieval monasteries dotted around the island include those of a thirteenth-century convent where Princess Margaret (Margit) was dedicated to God at the age of nine, according to a vow made by her father King Béla IV. She died there at the early age of twenty-eight. Today the island is a verdant paradise of splendid wooded parkland. The Danubius Grand Hotel Margitsziget at the north end of the island is a must. This beautifully renovated establishment offers an exceptional combination of calm, comfort, and first-class thermal spa facilities. Guests can enjoy a leisurely breakfast on the balconies that overlook the great expanse of river on one side or the green woods on the other, watching the morning visitors stroll past before joining them to explore the island.

Óbuda Island (Óbudai-sziget) is another part of Budapest that city dwellers visit to get away from it all. It is a little more difficult to get to than Margaret Island: you have to follow the quays on the right bank of the Danube and go under the Árpád Bridge. Pass the impressive port installations currently under development, then take a little metal footbridge across a branch of the river. The island is covered in vegetation nearly all year round, and is a favorite spot for open-air events, such as the Sziget music festival, one of Europe's biggest—a kind of Woodstock, held every August, which attracts large audiences of young people from Budapest and much farther afield. Óbuda Island is gradually coming to symbolize a modern, trendy lifestyle–you can play golf or tennis, or go horseback riding or boating there, whereas Margaret Island is generally

On Obuda Island, the open-air café Ládik Csárda (below) has recently opened near the pier. An ancient willow tree provides refreshing shade in which you can enjoy hot fish soup, even in the heat of summer.

Margaret Island has a certain nostalgic elegance, with its many species of trees and flowers planted in orderly rows. This impression is enhanced by the various "follies" dotted around the island: a neo-Romanesque chapel at the end of a walk featuring the busts of famous Hungarian artists, an open-air theater where young people enjoy energetic sessions of traditional dance, or an extravagant water tower. The Grand Hotel Margitsziget (left) makes a perfect base from which to explore the island.

preferred for the more popular sport of cycling (alone or in cycle-cars designed for families). There are special areas for children's activities.

Enchanted by these islands, the visitor may decide to venture farther upriver toward the old town of Szentendre on the right bank of the Danube, which faces the island of the same name. An expressway that runs for part of the way alongside the ruins of the Roman town of Aquincum to the north of Budapest takes you to the town. The steep cobbled streets of Szentendre are home to many artists, and still more have settled around the Pilis Mountains, with their spectacular views of the town and of the lazy course of the Danube. The town owes its prosperity in large part to the community of Serbian traders who settled there in the seventeenth century, driven out of Serbia by the Ottoman advance. It is a bewitching place, with an atmosphere all its own, perhaps due to the beauty and diversity of its churches (several of which are Serbian Orthodox), to the variety of its museums, or to the pleasant way of life that is almost palpable when strolling in the streets on a weekday. As Claudio Magris—whom we will often have occasion to quote in the course of our trip along the Danube—so aptly wrote in *Danube*: "Szentendre is a Montmartre of the Danube. The colors of the houses and the pictures on show in the streets filter off into those of the river, while a light, liquid gaiety enfolds the dawdler and draws him gently along the picturesque alleys which move down towards the river-banks in a tranquil flow."

One of Szentendre's many artists is Ádám Farkas, a well-known sculptor who has exhibited practically everywhere in the world and whom his peers recently elected president of the Academy of Fine Arts. He and his wife Anikó Rákossy (also a talented painter) have converted their family home to house their respective studios and their children's works—especially those of Zsofi, a sculptress who is following in her father's footsteps. Visitors to the lovely old house on the river's edge receive a delightful welcome.

The nearby Hungarian Open-Air Museum (Szabadtéri Néprajzi Múzeum) is exceptional in more ways than one. Scattered over an area of several acres are buildings representative of every style of Hungarian architecture: wonderful examples of religious or rural buildings from Lake Balaton to the Northern Uplands, from the Great Plain to Zala County. It takes several hours to explore this extraordinary museum, but learning is fun when the history, geography, folk traditions, and lifestyles of a country are brought to life in such a simple and attractive way. It makes for an experience that can be enjoyed by adults and children alike.

Szentendre itself has an exceptional range of museums and galleries—about fifteen in all. Two of the most interesting are the Marzipan Museum (Marcipàn Múzeum) and the Margaret Kovács Museum (Kovács Margit Múzeum). The first, run by the Szabò family, who have specialized for several generations in the art of making attractive, tasty marzipan delicacies that appeal to young and old alike, is a must for the sweet-toothed. The second pays homage to the extraordinarily sensitive artist Margit Kovács with an exhibition of the ceramic figurines and scenes that were her life's work. For Claudio Magris, "in the figures of Margit Kovács suffering is dumb and inexplicable, the sorrow of a great motherhood, which creates both life and pain. But in that silence there is an unshakable dignity even more mysterious than sorrow, the enigma of existence and even of happiness in spite of tragedy."

No visit to Szentendre is complete without taking time to discover the famous painters such as Béla Czóbel, Károly Ferenczy, or Lajos Vajda who lived here in the past. The beautiful houses they lived and worked in have now been converted into museums. Memories of the old trading families who once made the town so prosperous also pervade the place. Near a charming church in the heart

The little town of Szentendre (facing page) is a popular tourist attraction. It is located at the foot of the Pilis Mountains (which are particularly rich in game), and the old part of town overlooks the Danube. The traditional tolerance of this region has made the town home to a great number of churches of various denominations; its present aspect owes much to the orthodox community of Serbian origin. Szentendre has been a haven for artists for over a hundred years, not forgetting the dyers, examples of whose traditional craft can be seen in villages throughout Hungary (facing page, bottom left). Many small museums in the town feature the works of local artists .The popular Hungarian ceramist Margit Kovács was a local artist who brought her subjects and characters to life with extraordinary intensity (right, top). The more contemporary work by sculptor Ádám Farkas is the result of this artist's love of nature and highly selective use of stone (right, bottom).

Many works by sculptor Ádám Farkas and his painter wife Anikó Rákossy are displayed in their home, together with works by their artist friends, members of the Szentendre School. The pleasant atmosphere of the place is enhanced by a veranda which opens onto a large garden with trees and flowers which have been cultivated over several generations.

A beautiful house, hidden behind the foliage of a Szentendre alleyway, contains a splendid collection of antique furniture put together by an antique dealer who descended from a very old Swabian trading family. New pieces have been acquired since 1990, and many unique items are currently on display—magnificent examples of the Copf or Biedermeier tradition. The icons that adorn the walls indicate the influence of Serbian culture on the history of this little town.

The town of Visegrád is steeped in history; it even inspired the name of the Central European alliance signed after the fall of the Berlin Wall, in reference to the historic Visegrád group of 1335. The Royal Palace (facing page) was built at the foot of the hill during the Renaissance, with the help of Italian artists. After undergoing the Turkish occupation and falling into ruin, it was rediscovered during the last century, and elements such as the red marble Hercules fountain (left, bottom) were restored to their former splendor. The lions themselves seem to be slumbering, waiting for the palace to recover its former glory.

of the old town is a pretty eighteenth-century house, almost hidden in the lush vegetation that covers its walls and overflows from its garden. The property belongs to an ancient Swabian family who have lived here for three centuries. It houses a rare private collection of Hungarian furniture, painstakingly collected and preserved during the last century by several generations of antique dealers.

There is so much to see in Szentendre that visitors can return time and time again and never tire of exploring the town.

Following the Danube

After this incursion into the outskirts of the capital, carry on farther to explore the length of the Danube with its varied landscapes and attractive blend of historical sites and folk traditions. Here, where the river laps against the ancient banks of the towns it passes, you will find echoes of French poet Arthur Rimbaud's "Europe with its age-old parapets." In the words of Claudio Magris, "The Danube threads towns together like a string of pearls." Komárom, Esztergom, Visegrád, Vác, Szentendre, Budapest, Ráckeve, Dunaújváros, Paks, Kalocsa, Szekszárd, Baja, Mohács: these towns punctuate the lazy course of the river. Hungarian poet Endre Ady described the Danube as running "verbosely beneath titanic bridges."

Continue north along the road from Szentendre as it runs alongside the Danube Bend (Dunakanyar) to Visegrád. Visegrád occupies both a strategic and a spectacular position; its hilltop citadel affords a breathtaking view over the Danube Bend. This former royal capital is a monument to the past when Hungary was ruled by the Angevin and Luxembourg dynasties in the Middle Ages, then by King Matthias Corvinus, whose court was among the most sumptuous in Renaissance Europe. A visit to the ruins of Visegrád's hilltop citadel is a must for Hungarian schoolchildren. The view of the majestic river flowing far below is an inspiring sight, seeming to bring to life the din of distant battles and tournaments. The scenery, with the Danube Bend and mountainous massifs in the background, is superb. The Royal Palace (Királyi Palota) on the right bank has been skillfully rebuilt by Hungarian architects and craftsmen and preserves traces of its former splendor, such as the red-marble Hercules Fountain built for Matthias Corvinus,

From Visegrád to Esztergom, the Danube flows between the forest-covered slopes of the Pilis and Börzsöny Mountains, full of abundant wildlife. The river narrows here, and its swirls and eddies are as treacherous as those of an Alpine river. These wild waters seem to reflect another facet of the proud, rebellious Hungarian soul.

Visitors to Esztergom are greeted by an imposing sight: the huge Saint Adalbert Cathedral, symbol of spiritual power and seat of the Archbishop and Catholic Primate of Hungary. For centuries, Hungary was a bastion of Christendom against the Ottoman Turks until the imperial army of the Habsburgs liberated Buda in 1686. The Hungarian tradition of resisting foreign domination was personified and upheld in the twentieth century by the indomitable Cardinal Mindszenty, who refused to cooperate with the Soviet regime, or even to be buried in Esztergom as long as his country remained under the control of a system he despised. His ashes were only finally brought home to Esztergom in 1991, once the Communist era had come to an end. The magnificent cathedral preserves its stately silence much of the time, except on ceremonial occasions or times of pilgrimage, when it wakes from its slumbers to magnificent scenes of pomp and circumstance. Visitors can admire the cathedral's magnificent treasure, then visit the nearby Christian Museum (Keresztény Múzeum),

The dimensions of the Royal Palace impressed the distinguished guests who were invited to Visegrád by King Matthias and Queen Beatrice; indeed one of them described it as "heaven on earth." There are still traces of the fountains, courtyards, and loggias which must have contributed to this impression of splendor.

The town of Esztergom grew up on hills that overlook the Danube. It was long the religious capital of Hungary, and boasted one of the royal palaces which were so common in the later medieval period. Today's visitors can admire its well-restored ruins, set among fabulous scenery.

The huge basilica is as awe-inspiring as the "Esztergom Mass" composed by Liszt for its consecration. The chapel, in red marble from the north of Hungary, evokes all the refinement of the Renaissance, introduced into Hungary by King Matthias's Italian wife, Queen Beatrice.

whose remarkable collections give some idea of the wealth and influence of the Hungarian Church in the fifteenth and sixteenth centuries.

The rebuilt Royal Palace (Királyi Palota) also conjures up the town's royal and religious past. A remarkable collection of bells of all sizes is displayed in the palace outbuildings. Visitors can return to the present day by taking a stroll along the riverbank to the newly reconstructed bridge between Hungary and Slovakia, a symbol of both countries' political determination to heal the scars of the conflicts that broke out in the aftermath of the Treaty of Versailles (1919) and during the Cold War. Present-day Esztergom is a historical border town, whose cathedral "beams forth a glacial temporal power, or insolence" (Claudio Magris). It reflects all the brilliance of the Hungarian past, yet looks serenely ahead to the changes the future may bring.

South of the capital, there are ample opportunities to discover the different ways of life of the villages and towns along the river. Kalocsa is traditionally known for its paprika plantations and for the brightly colored clothing worn by its inhabitants, Szekszárd for its vineyards, and the Sárköz region for its local crafts. There is a remarkable floodplain forest in Gemenc, and Baja is a town of fisheries, noted for its delicious fish soups.

Among Hungary's renowned wines, those from Szekszárd are high on the list. Work was undertaken in the nineteenth century to regulate the flow of the Danube at this point, and as a result this little town is now separated from the river. Szekszárd may not be unforgettable in itself, but after stopping for lunch in the pleasant underground room of the Fispán Étterem restaurant, you should climb the hill in the heart of town to enjoy an exceptional view of gently undulating vineyards dotted with the vine workers' pretty cottages. The cobbled streets of nearby Sióagárd are lined with wine merchants' shops and cellars covered in ancient dovetail tiles. The local wine growers give visitors a warm welcome, inviting them to penetrate the mysteries of their craft. If you visit an old cellar you will often be able to taste these pure, unpretentious wines, worthy of the *kadarka* vine from which they are produced.

The village of Decs, not far away in the direction of the river, is well worth a visit. Decs is at the heart of the tiny Sárköz region, forty square miles in area, where deep-rooted customs continue to thrive. Its country museum (*tájház*) is housed in a wealthy stockbreeder's traditional home with a long, white-pillared veranda in front. In one room, a group of villagers dressed in brightly colored outfits sing and dance enthusiastically. In the next room there is a beautiful display of typical local craftwork. The little doll museum and painted egg collection in a nearby house complete this picture of traditional Hungary. Model figures dressed in appropriate costumes depict the region's ancient and modern crafts.

The age-old Gemenc forest, world famous for the rich biodiversity of its fauna and flora, lies on a floodplain crossed by branches of the Danube and its tributaries. It is one of Europe's last great nature reserves, where large mammals such as magnificent stags and wild boars, great birds such as herons, black storks, and cranes, and rare tree and plant species are to be found. Visitors can explore its protected paths in horse-drawn carriages, whose slow rhythm seems in harmony with the very heartbeat of the forest. On the farms and hunting lodges scattered around the edges of the forest there are animals rarely seen elsewhere, such as the wooly, black Mangalica pig, whose fat is said to be cholesterol-free.

The people of Hungary have a high level of environmental awareness, as is apparent in the relationship they maintain with the river and the activities it has generated, an important source of income

There are many surprises in store when you explore the regions along the Danube south of Budapest. The landscape is quite unspoiled, especially in the Gemenc Forest, which you can visit in a horse-drawn cart (right). The local vineyards produce wines that have been much appreciated since the Middle Ages. In Szekszárd (facing page) and the neighboring villages, local people have exploited the land for centuries, dividing it into separate plots; each wine grower constructs a wine storehouse in the middle of his vineyard—a symbol of his love for the land. The wine-tasting ceremony can be a memorable occasion, when organized by the master of the local Bacchic brotherhood, elegantly dressed in black and assisted by a young woman from the village.

Rural customs are thriving in the Szekszárd area, where many people still live in the heart of the huge Gemenc Forest and the traditions of the little Sárköz plain are still strong. Folk dances have not died out, and you can admire traditional dance costumes at a charming museum in the village of Decs. Rural homes are still constructed in keeping with traditional proportions.

The Gemenc Forest is traversed by various branches of the Danube, resulting in a rich ecosystem with exceptional flora and fauna. Under the Habsburg monarchy, the mighty stags of the forest attracted royal hunters, who stayed in beautifully ornate wooden hunting lodges, sometimes featuring carved horses' heads. Some of these constructions have been restored, and they make a picturesque sight.

Kecskemét is a wealthy *puszta* town whose many remarkable buildings reflect the influence of Art Nouveau on Hungarian architecture. The Ornamented Palace and Town Hall (right) designed by Ödön Lechner illustrate the enrichment of this decorative art with traditional Hungarian folk motifs.

for the region. In the neighboring town of Baja, the annual July Fish Soup Festival illustrates the strength of these links. Gourmets, food lovers, fishermen, and cooks gather together in a cheerful, convivial atmosphere, where everyone is welcome to sample the tasty, heart-warming soups simmering in large copper cauldrons over open fires.

The description of the Danube by the great Hungarian poet Attila József still holds good today: "cloudy, wise, and great." If you follow the river as it flows southward through Hungary you will eventually arrive at the town of Mohács, near the Croatian and Serbian borders. Here, the lazy course of the river is dotted with little islands joined to the bank by stone causeways. Jetties moored to the riverbank enable fishermen to advance into the middle of the river without getting their feet wet.

Among the many tragic events that have punctuated the history of Hungary was the battle of Mohács in 1526—described by Claudio Magris as one of those battles that "for centuries seals the destinies of a people"—when the Ottoman Sultan Süleyman I (the Magnificent) defeated a Hungarian army one-fourth the size of his own. The young Jagellonian King Louis II, the last independent king of Hungary, was killed, and for the next century and a half, Hungary was ruled by the Ottomans, who left their mark on the country's architecture, gastronomy, and bathing traditions.

At the exit to Mohács in the direction of the border, a memorial park commemorates the great battle with strange, carved wooden posts that symbolize the decimated army. Claudio Magris gives a moving description: "Those rash, ingenious carvings hint at the heads of men and of horses, the manes of dying steeds, huge turbans, deadly maces crashing down, faces contorted by agony or ferocity, crosses and crescents, slaves beneath the yoke, heads rolling to the feet of Süleyman the Magnificent."

Mohács is also famous for its terrifying *busó* masks, made from painted willow wood, horn, wool, and other natural materials. Skilled craftsmen work throughout the year to make these ferocious masks, which seem to symbolize rage and destruction: it is as if the town's tragic past has infused it with an eternal atmosphere of sadness. Every year, on Septuagesima Sunday, the third Sunday before Lent, the masks are paraded around the town, past the low, brightly colored houses, to the strident accompaniment of rattles and bells. The parade ends with a huge bonfire, on which a coffin—said to contain the remains of the cold season—is burned, symbolizing the death of winter and the arrival of spring.

Kecskemét and Csongrád, cities of the plain

Visitors to Kecskemét, which lies on the Great Plain between the Danube and the Tisza, should explore this lovely town on foot to appreciate all its charm. German composer Johannes Brahms considered it "the prettiest town in the world," and it featured in one of his songs. Musician Zoltán Kodály was born in Kecskemét in 1882 and remained attached to the town his entire life. Nowadays, students come from all over the world to the Kodály Institute, housed in a former Franciscan monastery, where they can study the teaching methods invented by the famous musician.

The many and varied church steeples testify to the wealth of this market town, which was long an important center for trade. In the late nineteenth century, Kecskemét flourished as the capital of Bács-Kiskun County, and many beautiful palaces and public buildings were built. A former synagogue is home to the collections of the privately run Photography Museum, which includes works by some of the most famous Hungarian photographers, from the earliest daguerrotypes to photographs by world figures such as Lázló Moholy-Nagy, Endre Kertész, Robert Capa, and Brassaï.

One of the most poignant places on the Great Plain is the Memorial at Mohács, a litle town on the Danube in the far south of Hungary near the borders with Serbia and Croatia. In 1526, the Hungarian army led by young Jagellonian King Louis II was defeated by the troops of Süleyman the Magnificent; subsequently Hungary was to endure Ottoman occupation for a century and a half. The disastrous battle is taught in every Hungarian school, and children learn of its consequences for their country: the depopulation of the center, autonomy for the northeastern province of Transylvania, and reconquest by the Habsburgs from the west. During the nineteenth century, the ambition of Greater Hungary was to eradicate the traces of this national trauma. The great wooden totems in the Memorial Park are a simple and moving expression of the implacable cruelty of this tragic battle.

Reed-thatched roofs on rural houses are a common sight in Hungary, and this tradition is currently undergoing a revival in many hamlets as the raw material, which is freely available from the marshes of the Tisza, is elegant in appearance and relatively simple to use. The wooden steeples of country churches are also a characteristic feature of local building traditions.

The Ornamented Palace (Cifra Palota) is a wonderful example of the decorative inventiveness of the architects of this period. The façade is embellished with motifs that evoke traditional folk tales or the intricate embroidery still produced by old local families, and its colorful reliefs bring out the elaborate contours of the bronze-ribbed windows. In comparison, the Secessionist-style building of the József Szinház Theater (Katona József Szinház) is more massive in appearance. A monumental pair of male figures graces the portal of this theater, which is renowned all over Hungary for the quality of its program. The most extraordinary building in Kecskemét, however, is the Town Hall. Designed by architect Ödön Lechner in Art Nouveau style, and completed in 1895, its huge pink façade stands out on Kossuth Street. Above the magnificent portal is a neo-Gothic balcony, decorated with little bells. The gables are reminiscent of the medieval Flemish houses of Bruges or Ghent. Every detail harmonizes with the overall perspective, from the graceful bronze statues adorning the chimneys to the willow tree whose branches stand out against the pink façade of Lechner's unforgettable masterpiece.

The nearby town of Csongrád, on the banks of the Tisza, is off the usual tourist track. Its many trees and flowers, wide avenues, attractive buildings, and scenic riverbanks seem to hark back to Hungary's golden age. The local history museum (Tari Lázló Múzeum) is named for a former resident of Csongrád with a scholarly passion for collecting and preserving vestiges of the town's past, from Bronze Age artifacts to traditionally embroidered garments. The Art Nouveau façade of the high school, embellished with majolica tiles and traditional motifs, epitomizes the tranquility of this town beside the river Tisza, bordered with willows and dotted with islands. As it continues on its peaceful way across the Great Plain, the Tisza washes up against an old fishing village with well-tended thatched cottages, one of which has been converted into a little museum, the Múzeum Ház. Here visitors can observe a meticulous reproduction of the traditional country lifestyle, in which fishing has, since time immemorial, played an all-important role. A mulberry tree spreads its bountiful shade over the patch of garden, aglow with the autumnal colors of dahlias, button chrysanthemums, French marigolds, and red-leafed saxifrages. Inside the house, there is a faithful portrayal of family life as it used to be.

A springtime excursion on and around the Tizsa

The eastern banks of the Danube open onto the vast expanse known as the *puszta*, "the great Hungarian plain par excellence, bounded by the mountains of Transylvania over a hundred leagues away," as Jules Verne puts it, in *The Danube Pilot*. This is the harsh yet magnificent environment that attracted Árpád and his Magyar followers to conquer Hungary in the tenth century C.E. The Mongol and Ottoman invaders who followed in their footsteps in the thirteenth and sixteenth centuries cut down the forests, thereby depriving nearby villages of their livelihood. People drifted away, and the villages were abandoned. The surrounding area became fallow land, known as *puzsta* (wilderness). In Claudio Magris' words, "In this empty, uncaring landscape, life flows negligently by, moving towards infinite distance like a herd of cattle. The only thing that happens is that time passes. The years, says one of Petõfi's poems, flash by like a flock of birds after a gunshot." But the *puszta* has worlds of its own, where age-old customs continue to thrive. The wild landscapes of the Cumania region, home to a diversity of animals, are unique in Europe.

The Tisza is the thread that links the water to the land and the world of the *puszta*. The many lakes and meanders of "this lazy Magyar Nile" (as it was described by novelist Kálmán Mikszáth) are abundant in fish. Indeed, Claudio Magris relates a saying that the river is composed of two-thirds water

Csongrád seems to be gently slumbering on the banks of the Tisza, but it still has the power to charm with its wide shady avenues, beautiful buildings from the Baroque age or the late nineteenth century, and traditional village houses.

At Bugac, the *csikos* in their traditional outfits demonstrate extraordinary complicity with their splendid well-trained horses; beautiful white cattle with lyre-shaped horns also live on the puszta.

and one-third fish. There are many different species, including carp, pike, and perch. In 1999, environmental disaster struck: cyanide waste escaped from a holding reservoir at a gold-smelting plant in Romania into a tributary of the Tisza, the Szamos. After huge numbers of fish appeared, floating belly-up in the Tisza, it was feared that the hugely toxic pollution would eradicate all river life for a long time. Fortunately, however, the river was able to recover very quickly thanks to skillful management of the catastrophe. Barrages and small reservoirs were built to limit the contaminated water to a small section of the river north of Lake Tisza (Tizsa-tó). The lake itself was, thankfully, unaffected by the disaster.

You can explore this vast, shallow lake with its exceptional fauna and flora by taking a trip in a flat-bottomed boat from the town of Tiszafüred. It is a pleasant and relaxing outing, sailing among the reeds, water-lilies, and various aquatic plants, watching the shadowy fish flitting by under the surface, sometimes disturbing the great wading birds that take off heavily, sending fine ripples across the lake's smooth surface. Only the sound of birdsong from countless birds hidden among the grasses breaks the silence. You may spot a roe deer and its faun scampering along a dike, but there are no signs of human presence except for the occasional reed-thatched hut. When you finally return to dry land it will take some time for your senses to recover from the magical experience of the lake.

The earth is often poor and infertile in the dusty *puszta*, but human tenacity has enabled men and women to exploit this sandy, marshy soil by irrigating land and planting poplars, willows, or acacias to prevent the land from eroding too quickly. What was once a desolate area has grown green again. There are two great National Parks: the Hortobágy and the Kiskunság (or Cumania, so dear to the heart of the poet Sándor Petõfi). Here, the *puzsta* is just as Jules Verne described it, an "infinite stretch of deserted moors, of vast pastures, of huge swamps aswarm with waterfowl."

It is easy to imagine how these Asian-style steppes beneath their changing skies must have appeared to the first Magyars who came from the distant plateaus of Central Asia many hundreds of years ago to end their wanderings in the Carpathian Basin. Strict regulations concerning the management of these national parks have preserved them from agricultural exploitation, and the age-old pastoral way of life has survived. Here are skillful horsemen (*csikós*), shepherds (*pásztor*) with their embroidered, fleece-lined sheepskin jackets, herders (*gulyás*) in charge of the lovely white cattle with lyre-shaped horns, and swineherds (*kondás*), whose unusually fierce-looking pigs have black, wooly coats. The only character missing is the legendary highwayman (*betyár*), who featured in the novels of romantic writers, for whom the *puszta* had an exotic image similar to that of the American Far West.

For Hungary has its cowboys too—and their remarkable horseback-riding skills can be admired at the equestrian demonstrations held on the *puszta* of Bugac, near Kecskemét, in one of the last protected areas of the Great Plain. The authorities of the Kiskunság National Park (Kiskunsági Nemzeti Park) organize these displays, in which the *csikós* perform amazing feats on horseback. The riders seem to be as one with the horses they have bred, watched over, and trained, in keeping with the spirit of the ancient customs of the *puszta*. The *csikós* wear traditional costumes: black waistcoats over white tunics tied at the waist with ornate belts, and black felt hats adorned with feathery plumes of grass from the plain. Whip in hand, they shout to encourage the horses that gallop across the plain. Then one of them, no doubt the most gifted, grabs a passing horse and leaps on, to ride it standing, bareback, using his reins to guide as many as five horses as they race along. This spectacular stunt is

Wood carving is an ancient Magyar tradition and today's craftsmen are reviving their ancestors' skills. Masters of organic architecture have contributed to this revival with their skillful contructions. A fine example is the superb Kakasd church, in the vicinity of Szekszárd; its narthex consists of a series of five ornate wooden panels, echoing the curious design of the church tower.

called "Five-in-hand," and requires an exceptional sense of balance and great skill in driving a team at top speed.

Meanwhile, the various animals characteristic of the Kiskunság region go calmly about their business. Enormous white dogs guard the magnificent herds of gray, longhorn cattle and spiral-horned sheep. Only a few buffalo in the middle of the herd stamp and snort and generally show signs of aggression toward curious onlookers. A big well, a distinctive feature of the Great Plain, stands out against the horizon. Reed-thatched stables, the horse-drawn carriages crossing the plain, and the little country-life museum, with its display of festive harnesses to decorate the plow teams on religious occasions, all create an atmosphere in which past and present, real and imaginary, are indistinguishable.

Among the rare inhabitants of the *puszta*, the shepherds live in harmony with their flocks.

To discover the unique lifestyle and traditions of the Great Plain, a visit to the Hortobágy Shepherds' Museum (Hortobágyi Pásztor Múzeum) is as interesting as it is informative. This museum, near the town of Debrecen in the northeast corner of the Great Plain, displays the customs and traditions of the inhabitants of the *puszta* in fascinating detail. Likewise, the nearby Round Museum (Körszinmúzeum) is devoted to the natural life and farming traditions of these regions, such as the clear-eyed Racka sheep with their long, twisted, horns famous for the quality of their wool, and the famous, high-spirited little Nonius horses, trained from birth to obey their riders' every whim. The annual Hortobágy International Equestrian Days are an opportunity to admire them. Sheepdogs, such as the *komondor* with its corded coat, the long-haired black or white *puli*, the long-muzzled *pumi,* and the sturdy white *kuvasz* keep a vigilant watch over these protected species. Each great sheepfold has one of these loyal companions, also present at shearing time, keeping a close eye on his charges. In *The Danube Pilot*, Jules Verne describes the animal life on the plain: "This *puszta* is like a table that is always generously laid for a multitude of four-legged guests, thousands and thousands of ruminants, among the great riches of the kingdom of Hungary."

A stormy sky over the Hortobágy *puszta* adds a sense of the infinite to this strange, deserted landscape, famous for its mirages.

You may see a rider galloping toward you out of the mist—but it is probably only a mirage, one of the *délibáb* for which the *puszta* is renowned. You may be lucky, however, and spot the rare great bustard—the biggest bird in Europe—nesting among the tall grasses, or one of the flocks of beautiful white-breasted geese, for whom the park is a favorite nesting place. And when the sky turns a radiant, glowing purple in the evening and the well stands out clearly silhouetted on the cloudy horizon, then the *puszta* begins to vibrate with the song of the birds and the hum of a myriad of insects that sense the approach of nightfall.

Traveling woodcarvers express their art with roughhewn portraits (left, top). They are distant heirs to the proud Magyar conquerors, whose sturdy horses brought them from the steppes to the Carpathian basin.

Since the recent celebrations in commemoration of the birth of the Hungarian State, every village and town on the Great Plain boasts its wooden statues, carved from the block of willow trunks (above).

Figures of warriors, craftsmen (left, bottom), or characters from Finno-Ugric mythology people the dreams and representations of artists from the east. Their style is simple and unaffected.

Rural architecture on the Great Plain obeys certain precise rules with results which can be admired in the villages. Some of these rural edifices have been reconstructed in Hungary's open-air museums. Thatched roofs, gabled walls, arcaded verandas and wells are the principal features.

THE NORTHERN UPLANDS: HILLSIDES AND VINEYARDS

The prince of Transylvania, whose residence stood beside the Bodrog River overlooking Sárospatak, promoted wine production in the Tokay region. The rows of planted vines on the southern hillsides of the Zemplén Mountains breathe an air of slumbering tranquility. The rich amber color of the sweet local wines is seen to best advantage in cut crystal glasses.

A range of small mountains in northern Hungary, along the Slovakian border, marks the beginning of the Carpathian Mountains, the mountain chain that describes a vast circle from Hungary to Slovakia extending as far as Romania to the east and the former Yugoslavia in the south. It is one of Europe's most mysterious regions, with many surviving traditions and customs. The fabulous tale of Count Dracula in his Bran castle, made famous by the English writer Bram Stoker and by the movies inspired by the myth, are rooted in the history of the region.

The highest peaks of the Carpathians are not actually in Hungary but in Romania and Slovakia. The slopes of the Hungarian uplands, at lower altitude, are covered in beech forests. An excellent tourist industry has developed here, based on the region's natural resources. It can easily be explored from Budapest by following a line that starts from the Danube, north of the capital, and runs along a succession of mountains from the Börzsöny, Cserhát, Mátra, Bükk, and Zemplén ranges to the Tisza basin and Tokay vineyards. The highest summit in Hungary, the Kékestet, rises to 3,622 feet (1,104 meters) in the Mátra Mountains. Hungarians are extremely fond of this part of their country. Its popular name, the Northern Uplands, evokes an earlier era when Greater Hungary included parts of Slovakia as far as the Polish border as well as the province of Transylvania in present-day Romania. The residents of Budapest love to visit the region for outdoor activities—long hikes through the forests, fishing, hunting, and (when there is enough snow to operate the relatively rudimentary ski lifts) winter sports.

The history of this part of Hungary is linked to that of the former principality of Transylvania, with one of its capitals located in Sárospatak. It has always been a proud region, with a strong tradition of resisting oppressors, be they the Ottomans in the fifteenth and sixteenth centuries, or the Habsburgs during the ultimately unsuccessful war for independence led by Prince Rákóczi in the early eighteenth century.

The exceptional soil of this hilly region is particularly well suited for growing grapes. The wines of Eger and the Bikavér (Bull's Blood) are renowned, and Tokay Aszú was famed throughout the world as early as the reign of King Louis XIV of France, who insisted it be served at his table. Fall is an exceptional time of year to wander from vineyard to vineyard, exploring some of the country's most beautiful landscapes as you enjoy the Indian summer, known locally as the "old ladies' summer," or *vénasszonyok nyara*.

Cities of art and resistance

To reach the Northern Uplands from Budapest you head northeast along the M3 expressway. Soon after leaving Budapest, stop at the town of Gödöllu to visit the former royal palace, a favorite residence

Over the years, Queen Elizabeth of Hungary, the beloved Sissi, stayed many times at the Royal Palace of Godollo. Now restored, the rooms are decorated with rare Herend porcelain and large gray ceramic stoves. Chandeliers of interlacing filigree hang from the ceiling and the mirrors on the walls reflect the elegant furnishings.

of the lovely Sissi, Empress Elizabeth of Austria who also became Queen of Hungary in the late-nineteenth century. Wife of the Emperor Francis Joseph, she is still beloved by Hungarians for the support she gave to their nationalist pride, which she demonstrated by staying for months at a time on this magnificent estate. Surrounded by a court of Hungarian magnates with whom the empress—a famous horsewoman—hunted and went riding, she and Francis Joseph enjoyed happy times here. A complete renovation of the palace was begun in 1995, and although the patina of centuries past is now gone, the rooms that are open to the public have been refurnished from the national collections, allowing visitors to glimpse something of the court atmosphere during the reigns of the last Habsburgs.

Large portraits of the imperial family and pieces of furniture from the Museum of Applied Arts in Budapest help us to imagine life in the palace as it would have been during the last years of the Dual Monarchy. Here we see Emperor Francis Joseph's sitting room, complete with Biedermeier furniture.

The palace was constructed for the Grassalkovich family in the eighteenth century and transferred to the Hungarian state during the Austro-Hungarian compromise of 1867. The great architect Miklós Ybl was commissioned to restore the buildings, which the state donated to the emperor and empress of Austria on their coronation as sovereigns of Hungary. For three decades, the Gödöllu palace was at the heart of Hungarian celebrations of the Dual Monarchy, but it lost some of its soul with the tragic death of Sissi, who was assassinated in Geneva in 1898. Francis Joseph subsequently spent little time here, and neither did his successor, Charles IV, who inherited it at the height of World War I. The Hungarian regent, Admiral Miklós Horthy, used the palace as his summer residence in the interwar period, but the property suffered severely and was sacked during the German occupation. It was then transformed into a military hospital by Soviet troops, who burned what remained of the furniture.

When the Hungarian Office for the Protection of Historical Monuments decided to start restoration work in the 1990s, the site was in ruins; all the roughcast finishing had fallen off and the immense rooms were desperately empty. Visitors today can admire the success of the restoration program. The plastered façades have been returned to their original pastel tones, the building has been reroofed with old tiles, and the gold-leaf stucco decorations of the reception rooms have been impeccably restored to their former Baroque glory.

The approach to the palace is across a small stone bridge that leads to the majestic main entrance topped with a dome and adorned with a wrought-iron balcony supported on red-marble pilasters. Some 18,300 square feet (1,700 square meters) have been reopened to the public, recreating—albeit imperfectly—the splendid lifestyle of the Habsburg monarchs. Each room has been furnished to illustrate its historical function: on show are the drawing room and office of Francis Joseph and those of Queen Elizabeth, as well as her bedroom and dressing room, the small crown room, the banquet hall, and the room reserved for the aide-de-camp. The gardens are gradually regaining some of their charm, but it will take many years to restore them to their original design. A stroll through the 74-acre (30-hectare) park gives the visitor an idea of the complexity of the palace, which consists of seven overlapping wings. It's easy to imagine the celebrations that took place in the U-shaped courtyard in an earlier era.

The Gödöllu tea room is fitted out in similar style to the palace; it is a delightful place for a break following a tour of the palace's rooms and garden (presently under restoration). The visitor who has had his or her appetite whetted by the culinary pleasures of the capital will enjoy the pastries on offer here—delicious confections of marzipan and colored icing, flavored with coffee or liqueurs.

The Eger vineyards are famous for Bikavér wine, a blend of several grape varieties aged in ancient cellars. Thummerer is one such vineyard; sculptures by the wine producer's wife lend an artistic air. Nearby is the Noszvaj château, built in neo-classical style in the early nineteenth century by the Szepessy-de-la-Motte family.

After this plunge into the last days of the Dual Monarchy, continue your journey toward Eger, one of the most beautiful cities in Hungary. The road leading from the expressway exit at Füzesabony winds through extensive vineyards. When the weather grows crisp in the fall, the leaves of the vines turn a lovely red. The grape varieties grown here are used to make the famous Egri Bikavér (Bull's Blood of Eger) and Egri Leányka (Eger Maiden)—the latter a delicious medium-dry, fruity white wine.

The Eger tourist office (Tourinform) organizes tours of the vineyards followed by wine tastings. Thummerer, a vineyard stretching out along the Bükk hills northeast of the city, makes some of the best wines in the region. The vinification process introduced in recent years has resulted in highly sophisticated red, white, and rosé wines. The classic grape varieties—Merlot, Cabernet Franc, and Cabernet Sauvignon—form the bulk of the production, but there are also a number of local and regional blended wines, including Egri Bikavér, Egri Leányka, and Egri Királyleányka (Eger Royal Maiden).

Noszvaj, another wine producer not far from Thummerer, is worth a visit. The beautiful manor house in French neoclassical style belonged to the Szepessy-de-la-Motte family and is now open to the public. A wrought-iron gate surrounds the garden in front of the charming building. The frescoes in the large drawing room are good examples of the Rococo *trompe l'oeil* decoration that often decorated the staircases and reception rooms of elegant late-eighteenth-century Hungarian mansions. The nearby village also has some interesting houses built into former quarries or abandoned caves.

The city of Eger no doubt gains its lively, cheerful ambiance from its links to the wine industry. Start your exploration of the historic heart of the town with the lovely Baroque homes lining the main pedestrian square, named for István Dobó, a hero in the resistance against the Ottomans. This section of the city slopes gently down toward the medieval fortress, which was originally constructed by the Hungarians, and then expanded and fortified in the sixteenth century by the Turks. Bright geraniums on the balconies set off the old rose color of the elegant Szenátor Ház hotel and restaurant, founded in the mid-eighteenth century. Several rooms face the Dobó Square, which contains a bronze sculpture celebrating the occasion in 1552 when a Hungarian force held off a Turkish army six times its size (the town eventually fell to the Turks in 1596 after a brief siege of just one week). Men and women fought side by side. According to legend, the Hungarian soldiers drank wine straight from the casks; the wine stained their lips so red that the attackers believed that they drew their strength from drinking the blood of their victims (other sources say it was because they drank bull's blood, hence the name of the wine).

In the late eighteenth century, Eger was placed under the authority of Bishop Károly Eszterházy. He was responsible for building the Lyceum (Líceum), intended as a university, and he commissioned the greatest architects of the era to design a structure that would be a worthy reflection of the Church's power in Hungary. The building's courtyard—certainly one of the most beautiful enclosed spaces in Hungary—is magnificent. The main entrance is decorated with trompe l'oeil frescoes and a ceiling painted with Baroque garlands, created by the most famous Austro-Hungarian artist of the late Baroque era,

This proud sculpture commemorates István Dobó, the heroic defender of Eger. Dobó led a successful resistance against a much larger Turkish army at a time when Eger was the only city in the country holding out against the Ottomans. The elegant Baroque fronts of the houses in the background give a foretaste of Eger's attractive streets and squares. As a base for exploring the city, the small Szenátor Ház hotel (top) is ideally situated in the town's pedestrian area.

Dd
Ee
Ff

The library of the Eger Lyceum has ceiling frescoes depicting the Council of Trent, and exceptional wood paneling carved by Thomas Lotter between 1778 and 1780. Bishop Károly Eszterházy founded the Lyceum as a university with four departments, and built the library to house the books he collected. Today the library possesses 130,000 volumes, including 34 medieval manuscripts, 94 incunabula, and the only signed letter of Mozart's in any Hungarian collection. Some of the works illustrate the international nature of European scholarship during the Enlightenment —for instance, there is a study of ornithology written in French by English authors and published in Nuremburg. From the top of the building there are spectacular views over the city and nearby basilica.

The iron grille on the County Hall (Megyeháza) (facing page, left, top) is a masterpiece of Hungarian Rococo. It features the coat of arms of the county of Heves, together with those of the bishop who commissioned the work, surrounded by vine leaves and grapes. More fanciful is the stork holding a serpent in its mouth. A statue of Saint Stephen, Hungary's patron saint and first crowned king, stands in benediction beside a fountain (facing page, right), which—fed by an underground stream—provides cool water all year round.

Franz Anton Maulbertsch. It was one of the very last works he produced. The most spectacular part of the Lyceum, however, is the sumptuous library, with a trompe l'oeil ceiling fresco by Johann Lukas Kracker representing the Council of Trent (1545–63), a symbol of the supreme authority of the Roman Catholic Church. Bishop Eszterházy's collection of books initially numbered 20,000 volumes; today there are 130,000.

A climb to the top of the tower brings the visitor to a room that serves as a camera obscura. Light coming through a small hole in the roof is reflected by a play of mirrors onto the walls, projecting a panoramic image of the city all around you. The sight of the town deployed in front of your eyes is truly amazing: the immense neoclassical basilica appears in its entirety, along with the spires of the Minorite Church, the bishop's gardens, the castle and its powerful walls, and the Lyceum itself. The dark streets and bright monuments form a living portrait of the city, with pedestrians strolling past buildings and people going about their daily business. The view is well worth the effort of climbing and descending the steep set of stairs.

Before stopping to eat in one of Eger's many restaurants, take a short detour to the County Hall (Megyeháza) to admire the elaborate ironwork of the main gate created in 1758 by the German blacksmith Heinrik Fazola for Bishop Eger Barkóczy. The nearby White Deer restaurant (Fehérszarvas Étterem) is a good place to eat. The service is friendly, the regional wine list extensive, and the cuisine inventive, with specialties such as smoked trout with lemon and apples, accompanied by an Egri Leányka 2001, or venison fillet with mushrooms and cranberries, served with a Cabernet Sauvignon 2000 from Tibor Gál. If you decide to spend a second night in Eger, the Garden of Talismans and Tulips Restaurant (Talizmán-Tulipánkert Étterem) is another well-known restaurant, and comes as an especially welcome sight after a long day of exploring the city or the nearby vineyards. It's located in a neighborhood known as the Valley of Beautiful Women (Szépasszony völgy), which is a short way from the center. The streets end in vineyards, creating a decidedly rural atmosphere in the midst of the city. The restaurant's sommelier can suggest a large selection of wines as part of a sampler meal created so that diners can taste the various wines produced in the region.

You don't need to make a long stop in Miskolc, the large industrial city in the northeast region of the country, but the baths in the natural caves of Miskolc-Tapoica are definitively worth a detour. With their turquoise-blue waters (beautifully lit up) and walls of sheer rock, you might think you were swimming in a cave on a Mediterranean island. Every Sunday the baths are crowded with people who come here for a dip before taking a stroll through the public park that surrounds the site.

On leaving Eger continue northeast to the industrial city of Miskolc, whose main tourist attraction is the thermal resort of Miskolc-Tapolca (Termál Barlangfürdu), containing bathing grottoes and several interconnected warm-water pools. It's a temple of kitsch, where gargoyles spew out water over bathers and a statue of Venus emerges from the pool in the main lobby, decorated with colorful tiles. A large, well-maintained public garden outside the baths provides a more natural setting.

The old city of Sárospatak, beyond Miskolc in the direction of the Ukrainian border, is worth a longer stay. Its history is similar to that of Eger; it, too, was a stronghold struggling to maintain its Hungarian identity throughout the centuries of Ottoman occupation and reconquest by the Habsburg dynasty. It is the birthplace of Saint Elizabeth (Szent Erzsébet) of Hungary and became part of the royal domain in the eleventh century. It then entered a prosperous period when the arrival of Italian merchant families stimulated the town's development. The Rákóczi family owned a fortified castle and large estates here until Ferenc Rákóczi II, prince of Transylvania, was forced to flee his domains in the late seventeenth century. This was during the wars against the Turks when Rákóczi entered the struggle between those who supported the alliance with Austria and the nationalists who wanted to recreate the Hungarian state once the Ottomans were defeated. Rákóczi, a patriot, led a rebellion against the Habsburgs and fought the Austrian army for nearly eight years, from 1703 to 1711. Ultimately defeated, he fled to Russia, to Poland, and then to the court of Louis XIV of France, who had supported his efforts for a time as a way of opposing the Habsburgs. Rákóczi was to die, twenty-five years later, on the shores of the Sea of Marmara near Istanbul, after requesting asylum from the Ottoman court.

Look carefully at the statues of Sárospatak in the streets leading up to the castle of the Rákóczi princes—as well as historical figures you'll find a group of tipsy drinkers, a reminder that Sárospatak lies at the center of the Tokay wine route.

Rákóczi's unusual destiny still feeds the local legends of this Hungarian province, which was detached from Transylvania and became part of Romania in the wake of the Treaty of Versailles. In his time, the prince promoted the vineyards on his lands and helped to establish the fame of the Tokay vintage by sending bottles of the wine to the court of the Russian czar as well as to the king of France. The Rákóczi castle is an impressive dwelling that combines medieval, Renaissance, and Baroque architecture; the loggia and courtyard in particular show the influence of Italian style. The fifteenth-century keep offers a remarkable view of the town of Sárospatak nestled below in a bend of the Bodrob River, a tributary of the Tisza, and over the gardens stretching out between the moat and the castle enclosure. Old trees encircled with iron railings, creeping tamarisk, and large ash trees form a lush setting around the old castle and the traditional houses below. The castle itself contains some lovely pieces, including elegant Renaissance furniture, a Turkish room lined with glazed green ceramic tiles, and large rooms such as the banquet hall with wide windows and a loggia from which the prince could greet his guests.

Architectural traditions remain strong in Sárospatak, sometimes called the "Hungarian Athens" because it has been dedicated to the arts and learning since medieval times. For instance, buildings in the contemporary Organic style carry hints of the superb Renaissance detailing of the Rákóczi castle.

Sárospatak is a small town with pleasant strolls by the river and along the wide, shaded streets. The library of the Calvinist College (Református Kollégium) is one of the largest in Hungary, with some 20,000 volumes in a number of different languages: Greek, Hebrew, Latin, and Hungarian. The town has long been an intellectual center. In 1568, the principality of Transylvania was the first European state to enact laws guaranteeing religious freedom. Protestantism, which spread through much of this part of Europe, gained a hold in Sárospatak, which has been called the "Hungarian Cambridge" and the "Athens of Hungary." In the seventeenth century the Rákóczi family used their own printing press to publish works by the Czech humanist and scholar János Comenius, who wanted to reorganize teaching methods in this part of the country.

As well as old buildings, there are many fine examples of contemporary architecture in the town, and several recent buildings have been praised for their original designs. In the 1980s, the famous architect Imre Makóvecz created the highly acclaimed Cultural Center (Muveludési Háza) in what is sometimes termed the Organic style. Children's outdoor games, totem poles, and wooden sculptures are dotted all around the building, in an architectural statement that affirms the vision of an urban life in

which nature, wood, and artistic design are essential elements. Somewhat farther away is the teachers' training college (Tanító Képzu Intézet), one of the finest examples of early-twentieth-century Secession and Art Nouveau style in the region. The exuberant yet classical lines are a tribute to Hungarian diversity and imagination.

Sárospatak is one of the capitals of Tokay wines, and is home to many wine producers. It is a great point from which to start a tour of the surrounding Tokay region.

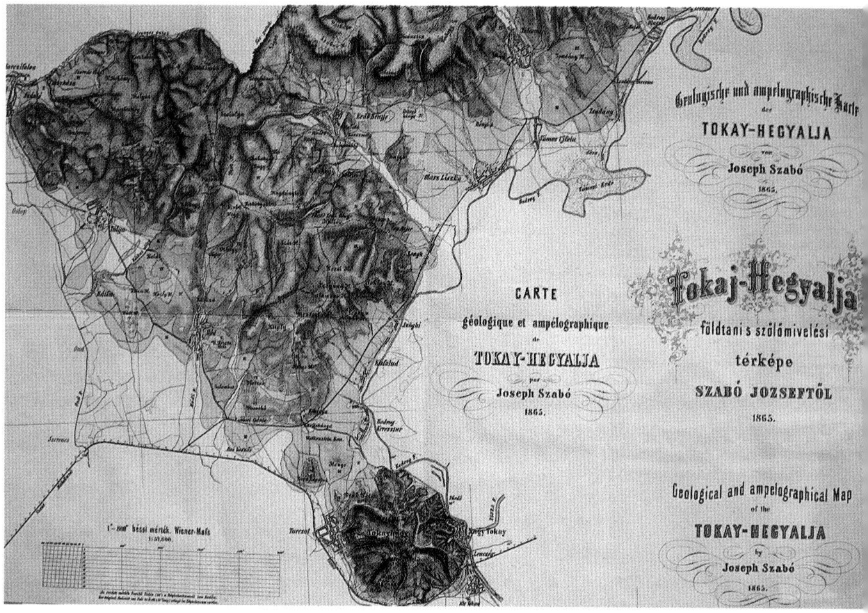

The secret of Tokay wines

Tokay—"wine of freedom," according to the title of a recent book by László Alkonyi—is the pure expression of the land of the same name that has always been famous for the quality of its wine. Hungarian historians believe that Tokay was probably the center of Attila the Hun's empire in the fifth century, and legend has it that he chose this area for its vineyards, which were already producing fine wines. During medieval times, Tokay wines were exported throughout all of Europe. Although the Turks never controlled Tokay itself, wine production nevertheless declined during the Ottoman occupation of Hungary. In the second half of the sixteenth century, a new Protestant aristocracy emerged in the principality of Transylvania, which—as we have seen—had considerable impact on intellectual and commercial affairs. During the seventeenth century, Prince Ferenc Rákóczi II organized a vast sales and distribution network for the wines of Tokay.

The famous mold *Botrytis cinerea*, often known as "noble rot," occurs in grapes that are left long on the vine. Winemakers discovered by accident that grapes harvested late in the season, after they had contracted the mold, produce a sweet wine. The Tokay winemakers gradually improved their vinification techniques, and the Tokay Aszú (*aszú* being the Hungarian word for the mold) acquired a unique reputation. By the early eighteenth century, when the remote province of Transylvania had become part of the Austrian Empire, the wine cellars of most of the courts of Europe, including those of Louis XIV, Peter the Great of Russia, Frederick the Great of Prussia, and Gustav III of Sweden held considerable reserves of this valuable wine. The French king praised it during a dinner at Versailles in 1703, held in honor of Prince Rákóczi, with a statement that could be taken as an advertising slogan: "The wine of kings and the king of wines" (*Vinum regnum, Rex vinorum*). The wine's reputation was made from this point on, and not only among royal patrons. The literati were also fervent admirers: Voltaire, Diderot, Goethe, and Alexandre Dumas all praised the virtues of this elixir. And so did churchmen. When Pope Benedict XIV received several bottles of Tokay Aszú from the Austrian Empress Maria Theresa, he exclaimed: "Blessed is the queen who sends this to me, blessed in the land from which it was created, and blessed am I, who drink it." It became part of papal tradition; Pope Pius IV also expressed his enthusiasm for Tokay: "This is a wine fit for a pope."

The *eszencia*, or "essence"—the juice produced by grapes affected by the "noble rot" and stored for some time in vats—used to be sold in pharmacies for its medicinal properties. This golden sweet wine has a delicate and exceptional balance of sweetness and acidity and can age for a long time in barrels. In an earlier age, it did not have any of the unpleasant aftereffects of many other white wines. It was even

The region around the hillsides of Tokay, the *Tokajhegyalja*, stretches across the southern slopes of the Zemplén Mountains. Famous winemakers such as the Château Pajzos have replanted the old vineyards with the appellation's traditional grapes. But the weather plays the decisive role in producing the "noble rot" (*botrytis*), which is the secret to the greatest Tokay wines. Winemakers store the *exzenci*, or "essence," of these grapes in translucent bottles.

recommended by doctors as a treatment for gastric or nervous disorders. The wine came to be intimately linked with the turbulent history of this part of Europe; its fortunes rose during times of peace and fell during times of war.

Today, the Tokay wine region is organized into several large domains. In the last ten years, these owners have invested considerable sums in modernizing production and vinification equipment. Smaller vineyards are also open to innovation, but these winemakers above all are dedicated to producing wines according to traditional methods. These consist of steeping the *aszú* grapes in a dry white wine and letting it age in partially filled old oak barrels for several years. The wine is obtained after filtering. The Tokay Aszú oxidizes slowly in contact with air and the wine takes on the characteristically smoky taste of yellow or "straw" wines.

But the range of wines produced in the Tokay region is not limited to sweet wines; indeed, the same domain may contain vineyards that face in different directions, so that the cellar master is able to create a diverse selection of labels each year: the eminent Tokay Aszú, the sweet or dry Tokay *szamorodni* (blended wines made with grapes that have achieved different states of maturity), late single varietal harvests, and blended or varietal dry white wines. The Tokay Aszú wines themselves include eight different names, each characterized by the quantity of residual sugars and the vinification process used. There exist the Aszú with three, four, five, or six *puttony* (a *puttony* is a bucket containing 136 liters of the *aszú* grapes that are added to the barrel of wine or fermenting must); the *aszú eszencia;* and even the pure *eszencia*; as well as wines from second pressings such as the *máslás* and the *fordítás*. With all this in mind, it is understandable why it is hard to obtain a clear and simple overview of the Tokay wines.

After visiting the extraordinary underground galleries that form the Rákóczi cellars in Tokay, a wine tasting and lively discussion with the cellar master rounds off your enjoyment (preceding pages). The cellars of Úri Borok in Mád, run by a young winemaker, are more modest in size but are also characteristic of the region.

Mount Tokay, the hill that overlooks the village of Tokay, is one of the most remarkable sites of the wine region. Swept by the winds from the great plain that are checked by the Zemplén mountain range, this hill (slightly over 1,600 feet/500 meters high) has been covered over the centuries by sediments of loess, clay, and limestone. These layers form an excellent filter for rainwater and retain the mineral salts that vines need to grow well. The Bodrog River flows into the Tisza at the foot of the hill, and the morning fog that forms in autumn over these rivers favors the early development of the *botrytis* mold. Villages near Mount Tokay—Tarcal, Bodrogkeresztúr, Mád, and, of course, Tokay, along with Tállya farther to the north—constitute some of the best grape-growing land in the Tokay appellation. Domains such as Disznóku, Hétszulu, István Szepsy, Gróf Degenfeld, Royal Tokay Wine Company, János Arvay, and Vince Gergely (*Úri borok*), to name a few of the best known, offer wines of exceptional quality.

Traveling toward the northeast along the banks of the Bodrog, you'll come across another group of remarkable villages that also stand out in this appellation: Tolcsva, Erdubénye, and Erduhorváti. Here the volcanic soil and harsher climate require sturdier varieties of grapes. The wines of Oremus, Château Pajzos, and the Cooperative of Tokay (Kereskeduház) are appreciated far and wide. Finally, the wines produced by Château Megyer, near Sárospatak, situated on clay and limestone soil, are extremely diverse and are characterized by a generous bouquet. A number of these domains have combined their marketing operations in order to make the most of the new opportunities provided by Hungary's approaching entry into the enlarged European Union as well as the opening up of new markets in Asia. Château Megyer and Château Pajzos now operate under a single management structure. With nearly 420 acres (170 hectares), this enterprise is now the leading domain within the appellation.

The winds that blow across the Great Plain, picking up particles of soil, deposit their load on the Tokay hillsides. This sedimentary loess, laid down over the centuries, forms an arid soil that is ideal for growing certain local varieties of grapes, such as the *furmint* and the *hárslevelű*. Many young vines have been planted on the Hétszulu domain (formerly the Emperor's Domain until its privatization in 1991) on the hillsides of Mount Tokay. You will find the Rákóczi cellars behind a lovely iron gate in the village. One of the bottles used for the sweet *aszú* wine stands on an immense vat. The owners of the Dessewffy castle have just restored the building as a guesthouse.

The mountainous region in the northeast, the foothills of the Carpathian Mountains, is full of surprises. Village life revolves around the wine industry, and tradition remains strong; children still learn the folk dances that Bartók recorded one hundred years ago.
In Hollóku, a village in the Cserhát Mountains, a clarinet player gives an impromptu performance of the old folk songs played during village festivals. Nothing seems brash or out of place in the villages of the Zemplén Mountains; the one-story homes are ocher in color and often have arched verandas overlooking small gardens or simple wooden sculptures.

To begin to understand the mystery of the Tokay appeal you should visit some of the main wine cellars. Many have miles of galleries dating from medieval times, and the vaulted ceilings above the long lines of barrels are covered in a thick gray mold produced by the evaporation of the esters contained in the aging wines. The bacteria in the air are important factors in maintaining the correct atmospheric conditions for the wine; they also amplify the tones of smoked wood, candied fruit, and spices that are the distinguishing mark of the great Tokay Aszú wines. The historic cellars of the Rákóczy in Tokay (Hétszulu) and in Sárospatak (Château Megyer), or the more modern Disznóku in Mád are particularly impressive. Visitors can enjoy wine tastings conducted by highly qualified cellar masters and winemakers. The passion of those who make the wine is transmitted to those who drink it, because when you taste a Tokay wine you are absorbing the centuries of patience, expertise, and love devoted to the creation of one of the best wines in the world.

Exploring the Carpathians

The mountainous region that stretches from Budapest to the borders of Slovakia and the Ukraine is one of the most untamed areas of Hungary. Hungarians themselves view this region as a place to rediscover nature and participate in outdoor activities. Strong cultural traditions survive in villages that are remote from major routes. At Easter, for example, or during harvest festivals, traditional celebrations are still a vital part of village life.

The succession of hills, villages, and deep forests extending from the Zemplén hills around Tokay to Hollóku in the Cserhát range are a particularly attractive landscape. The wine lover who wanders from one village to another across the Tokaji Hegyalja, as the region between Sárospatak and Tokay is known, will be surprised by an unending stream of fresh discoveries.

At Tolcsva there is a wine museum with a number of extremely old bottles of *aszú*, known for their capacity to age well: a recent wine auction in London featured several bottles of Tokay Aszú brought up from a nineteenth-century shipwreck and apparently still quite drinkable. In Tolcsva there is, next to the former castle of the Rákóczys, a Baroque chapel; it is topped with a wooden turret decorated with the kind of arches that are typical of the Hungarian Uplands. But the real highlight for the visitor is the remarkable restaurant us Kaján, recently remodeled and opened by a French couple who have chosen to live in the Hungarian countryside. After working for a time selling wines, Pascal decided to settle down in the midst of a vineyard. With his wife Anna, he purchased a series of farmhouses, which they decorated, blending their own personal taste with the traditional style of the region. The restaurant contains a series of rooms each of which is in a different style—bourgeois, Bohemian, rustic—and the objects and paintings in each room are for sale. The quality of the food is equal to the meticulous interior décor, and diners flock here from neighboring towns, and even from as far away as Budapest and abroad.

From Tolcsva, the road winds through vineyards toward the village of Erdubénye. The *hárslevelu* grape grows well on the steep slopes of the Zemplén hills, a testimony to mankind's obstinate efforts to

It takes some time to get to know the Tokay wines. Only after you can distinguish one grape variety from another, understand the subtle distinctions in the gradation of the sweet wines, and fully appreciate the late grape harvests, will the vineyards start to reveal their mysteries. The vineyard owners are happy to help you on this quest for knowledge. Over the last decade the Disznóku domain, at the western edge of the appellation, has invested considerable sums in reviving this traditional *grand cru*. The wine cellar (left, bottom) is a technological and aesthetic success—the architect's concern for design has even extended to the tractor barn (left, top). Sometimes a traditional home, or *kurya* (facing page), sits amid the vineyards, awaiting the arrival of craftsmen to bring it back to life.

cultivate difficult land that nonetheless produces a remarkable wine. Erdubénye is certainly the most well-maintained town in the region. The houses are tastefully decorated with old tiles, and the attractive colonnaded entranceways are sometimes covered with vines. From time to time you can catch a glimpse of a lovely garden through the gates. There is a series of graphically naive wooden sculptures near the church: one depicts Saint George slaying a mildly ferocious dragon; another portrays a tender-looking queen with bent head; a third is of a languid Margita. During religious celebrations, the young girls of the village, wearing colorful costumes, dance to music performed by a small band of local musicians, one of whom plays the *ütugordon*, a large stringed instrument; he uses the bow to sound the strings and also to strike the heavy wooden body, which resonates like a percussion instrument.

Be sure to visit Tokay itself to admire the vineyards that climb up the hillside overlooking the small town. Stroll along the pedestrian streets lined with brightly colored Baroque houses and take a look at the Bodrog River—at times peaceful, at times tumultuous—just beyond the historic center. There is a landing stage here for the small comfortable boats that ply the river as far as Sárospatak in the spring and summer. Flocks of colorful birds take flight at the noise of the engines and you may see a beaver or an otter swimming silently in the rippling green water near the docks.

The road from Tokay to the village of Mád runs alongside the Disznók vineyards. The cellars were constructed in 1995 by the architect Dezsu Ekler in the Organic style, and are a technical and aesthetic marvel. Call in for a simple but delicious lunch at the Yellow House (Sárga Ház). Afterward, the friendly cellar master, László Mészáros, will take you on a tour of the production facilities. Although Mád does not have any exceptional sights, it does have a certain appeal. People have begun to rebuild some of the old abandoned homes and to repaint their colorful façades; you get the sense that everyone wants to spruce up this small town and return it to its former splendor, when it was among the most famous towns in the Tokay appellation. The vine growers work their land with this aim in mind, and early results are already visible in cellars like that of Vince Gergely, which fosters a blend of tradition and modernity. Here the "noble rot" creeps over everything so that winemaking equipment and any other stone and metal objects seem as one with the walls, which the mold has attacked for centuries. Treasures slumber in the barrels of *eszencia* and the bottles of *aszú-eszencia*.

One of the most beautiful roads in Hungary crosses the mountains to the north. From Miskolc, it leads to Eger, then Hollóku, the loveliest way round, but also the longest. The Bükk National Park (Bükki Nemzeti Park) stretches over a vast tract of forest north of Eger. The best way to reach the park is to take the road from Miskolc past the lovely medieval Diósgyur castle, unfortunately in a very run-down part of town. Constructed in the time of the Angevin dynasty during the fourteenth century, the castle later played a major role in Ferenc Rákóczi's independence uprising. It was then left empty and fell into ruins; restored in the last few decades, it now hosts folkloric events and cultural performances.

Farther along, a huge enchanting castle rises up on the banks of a lake. This is one of Hungary's most spectacular hotels, the Palace (Palota) Hotel. The best way to see this immense building is to head toward Szilvásvárad. Some little way farther on, the palace suddenly appears out of nowhere, standing tall over the calm water of the lake. If you want to see the entire building, go around behind it to get a sense of its size, then view it from the well-tended small rock garden. Every possible style seems to be mixed together in this hotel, which was built between the two World Wars as a tribute to the provinces lost under the terms of the Treaty of Versailles. It combines Renaissance, Baroque, and Ottoman influences—the latter in the form of a Turkish bath—with a gabled façade that would look well in Bruges,

One of the most romantic hotels in all of Hungary is located in the beech-covered Bükk Mountains. The Palota de Lillafüred Hotel was built between the two World Wars in a style consciously harking back to the Greater Hungary that existed before 1914, and its stained-glass windows record some of the most glorious events in the country's history. The lobbies, dining rooms, and the rear façade are a riot of medieval styles, resembling a Hollywood movie set. The towers of the hotel cast a somewhat sinister shadow onto the calm waters of the lake.

The medieval castle of Diósgyur stands proudly at the edge of the Bükk Mountains. Once surrounded by forest, it belonged to the Angevin dynasty, which held the crown of Hungary in the fourteenth century.
In Szilvásvárad, Lippizaner horses walk freely through the streets to their stables after giving a dazzling dressage display in the riding ring. A flock of noisy geese by the roadside is a reminder of Hungary's great gastronomical traditions.

a bell tower, and domes—all these features making reference to the diverse religions of Hungary. Walk along the road for extraordinary views of the forest.

When the beeches start to turn gold in the fall, you can see a sea of trees swept by the strong north winds. The trees sway, the leaves are scattered, and you may catch sight of a large deer springing across the road. The sun plays hide-and-seek with the clouds, and in the winter, the bare branches of the large beeches cast geometric patterns of shade across the footpaths. Down below, you may spot a light green field of alfalfa that stands out brightly against the hillsides. Virtually no one lives in this vast expanse of trees, and there are no houses—an occasional observation tower is the only sign of any human presence. As you walk through these mountains, you'll feel as if you're exploring the birthplace of mankind itself, faced with an untamed and sometimes hostile environment.

This is also a region of horses. When traveling through Szilvásvárad, don't be surprised to see a procession of Lippizaners blocking the entire street. They have probably just finished a performance in one of the riding schools, where future buyers come to judge their qualities. Elsewhere, near the forest, a carnival-like atmosphere reigns as carriages, drawn by two, three, and even up to seven horses, trot along the paths. (There is also a charming small train from Szilvásvárad that winds through the area.) The owners of the horses and carriages, along with their stable boys, give their horses lots of tender loving care; the animals are brushed to a lustrous sheen and curried regularly, and are magnificently decked out with burnished leather harnesses. They are trained to race or perform in equestrian shows. The Hungarians' love of horses goes back to the days of the country's earliest defense. The passion continues to this day—you can see it reflected in the sparkling eyes of young children as they admiringly watch the impressive steeds pass by.

The small town of Parád in the Mátra Hills is another famous equestrian center. But before going there, make a detour to see the well-preserved limestone and red-sandstone Romanesque abbey of Bélapátfalva, which stands on the top of a limestone cliff. The Cistercians usually chose isolated sites for their austere churches. The simple architectural motifs—ornamental foliage on the main doors, rose windows on the façade—underscore the majesty of the structure. Three crosses, bearing painted wood sculptures of Christ and the two thieves, standing isolated amid this grandiose landscape, accentuates the feeling of abandonment and vulnerability. When the composer Hector Berlioz was traveling through this region of Europe in 1846, he was struck by exactly this feeling and later wrote words for Faust describing the emotion he had felt:

Immense, impenetrable, and proud Nature,
You alone can soothe my endless ennui...
Yes, blow, hurricanes, cry, deep forests,
Collapse, rocks, torrents, hurl down your waters!

It's worth making the effort to climb up the mule track leading to the ruins of the castle at Sirok, which once controlled the pass where the Bükk and Mátra ranges meet. From this eagle's nest, on a clear day, you'll be rewarded with a marvelous view of much of the Hungarian Uplands.

In the Mátra Hills near Budapest a large number of paths run through the unspoiled forests, especially in the region of Mátraalja. From Recsk, the road winds through the chain of mountains. The small thermal spa of Parádfürdu is just one of many hot springs dotted throughout these mountains. The large building at the entrance to the town is a spa hotel, the Erzsébet Királyné Park Hotel, constructed in 1893. Its architectural style looks as if it were borrowed from the Normandy coast of France, with its immense

The Mátra Mountains near Budapest are a great place to enjoy nature and wildlife. Although the major paths are signposted, it's easy to get lost in the deep forests—all landmarks quickly disappear if you decide to follow the track of a deer through the undergrowth. The beech trees lose their leaves in October, and the autumn sun sculpts a sharply defined relief on the steeply sloping hills. The Bélapátvatva Abbey, at the crossroads of forest, fields, and cliffs, is one of the very few Romanesque buildings to have survived in Hungary, a country that was in almost constant turmoil from the fifteenth century to the Baroque age. The exterior is built with alternating red and white bands of stone, and a rose window casts light into the dim nave.

This church with a traditional wooden bell tower, characteristic of country churches in the Palóc region, is situated in the center of the small village of Hollóku. Its simple, unadorned structure reflects a deeply rooted but understated piety.

half-timbered façade with wooden balconies facing the garden. The covered porch, however, is a traditional element of Transylvanian architecture. The interior has been recently restored to meet the standards of a clientele that has become increasingly demanding in terms of the services expected from an establishment of this sort. Other buildings nearby have been renovated. One, a château that once belonged to the Károlyi family, later became a sanatorium, then a retirement home. The majestic building was meant to reflect the power of this family of magnates, one of whom was the president of the short-lived liberal Republic set up in 1945. Inside the gardens is an evocative manor house called Zsuzsannalak, or "Susanne's home." Without knowing the history of this building, it is easy to imagine that it was built for a woman loved by one of the former lords of the manor.

Parádfürdu is gradually being restored to its former state, as is the nearby town of Parád, famous for its Carriage Museum (Kocsimúzeum). Housed in the stables that formerly belonged to Count Károlyi (Cifra Istálló), this elegant building is enclosed with a covered brick entry and has three wings, each with a square corner tower. All the roofs were retiled using old tiles from the region. Here again, the use of wood in the façade gives a particularly welcoming look to the building. The whole panoply of Hungarian horse-drawn vehicles is displayed inside (the English word "coach" comes from the Hungarian *kocsi*). Among the various calashes, wagons, and coaches, some of the more unusual vehicles include the carriage constructed to carry the president of the parliament at Hungary's Millennium celebrations in Budapest in 1896. Created by the Kölber Brothers Company, it was decorated with great taste—as revealed by a recent restoration—and the politicians riding inside it must have found it comfortable.

Visitors to the region can now enjoy top-notch hotels. The recently opened, luxury Karolyi Kasteli Hotel in Parádsasvár, for example, may be somewhat overdone, but it is a charming establishment that deserves its five-star rating. Before returning to the plain, make a trip to the top of Hungary, to the town of Galyatetu, for one last look at these mountain ranges.

The Cserhát hills are smaller; indeed, their highest point barely exceeds 1,600 feet (500 meters). All the same, the small villages scattered throughout these hills have retained authentic traces of their local culture and *palóc* traditions, especially in embroidery and vernacular building styles, which survive in a number of places. The village of Hollókö, for example, demonstrates a firm determination to preserve and promote its unique regional identity. The gentle landscapes of the Cserhát hills form a perfect backdrop to this charming village of a hundred or so homes, which is now on the UNESCO World Heritage list. The main street is lined with large sandstone paving stones; the spic-and-span homes, all remarkably well preserved with attractive, tidy gardens, are painted an immaculate white, standing out against the corbelled roofs covered in dovetailed tiles.

A good place to stop after visiting the village is the Geranium Inn (Muskátli Vendéglu). You'll find delicious traditional dishes such as *palóc leves* (a filling mutton and vegetable soup) and *babgulyás* (beef and bean soup). *Hortobágyi palacsinta*, a meat-filled crêpe, is a good choice after these filling first courses, and you may want to top it all off with a *túróslepény* (yeast bread with cheese topping).

If you decide to continue into the heart of the Cserhát hills to discover the hidden treasures of the villages of this protected region, you should stop at the small village of Szirák, where you can stay in the magnificently renovated hotel belonging to the family of the Count Teleki-Degengeld. An imposing porch leads to spacious rooms, and the staff is welcoming and attentive. The castle's reception room is decorated with pencil sketches illustrating the poems of Ovid. This region is not known for bringing together regional popular art with the Rococo style of the large manor houses, but this hotel has achieved a perfect balance between the two.

In the villages of Parádfüred and Párad in the Mátra Mountains some of the elegant buildings that once belonged to the Károlyi family have been restored. The family château has been transformed into a retirement home (above); a manor house and the stables have been renovated and now form a Carriage Museum (facing page, far right, top).

The village of Hollóku is on the list of UNESCO World Heritage Sites for the unspoiled completeness of its traditional architecture. Its well-kept homes, covered with ancient overlapping tiles and set amid flower-filled gardens, provide a real taste of the rural life of the old Hungary.

LAKE BALATON: THE "HUNGARIAN SEA"

The region around Lake Balaton is a world of light and water. Sunlight plays on the waters of the lake, and sheds its evening glow on the carts that make their way home across the fields. Strings of paprika drying in the sun and colorful embroidered fabrics also add bright splashes of color.

The region of Lake Balaton, Central Europe's largest lake, seems to reflect the Hungarian soul better than any other part of the country. Its history and geography are interwoven with national traditions and culture. People have lived beside the lake for more than forty thousand years, and legend has it that the shores of the lake were the farthest point of the Magyars' westward advance in the ninth century. As far back as Roman times, colonists planted vines on the hills around the lake, which they knew as *Lacus Pelso*. The Slavs called it *Blatno* (stagnant marshy water), which became Lake Balaton. During the Middle Ages, many Romanesque abbeys and churches were built around the lake, some traces of which remain today despite the ravages of the Mongol and Ottoman invasions, and even the Habsburg reconquest.

Apart from the great lake itself there are smaller lakes such the Belsõ-tó, famous spas like Héviz, and little rivers that irrigate the region. Lake Balaton first became a vacation resort in the late-eighteenth century after the first spa was built in Héviz in 1795. From the 1820s onward, people went in ever-increasing numbers to take the waters at Balaton. The lake has also attracted yachtsmen for over a hundred years. Hungarian artists and members of the middle class aspired to settle among the great aristocratic estates around its shores, the most famous of which is the Festetics Castle at Keszthely. Any excursion along the lake's volcanic northern shoreline is bound to include a tour of these manor houses, which were renovated with loving care both during the Communist period and after the change of regime.

The area around Lake Balaton is part of the story of modern Hungary. Many Hungarian intellectuals now flee the polluted atmosphere of Budapest on the weekend and head for their weekend residences in one of the villages in the Káli Basin or around the little town of Szigliget, and the region is full of memories for the generation currently in office. In their dissident days, they played hide-and-seek here with the police of the János Kádár regime (sometimes their own fathers). They took part in many a risky venture, such as hiding a duplicating machine in the reeds, escaping dawn police raids through the back door of the family house, then sailing across the lake or meeting with friends at hideouts among the vineyards. For several generations of Hungarian intellectuals, Lake Balaton is therefore the stuff of legend.

Central Europeans have also long appreciated this "Hungarian Sea," coming here to enjoy the atmosphere of a seaside vacation. During the 1980s, East Germans used to meet their cousins from the West here, in what they considered to be a little Socialist paradise. During the summer of 1989, East German vacationers at Lake Balaton who wanted to cross to the West exerted such pressure on the Austro-Hungarian border that the Hungarian regime began to dismantle the once impermeable barriers, thereby signaling the rapid collapse of the Iron Curtain.

The lake shores are so spacious and varied that a whole range of sporting and leisure activities are possible there, from swimming, sailing, and fishing, to hiking in the hills and wine tasting. Lake Balaton is 48 miles (77 km) long from east to west. It is one mile (1.5 km) wide at its narrowest part, opposite the Tihany peninsula, and 8.5 miles (14 km) at its broadest, in its eastern stretches. The average depth is from 11.5 to 13 feet (3.5–4 m); it reaches its maximum depth of 36 feet (11 m) off the Tihany peninsula, at a spot that fishermen call the "Tihany Well." The regular hours of bright sunshine in this region heat the water to temperatures pleasant for swimming—between 73 °F (23 °C) and 79 °F (26 °C)—during the summer months, but Lake Balaton is also famous for the sudden, violent storms that sweep it from the northwest. Yellow flashing beacons warn vacationers that violent winds are forecast, changing to red when a storm is on its way.

The Lake Balaton region is an ideal destination for vacationers and tourists. Visitors can enjoy a taste of country life in the beautifully renovated local houses on the northern shore. The roads leading to the lake are dotted with restaurants or places of historical interest to visit before enjoying a swim in the lake or in the famous warm-water springs.

When strolling among the ancient trees in the landscaped grounds of the Pusztaszámor mansion, you arrive at a small lake. A strategically-placed bench is an invitation to sit and dream, as you contemplate a white neoclassical temple that casts its dazzling reflection on the water.

The attractive façade of the Pusztaszámor mansion gives onto the garden of this welcoming guest house.

Toward the lake and the Balaton region

The Budapest-Balaton highway takes you past Lake Velence (Velencei tó), which is another favorite weekend destination for city dwellers of all ages in search of a place to cool off away from the heat and stress of the city. Nearby, a dead-end road leads to the peaceful village of Pusztazámor, which is less frequented by tourists. On the roadside at the entrance to the village, a wooden Virgin looks out calmly from her bell-tower niche. The mansion built by the Barcza family in 1870 on eighteenth-century foundations is hidden from view. This property has been recently renovated and tastefully converted into an inn by its owner. The spacious lounge has English furniture, a beautiful positive organ, and many tasteful objects that have been collected by the current owner of the property. Its warm, family atmosphere is perfect for a relaxing weekend on the journey between Budapest and Lake Balaton. Each room has its own distinctive charm, but all are furnished in Biedermeier style and face a garden that slopes gently down to a little lake where guests can swim. On an island in the lake is a small neoclassic temple, a surprising but harmonious addition to this property with its air of elegant simplicity. The owner takes great care of his guests, and will organize concerts, wedding parties, or custom-designed tours of the region if asked. Gourmets will relish the elegant breakfast menu and, if necessary, you can arrange for a caterer to send in meals. This is one of the most highly recommended places to stay in Hungary today; it provides a delightful departure-point for guests wanting to explore Transdanubia and the Lake Balaton region.

Less than 30 miles (50 km) along the highway, west of Pusztazámor, Székesfehérvár, the former capital of Hungary, is well worth exploring. Industrial developments now surround it, but the old town is steeped in history and tradition. Saint Stephen, descendant of Árpád, the shadowy Magyar chieftain of national legend, established his dynasty on the marshes here around 998, and the kings of Hungary were crowned in this capital for almost five centuries, until Buda asserted its supremacy. In the heart of the old town on Coronation Square (Koronázó tér), where the royal basilica once stood, is the Bishop's Palace, one of the Hungary's most striking Baroque buildings. This type of architecture is actually known as *copf*, a Central European variation on the earlier Baroque style, dating from the late eighteenth and early nineteenth centuries. One of its distinguishing features is an abundant use of garlands as decorative motifs. From the palace, there is a stunning view over the town, featuring several impressive religious buildings, the Town Hall, and a beautiful house ornamented with finely worked stucco decoration as well as a magnificent Rococo corner balcony.

Opposite the beautiful Baroque Cistercian church, the Black Eagle Pharmacy (Fekete Sas patika) is likewise definitely worth a visit. The Jesuits built it in 1730, and it now houses a charming little museum containing an extraordinary collection of medicinal flasks, phials, pillboxes, and various other pharmaceutical containers, the oldest of which date from its foundation. The magnificently carved furniture is the work of Jesuits. Gilded cherubs in a wooden niche seem to keep a kindly yet protective watch over the premises. Beautiful items of pottery decorated with delicate traditional motifs are for sale at very reasonable prices at this delightful historical monument.

The royal town of Székesfehérvár is worth a prolonged visit. Step through its baroque doorways into fantasy worlds such as that of the Doll Museum. Tall, colored steeples harmonize with the walls of the town's historic buildings.

Also worthy of interest is the Doll Museum (Baba Múzeum) on the Megyeház utca, a steep old street lined with eighteenth-century houses. Each item in the museum is a unique and faithful replica of the everyday costumes and customs of a particular historical period. Porcelain figures and beautiful doll's furniture are arranged to create an extraordinary variety of charming scenes: a little girl's tea party, at which a small dog is devouring sausages stolen from the guests; a stylish lady trying on hats at her mirror; a melancholy girl playing the guitar; feverish preparations for an elegant, aristocratic ball. The evolution of Hungarian interiors over two centuries is represented here—a pleasant way for interested visitors to discover how the Hungarian middle classes lived in the late eighteenth century, or the extravagant lifestyle enjoyed by noble families at the time of the Austro-Hungarian Compromise in 1867. There are also touching scenes such as the sailor's return to his family after months, or maybe even years, away at sea, or the bride and groom at the altar. The perfect condition and accuracy of detail in this collection make this museum one of the most remarkable sources of information about daily life in Hungary, both past and present.

After visiting Székesfehérvár, take time for a refreshing break at a traditional country inn (*csárda*) on the road to Budapest. The fashionable Szárcsa csárda is one of those that do justice to Hungarian

5.

The Art Nouveau ornamentation of a storefront intrigues passersby in a street in the old center of Székesfehérvár. The fabrics displayed in the window are echoed on a panel which features a graceful dancer dressed in a gold-embroidered costume. Above the store sign is a sprightly elf, against a background of flowers.

The Black Eagle pharmacy (Fekete Sas) in the heart of Székesfehérvár is one of the oldest in the country. When its ornate shutters and doors are open, you can admire the mysterious powders, herbs, and ointments that apothecaries used to sell. A guardian angel watches over the room, whose many shelves are covered with a variety of little pots and phials. Another of the town's marvels is the Doll Museum, where many charming scenes portray antique figurines dressed in period costumes.

gastronomy. Its beautiful rooms are ornamented with copper utensils, pieces of wrought iron and a lovely center light of painted Herend porcelain, made not many miles away. There is also a large courtyard, which fills the restaurant with light on sunny days.

From Székesfehérvár you should take the highway to Gorsium. During the reign of the Emperor Hadrian, this Roman colony acquired the status of a town and became the capital of the Roman province of Pannonia. The Roman remains are situated in a lovely park, which makes Gorsium a delightful place to visit. The nearby town of Tác is home to Lázló Fehér, one of Hungary's greatest living artists. He lives in an enormous white house designed by the architect to meet his special requirements. It has a particularly haunting atmosphere. There is a huge white-walled studio for his paintings, and the family rooms have been furnished in minimalist style by an Italian designer in keeping with the Bauhaus spirit that accords with Fehér's own understated style of painting. His pictures feature the tiny silhouettes of figures lost in a dehumanized urban environment—like the ghosts of those who disappeared during the Holocaust, references to which impregnate the painter's entire oeuvre.

If you continue westward along the eastern shore of Lake Balaton you will arrive at Veszprém, capital of the wooded county to the north of Lake Balaton. Veszprém is an archbishop's see—one of three in Hungary—and from the eighteenth century onward each successive archbishop vied with his predecessors to add ever greater embellishments to the town. According to tradition, the archbishop of Veszprém crowned the queens of Hungary. There is an excellent view of the architectural layout of Veszprém from the rocky peak overlooking the lower part of town. The old town, perched on top of a rock overlooking a valley (Aranyos-völgy), still seems impregnated with a certain royal and religious elegance. Its façades are painted in the ocher or sienna tones of "Kakania"—the satirical, scatological name that the Austrian writer Robert Musil gave to the declining Austro-Hungarian Empire (from its title, Kaiserlich und Königlich—shortened to K und K—"imperial and royal"). There are plenty of interesting details to observe as you walk around the town, from the extravagantly Rococo Holy Trinity Column to a little fountain in the recess of a wall, or the statue of a pensive saint adorning an old house. The Eclectic or Art Nouveau façades at the bottom of the old town testify to the cultural vitality of Veszprém, a religious capital that flourished at times when the church was thriving, such as during the Counter Reformation and the Habsburg reconquest. The charming little Laczkó Dezsõ Múzeum is well worth a visit to learn about the traditions of the nearby Bákony Mountains and the customs of the various communities that have peopled the region for centuries. Nearby, the Bákony House is a traditional folk house that has been converted into a glassblower's workshop; it offers a particularly vivid picture of local life.

Contemporary painter Laszló Féher has a vast studio on the outskirts of Székesfehérvár, which seems surprisingly bare once you have grown accustomed to the ornamentation of Baroque and Art Nouveau buildings. Here the artist hangs several of his large paintings: realistic portraits whose eyes seem to stare in a perpetual questioning about human barbarity. But the simple pleasures of life can also be enjoyed in the friendly, traditional-style Szárcsa Csárda inn (above) at the edge of town.

An excursion from Veszprém to the little towns of Herend and Ajka offers an opportunity to discover some of the country's finest craft traditions. Herend porcelain has long been considered one of the greatest expressions of Hungarian craftsmanship. All kinds of designs can be found in the souvenir shops, ranging from the traditional to pieces that are rather florid and overly ornate. The manufacture of porcelain in Herend dates from the early nineteenth century, when a small factory was set up here that imitated the style and technique of Meissen, in Germany. The growth of this industry matches the economic development of Hungary. Herend porcelain has represented Hungary on

The atmosphere of Veszprém owes much to the rich religious past of the town. From the eighteenth century, the Church set out to embellish what is one of Hungary's three archbishoprics, and the town's religious buildings and extraordinary Christian Museum bear witness to this ambition. The cathedral towers stand out proudly over the rooftops of the old quarter.

several occasions at Universal Exhibitions and despite various ups and downs, porcelain production is now flourishing in Herend once more. Ajka is famous for its crystal. The nearby forests supply the wood needed to heat the great furnaces used by the glassblowers to work their paste. The modern-day designs produced in the Ajka factories are remarkable, and the quality of the work is worthy of the great tradition of this industry.

The road to Lake Balaton snakes through the hills to Nagyvázsony, once a fortified border town. Its main feature is the impressive Kinizsi castle, home to the legendary fifteenth-century general Pál Kinizsi, who was renowned for his military expertise and prodigious strength in the struggle against the Turks. An engraving inside the castle portrays him in all his splendor, executing a sort of war dance as he lifts a Turk off the ground with his teeth and brandishes a sword in either hand.

Country life on the lake's northern shores

The best time to visit the northern shores of Lake Balaton is a fine day in early summer, before the crowds arrive and the weather becomes too sultry, and the best place to start is the Tihany peninsula, which juts out into the middle of the lake. From the hilltop Benedictine abbey there is a splendid view, not only of the opposite shoreline (several miles away) but of the whole length of the lake. Down below is a charming terraced village, with reed-thatched, whitewashed cottages. These have been beautifully renovated, often by well-heeled city dwellers in search of a Bohemian lifestyle, and they represent a comfortable, simplified version of traditional rural architecture. As you wander through the village, you can stop at one or other of these houses and converse in English or German with the friendly owners, who are justly proud of the work they have done there over the years.

One fine example of such renovation is a blacksmith's house, well known for its remarkable wrought-iron gates. It was built in the 1800s, but abandoned for a long period before being enlarged and given a new lease on life by its owner, passionate about interior design, in recent years. The living room opens onto a vast lawn, with a superb, unspoiled view of Lake Balaton and the Inner Lake (*Belső tó*) of the Tihany peninsula in the background. The interior is equally charming, with beautiful bourgeois furniture locally made in the Balaton region, and original touches such as a curious collection of casting moulds and a painted clock. Outside the house is the little world of village craftsmen and shopkeepers, who display their wares in a small square bordered by thatch-roofed houses. Strings of paprika gleaming in the sun and tablecloths embroidered with traditional motifs add bright splashes of color to the scene.

Before leaving the Tihany peninsula you should make an excursion to the geological curiosity of the Inner Lake, some 82 feet (25 m) above Lake Balaton. A dirt track leads past a thatched tithe barn and green pastures where great white cattle with lyre-shaped horns stand out against the little lake—a traditional Hungarian picture-postcard scene. Sometimes a pair of horses trots past pulling an old cart. The atmosphere of this area is in sharp contrast with the crowded vacation resorts on the nearby shores of Lake Balaton. Visitors who want to spend some time in Tihany would do well to try the Park Hotel, in a discreet Baroque house set in a delightful park that slopes gently down to the lake. What the hotel lacks in reception facilities or air-conditioning is more than made up for by a large terrace, with a magnificent view of the lake, and a string of spacious drawing rooms.

The center of Veszprém is a car-free zone, where the gently sloping cobbled streets are lined with ocher mansions with tiled roofs. The peace of the inhabitants is rarely disturbed by flocks of foreign tourists.

In Veszprém, an elegant Secessionist style building features the County's coat of arms; elsewhere, windows reflect the influence of Art Nouveau. Storks nesting on a thatched roof near the lake make for a bucolic picture.

The Tihany peninsula is an ideal spot from which to view the whole of Lake Balaton. The road runs along the lakeside before climbing towards the abbey, whose present form dates from the eighteenth century. Guests who want a quiet holiday will appreciate the Park Hotel, a beautiful residence surrounded by trees, where they can relax in the shade of the columns or in the spacious grounds.

Heading west out of Tihany you go through the village of Örvényes, where a little bridge and water mill with moss-covered roof make for an enchanting bucolic scene. Among some of the finest unspoiled landscapes around the lake are the Badacsony Hills (Káli Medence) overlooking the volcanic Káli Basin. This is a wonderful place for hiking among the vineyards dotted with their charmingly pretty little cottages. The summit of the hill is over 1,300 feet (400 m) high, and the views out over the lake are superb. Halfway up is the Szent Orbán Borház, one of the best and most sought-after restaurants in the region. The rooms in this attractive restaurant have stained-glass windows, portraying scenes from the lives of local saints Vincentius and Martinus, and there is a lovely, inviting bower beneath an ancient vine. You can enjoy local specialties here, such as cooked ham with acacia honey, paté de foie gras with green pepper, or baked pike perch caught that very morning in the Balaton, served with new potatoes seasoned with a tasty herb sauce. The caraway and thyme aromas of a Badacsonyi olaszrizling 2000 wine from the Szeremley Huba label will do justice to the subtle flavors of this delicious dish.

Some of the best Hungarian wines come from the Badacsony Hills and the Kali Basin, but you would be well advised not to overindulge, as Hungary has adopted a policy of zero tolerance for drunk drivers, and the local police are most severe when it comes to inflicting the appropriate penalty. Many types of grape are peculiar to the region or have successfully adapted to it, and produce remarkable wines such as Kéknyelu (Blue Stem), Mustokály ottonel (Ottonel Muscat), Badacsonyi olaszrizling (Badacsony Italian Riesling), and Szürkebarát (Gray Monk). Szeremley Huba's many varieties of wine come from the best-situated vineyards in the region north of the Balaton.

The Badacsony Hill, of volcanic origin, is over 1,300 feet high (438 meters). You should climb to the top taking the stony paths that snake among the vines (following pages). On the way down, take a break in the little Szent Orbán Borház (above) to enjoy a delicious meal as you look out at the misty hills round about, one of which overlooks the village of Szigliget.

Every summer, many Hungarian intellectuals seek refuge in the peace and quiet of the tranquil little village of Hegymagás. Here, and in other villages in the vicinity, writers, artists, and journalists meet in each other's houses. These are simple one- or two-story structures with connecting rooms whose only adornments are the simple moldings and wood trim typical of the region. The roofs are tiled or occasionally reed-thatched. The interiors are generally sparse and elegant, with whitewashed walls, light-colored, wooden country furniture, and workrooms that open onto gardens full of fruit trees, where children gambol and frolic among the flowers and currant bushes—no doubt providing the occupants with plenty of artistic inspiration.

A favorite outing is to a nearby hill, *Szentgyörgy hegy*, which has all the ingredients that make this area so charming: a lovely Baroque house currently under restoration, a cellar selling the best Balaton wines, and a little church with a wonderful view of the lake and the nearby village of Szigliget. A short distance away are the ruins of a property belonging to the Esterházy family. The veranda of this building provides hikers with shelter from a storm, and is a haven where lovers can snatch a romantic moment.

When you leave this enchanting place, an excursion through the seven "hills" of the Káli Medence will give you an idea of the special atmosphere of this Hungarian Tuscany This relatively small area seems to capture the spirit of the ninth-century conquest of the Carpathian Basin by the Magyar

chieftain Árpád. In the nineteenth century, the Hungarian realist painter Mihály Munkácsy imagined the scene, with proud riders on horseback arriving at the foot of hills whose volcanic soils were already planted with vines dating from the Roman occupation. The landscape today is practically identical to that of a thousand years ago, the only sign of human habitation being a few pretty houses hidden in the woods.

One such house, in the hamlet of Káptalantóti, belongs to the famous Hungarian painter István Nádler. The artist is an heir to the Constructivist movement, and is also influenced by oriental meditation techniques. The large canvasses he paints are much sought after by collectors. During the Hungarian "old ladies summer" (Indian summer), friends from the neighboring villages gather among the paintings in his studio to taste the new wine made by one or another of the guests. Nádler's abstract paintings are well suited to the atmosphere of his house, which is typical of the region, with its simple furnishings, traditional painted furniture, Transylvanian seats, and wall coverings that add a splash of color.

Painter István Nádler and his wife Véra have a lovely house, hidden among luxuriant greenery. In summer and at grape harvest time, their home is a veritable retreat for their friends from the surrounding area.

A well-known journalist lives a short distance away, though her tiny home, like a doll's house, is difficult to find on the footpaths of Bare Hill (*Kopasz hegy*). The construction date—1833—stands out proudly against the white façade of the house, which is a veritable haven of peace, especially in winter when the old stove hums, fed with logs from the nearby chestnut trees. There are three agreeable rooms and a veranda that opens onto the woods—a lovely place to enjoy a leisurely breakfast as you watch roe deer scamper past. Nature lovers will be in their element in this area with its rare plant species, including several varieties of orchids. When out walking in the hills early in the morning, if you are lucky, you may spot stags, wild boar, roe deer, hares, pheasants, or woodcocks. Many of the local artists are sensitive to this splendid natural environment, and this sensitivity is reflected in their work.

Tamás Trombitás, for example, captures the essence of the Káli Medence's volcanic soil in impressive abstract sculptures that combine metal and neon lighting. These works are sometimes exhibited in the forest: an unusual open-air "gallery" that provides an ideal setting for the expressivity and sheer raw power of these works. Trombitás has spent the last fifteen years patiently converting a series of houses in the little village of Szentbékkálla into studios or living spaces encircling a romantic tangle of a garden. There is a large red-sandstone wall around the property, which recently acquired a new outbuilding with a vast nineteenth-century portico and columns. Parts of the roof and an inner dome are made of bricks and limestone, testifying to the building's great age. This unusual structure seems to draw its inspiration from the chaotic tumbles of huge, mysterious, primeval

The intellectual tradition on the Balaton's northern shores is reflected by the many members of the intelligentsia who come here to escape the stifling summer heat of Budapest. Some of them spend their days in beautifully renovated houses, such as the one belonging to painter and sculptor Tamás Trombitás, who has highlighted the traditional archways and inner cupola of his old house and designed a comfortable studio (facing page, bottom). A journalist from the capital owns a pretty little house in the woods, where folk art objects contribute to the charming atmosphere (right and below).

If you want to spend a few days in the hills around the Balaton, the Kali Art Inn in Köveskál makes a delightful place to stay (facing page). This is actually a hotel, set in a lovely garden, with rooms which have been personalized by young artists. The swimming pool and refined breakfasts are additional attractions. From Köveskál, in the heart of the volcanic Kali basin, the lakeside is within easy reach. A little traditional water mill in Örvényes (far left, bottom) is worth seeing as you leave the Tihany peninsula; and on the road from Veszprém to the Balaton there is a csárda with several farm animals which are popular with young visitors.

rocks scattered under the shady trees in the nearby forest, which attract visitors from far and wide.

The Káli Art Inn in the lovely village of Köveskál is an especially pleasant place to stay. This group of old farmhouses, renovated in local red stone, first opened in 1998 as a residential summer art school for young artists and their teachers. This initiative did not get off the ground, however, as it turned out that the artists lacked the financial resources to pay for their board and funding was hard to find, and so the owner decided to turn it into a hotel, embellishing the initially rather bare, spartan rooms with furniture and artworks by talented contemporary artists from the region. The food is excellent—try, for example, the memorably delicious lemon chicken served with eggplant *au gratin*. The breakfast is exceptional for a Hungarian hotel, with homemade jam, spicy bread rolls, fresh orange juice, and tea brewed to perfection. You should not leave this charming place without visiting the main building, a lovely big house whose ceiling is adorned with frescoes that hint at the building's original function as an officers' casino.

From Köveskál, you can make various excursions throughout the Balaton area. A particularly delightful destination is the hamlet of Szigliget, near Keszthély. This remarkable site is a favorite with those who love the wild shores of the Balaton, and is dominated by the ruins of an ancient fort from which there are fabulous views of the eastern part of the lake. In his poetic work *The Philosophy of Wine* (an Epicurean classic well known to true oenophiles), Hungarian writer Béla Hamvas gives a highly personal description: "I was thinking, then, of these things (namely, that wine-loving peoples live in the tradition of the golden age rather than that of universal history) on the enchanting summit of Szigliget hill. At my feet were vast gardens, and in the distance, Lake Balaton; just beside me, the wine in its flask, and when my thinking grew sluggish, I took a hearty swig."

The local houses are in keeping with the traditional aesthetic values of the region: rounded roofs covered with thatch made from the reeds that abound in the marshes (specially reinforced to resist storms), thick basalt walls, and simple whitewashed interiors. There is an official writers' residence here: a place to rest and work, in a former castle belonging to the Esterházy family. From the courtyard in the summer, the residents can be seen going calmly about their business. Szigliget is a fine example of the essential charm of this area north of the Balaton, with its combination of tranquility and genuine tradition. Outings to the lakeside resorts may have a certain charm off-season, but avoid them during the summer months—even here in Szigliget. The lawns beside the lake swarm with visitors, making it difficult to reach the water. In September, however, the temperature of the lake is ideal, and the pastel tones of late summer beautify the whole environment.

Another place that is full of charm at this time of year is the little town of Balatonfüred, the oldest spa resort on the lake's northern shore. Count Széchenyi introduced steam navigation to this part of the lake in the mid-nineteenth century. A peaceful, tree-lined promenade leads to the port, which is very popular with sailing enthusiasts. The promenade is named after Indian poet Rabindranath Tagore,

László Vass, a famous shoemaker and major collector of Hungarian contemporary art, owns a luminous villa near the lake. Its pure lines and sober interior make it an excellent showcase for part of his collection. The geometry and light tones of the living room serve to highlight abstract works by Anselme Kieffer, François Morellet, Véra Molnar, or Marta Pan.

winner of the Nobel prize for literature in 1913, who visited the spa to seek a cure for his cardiovascular problems (the medicinal properties of the radioactive sodium bicarbonate waters were discovered as early as 1632). Following the example of other famous visitors, Tagore planted a now flourishing limetree on the promenade, on which he inscribed this verse:

When I have left this earth, my tree,
Let your leaves, new each spring,
Murmur to the passer-by:
As long as the poet lived, he loved.

Nowadays, Balatonfüred is popular with many Hungarian businessmen because of its proximity to Budapest. The elegant shoemaker Lázló Vass, whose stylish, elegant men's shoes are appreciated all over Europe, has a country house here in which he keeps part of his exceptional collection of contemporary art, featuring works by Vera Molnar, François Morellet, Anselme Kieffer, Marta Pan, Ádám Farkas, and István Haraszty. The sculptures and paintings harmonize with the Italian-designed furniture in light-colored wood. Each room—dining room, drawing room, and owners' bedrooms—has its own special atmosphere, giving the house remarkable appeal. The villa's Italian decorator created an overall harmony between rooms, with living areas that are easily accessible and a veranda which lets plenty of light into the house. The terrace with its deckchairs is like an extension of the dining room.

Keszthely castle and the Héviz spa

One of the greatest Hungarian aristocratic families, the Festetics, held a prominent position in the west of the country for several centuries, particularly after the Turkish occupation. These wealthy magnates owned hundreds of thousands of acres of land on the western shores of Lake Balaton, and the family castle at Keszthely testifies to the splendor of a lifestyle that is difficult to imagine nowadays. This aspect

The long façade that gives onto the English-style garden of Keszthely castle reflects the practical considerations of the Festetics family for whom this splendid castle was constructed between 1750 and the late-nineteenth century.

of the glorious past of the Austro-Hungarian monarchy has fallen into oblivion after two wars and forty years of communism. However, in his extraordinary novel *The Dukays,* twentieth-century Hungarian writer Lajos Zilahy retraces the history of this era. He portrays the decline of the Dukay family through the experiences of a large cast of characters as they live through the dramas that befall their country. The saga is reconstructed from the real experiences of the Széchenyi, Batthyány, Károlyi, and Festetics families, and takes place in the vast domain of Ararat, which is the nerve center of the work (indeed it has been called the story's real hero). With its many thousands of acres and fifty-eight servants, it might well be the castle of Keszthely that Zilahy describes:

> The huge three-story castle, nobly compact and ponderous in the style of the Empire, stood forth proudly in the brilliant light, the monotony of its ocher-yellow walls relieved by the sun-faded Pompeian red of the shutters… its wings outspread, the ancient tower of the chapel at its center, as tremendous as an ocean liner, with countless windows.

The construction of the present residence at Keszthely took nearly one hundred and fifty years, from 1745 to 1887, although nowadays it resembles a great Victorian residence—an impression that is reinforced by its park, designed by an English landscape architect. A British charm predominates in the mahogany tones of the apartments, thereby demonstrating the evolution of Hungarian taste over one century: from French-style classicism (as in the castle of Fertőd in northwestern Hungary) to a preference for the Victorian. There are only two storeys, and the rooms that overlook the park are all of similar size, which meant that each distinguished guest could enjoy the same luxury.

A magnificent square staircase with scalloped ornaments leads to the series of second-floor rooms. In a smallish drawing room filled with perfect eighteenth-century furniture, there is a very sensuous painting of a buxom Venus surrounded by a host of cherubs. The more austere red room also contains magnificent furniture from the late eighteenth century, including a particularly fine Transylvanian writing desk with ivory inlay. The walls are adorned with family portraits of Maria Theresa, Joseph II as a child, and Marie-Antoinette. The luxurious Empire-blue drawing room is furnished according to the rather formal taste of the period, abounding in malachite heads, antique busts, ebony chests of drawers, and claw-footed tables and chairs. The more modest Biedermeier-style drawing room (pictured right), with its French and Hungarian furniture, has wall coverings adorned with little flower motifs from the early nineteenth century. It still contains much of its original furniture, thanks to the cultural awareness and presence of mind of a Soviet officer who had several rooms in the castle walled up to avoid pillaging by his own troops in 1945.

The castle's major attraction, however, is its great library. A Festetics prince of the early nineteenth century, György, founded the Georgikon College here to put into practice his enlightened educational philosophy,

The library (following pages) was patiently built up over the centuries by the castle's successive owners. Its remarkable architecture dates from the late-eighteenth century, when it was enlarged by the architects György Rantz and András Fischer.

HISTORIA
PHILOLOGIA

which was based on the principles of Socrates. Professors and students were free to borrow works from the library, which included volumes on jurisprudence, philology, theology, politics, genealogy, heraldry, and military history, not to mention more traditional subjects such as history, geography, science, philosophy, or music, arranged according to a complex system of classification. In 1820 the library contained thirty-five thousand volumes; by 1940 there were fifty thousand. The library fortunately suffered little damage during the war, and in 1948 it was named Helikon, in reference to the literary gatherings that György Festetics had organized there a century earlier. The classification system currently in use dates from this period, and now lists ninety thousand volumes. These include such treasures as four incunabula (books dating from the first fifty or so years of mechanical printing, before 1501), forty-eight others from the library having been transferred to the Budapest National Library, and the first complete Hungarian translation of the New Testament, dating from 1541. A huge crystal chandelier lights the magnificent library. Elsewhere in the castle, visitors can admire hunting trophies, a collection of weaponry, and a room where chamber music concerts are organized, frequently under the patronage of the great Hungarian violinist Vilmos Szabadi. Keszthely is one of the most impressive Hungarian stately homes, and undoubtedly the most authentic.

From the castle, a beautiful wrought-iron gate opens onto the spacious grounds with their ancient trees, ordered flower beds, neat box hedges, and well-pruned junipers. Part of this charming park is arranged like a Japanese garden, with a rock garden and a little bridge over a pond.

Away from this aristocratic atmosphere, the Héviz spa attracts all manner of visitors, from the local families who come swimming every Sunday to people from many parts of Europe who travel here to find relief from their ills in the mud and thermal waters of the spa, which are slightly radioactive and are known to have bactericidal properties. A wooden bridge decorated with geraniums leads from the lakeshore to an island, where a vast Transylvanian-style building with corner towers and pointed roofs welcomes those who come to bathe in the waters. At Héviz you begin to understand the importance that Hungarians attach to their ancient bathing traditions. Local beauties sunbathe on the lakeside lawn, little children paddle in the water with their grandparents, and the wooded surroundings help make it a very pleasant place.

Finally, before leaving Lake Balaton, the Balaton Múzeum, in a lovely neo-Baroque building in Keszthély, is worth a visit for its lively presentation of the history and traditions of this unique European lake. It contains reconstructions showing the former way of life of the fishermen and farmers and their families who earned a sometimes precarious living from the lake and its shores. Visitors are shown how to make reed-thatched roofs and various kinds of fishing nets, and are introduced to the lake's rich flora and fauna, in particular the numerous bird and fish species. This will inspire nature lovers to go a few miles farther on to the Little Balaton (Kis Balaton) reserve. This shallow wetland of thousands of acres of reed beds is a paradise for migratory waders. The reserve cannot be visited without a permit, but an observation tower on Kányavár Island (Kányavári sziget) can be reached by a wooden suspension bridge from Balatonmagyaród village. These waters were once part of Lake Balaton, and their protected environment gives an impression of what the great lake must have been like before the advent of mass tourism.

Any tour of the Balaton region must include the undulating countryside north of the lake. The houses dotting the fields have preserved their traditional charm, and elegant lines of trees divide up the landscape. In the fall, walnut and quince trees bear flavorsome fruits.
The Badacsony Hill is a favorite place from which to contemplate the lake as it shimmers in the sun, or watch as a sudden, violent summer storm goes sweeping along its length. The leafy terrace of the Szent Orbán Borház inn provides an unforgettable view of this extraordinary area, home to the largest lake in Central Europe.

TRANSDANUBIA, HEART OF BAROQUE HUNGARY

The most evocative of all Hungarian palaces is Fertőd, situated on the shores of Lake Ferto on the Austrian border. Once known as Esterháza, the palace was the magnificent home of the Esterházy princes and is now undergoing renovation to return it to its former glory. Its interiors were mostly destroyed during the upheavals of the twentieth century, but as restoration work proceeds the "Hungarian Versailles" is gradually coming back to life; the chandeliers and gilt decorations gleam brightly once again (preceding pages, facing page, and left).

At the end of the seventeenth century, the Habsburg dynasty took the leading role in the wars that ended the century-and-a-half occupation of large parts of Hungary by the Ottomans, and then strengthened its hold over the whole country. The capture of Buda from the Turks in 1686 by the imperial army marked the beginning of a new era for Hungary. The imprint of Habsburg culture was most strongly felt in Transdanubia (Dunántúl)—the region between the Danube in the east and the border with Austria in the west.

For the next two hundred years, the political issue for Hungarians was whether to support the Austrian alliance or join the fight for Hungarian independence. The loyalist party, the *labanc*, sided with the Habsburgs at every turn; the standard-bearers of the Hungarian patriots, or *kuruc*, were Prince Rákóczi, during the anti-Habsburg revolt of 1701 to 1711, and Lajos Kossuth during the ill-fated 1848 Revolution. The Austro-Hungarian Compromise of 1867, which brought into being the Dual Monarchy, did little to quell this opposition. Readers can discover the lively flavor of political debate in the early twentieth century from Count Miklós Bánffy's great novel *They Were Divided*, written in the 1930s and reissued in an English translation in 2001.

The Counter-Reformation, with its militant brand of Catholicism expressed through the medium of Baroque architecture, was a major factor in the Habsburgs' gaining of control. The great medieval feudal castles of the Magyar nobility—those proud symbols of resistance to Ottoman domination, then to the new Habsburg masters—disappeared. The buildings that replaced them, in the new "court" style of architecture, bound the feudal aristocracy into the nexus of power, so ensuring their allegiance to the Habsburgs and cementing the links between the Empire's various states and provinces. The Empress Maria Theresa and her successors, hereditary rulers of the German Holy Roman Empire and sovereign in their own kingdoms, ruled over a vast territory. Throughout the empire, even the façades of imperial and aristocratic residences came to be painted exactly the same shade of yellow ("Maria Theresa yellow"). That is how the *K und K* (*kaiserlich und königlich* – "imperial and royal") tradition was established in the heart of eighteenth-century Europe.

It is still apparent today in the principal towns of Transdanubia—Sopron, Győr, Veszprem, Pécs, Kaposvár, and Bábolna—which all share characteristic features that are familiar to anyone who has traveled in Central Europe. They result from an ordered approach to town planning and architecture, and from the presence of a large German population, descendants of those who were encouraged to settle in these towns to repopulate an area left deserted after centuries of incessant conflict. Religious art features strongly: a fine example is to be found on a little hill on the outskirts of Nagykanizsa, in the southwest area of Hungary, where a Baroque mortuary chapel stands in solitary splendor behind a serpentine wall. In addition, a tradition of equestrianism, a taste for stately classical music, and a respect for local heritage are the result of the merging of the imported Habsburg culture with the old aristocratic traditions of the Magyar people.

To make an excursion through this region of Hungary is rather like taking a voyage in H. G. Wells's Time Machine: at every stop, the explorer has to decide whether to remain in the present or be tempted back to the still tangible past. Those who enjoy going back in time should follow the tour of Baroque Hungary outlined below. One highlight of this voyage of discovery is the town of Fertõd, where the former palace of the Eszterházy family conjures up a glorious musical tradition. But there is one town that seems to bring together every age and aspect of Hungarian civilization. It mingles the Baroque with traces of Turkish occupation; it is as rich in vineyards as in remarkable museums; and its almost Mediterranean character is unexpected in Hungary. This is the town of Pécs, where a typically Hungarian lifestyle has successfully adapted to the realities of present-day living.

A tour of Baroque Hungary

When you head west out of Budapest along the M1 expressway to Vienna, one of the first exits leads to the little town of Bábolna. Emperor Joseph II founded a stud farm here in 1789, and Bábolna is famous for the purebred and half-bred Arabian horses it has produced since 1816. The stallion Shagya Senior, brought to Bábolna from Syria in 1836, sired a line known to specialists as the "Shagya Arabian," which was later officially recognized and quickly gained an international reputation as one of the finest Arabian horses. The beautiful stallion Malik Bey, christened by Queen Sofia of Spain in 1996, is one of the stars of the Bábolna Stud. On formal occasions, equestrian demonstrations are held in the lovely riding school, open to members of the public by reservation only. Horse lovers will also enjoy the nearby museum with its collections of barouches and saddlery.

Hungarians are passionate about their equestrian traditions, and take pride in their Lippizaners and purebred horses. The Bábolna stud farms are famous for the Shagya purebred line, which specialists call the "Bábolna Arabian." Visitors are able to attend regular dressage performances by the highly schooled stallions in the elegant riding arena.

The stud farm founded by Emperor Joseph II, housed in beautiful Baroque buildings within a garden, is entered through a magnificent stone archway. More than 700 horses, including 250 Arabians, are kept here. Each stallion has its name inscribed on a shield above its stable box. Some of these horses have achieved world fame.

The next large town you come to is Gyõr, the capital of Transdanubia. A town since Roman times, Gyõr owes its strategic importance to its position at the confluence of three rivers. It was made a bishopric in the eleventh century but was later occupied by the Turks. It became a significant crossroads in the eighteenth century. Gyõr's charm is hidden at first; to discover it, you should admire the view of the old town from the bridge over the river Rába on Vienna Gate Square (Bécsi kapu tér). The composition formed by the Baroque façades in the foreground, with the Carmelite church and the spire of the cathedral in the background, is like a beautiful stage set, an effect heightened by the decorative nature of a wrought-iron rococo balcony here, a beautiful green house with gabled roof there, the corbels on the elegant classical houses, and the flower stalls.

Behind the cathedral, an alley slopes gently down towards Széchenyi Square (Széchenyi tér), the heart of the old district. A symphony of color greets the visitor: the front of one house, its many balconies supported by atlantes (male figures) and cherubs, is painted a shade of old rose. The orange façade of another house is adorned with statues of Hungarian kings framing a small corbeled living room. Yellow ocher is omnipresent and many façades have recently been spruced up with a fresh coat of bright paint.

Gyor's old center has one of the most attractive and well-preserved ensembles of buildings in Hungary, rivaled only by Sopron and Pest. Many of its elegant eighteenth-century town houses have been restored. The Rába flows peacefully alongside the city walls before joining a branch of the Danube. From a small tree-covered island, you have a lovely view of the Vienna Gate Square (Bécsi Kapú tér) and the monuments around it. The cathedral towers over the old part of the city. Although it has been damaged over the course of time, it is worth a visit for the exceptional gold reliquary of King Ladislas I, dating from the fifteenth century.

The "Iron Stump House" on Széchenyi Square testifies to Győr's historic importance as a craft center; whenever a journeyman arrived in the town, he planted a nail in the trunk of this tree. The impressive churches in the square, and the Holy Virgin Column opposite the Church of Saint Ignatius, bear witness to the town's religious past. The Jesuit pharmacy, with beautiful ceilings adorned with Rococo frescoes, reflects the role played by the Jesuit order in Győr' history. The town is well worth a stay or at least a pause for lunch in one of the attractive restaurants on Vienna Gate Square, such as the Várkapu Étterem or the Gróf Cziráky Panzió. Easter is perhaps the best time of year for visiting Győr: spring comes early here, and visitors can enjoy pleasant weather while they admire the displays of beautiful painted eggs from all over Hungary on sale at the annual market.

One of the best departure points for a tour of western Hungary is the town of Sopron, a stone's throw away from the Austrian border. After World War I, the Treaty of Versailles stipulated that Sopron and its region should be part of Austria, but at a referendum held in 1921 the town decided otherwise, and it has been Hungarian ever since.

Sopron is perhaps the only town in Hungary that has retained most of its old buildings practically intact. Neither the Mongol nor the Ottoman invaders progressed beyond the outskirts of the city and its medieval buildings survived, to blend harmoniously with those of the Baroque period. The town has a strong cultural tradition: during the Renaissance, it boasted Hungary's first establishment for secondary education, a Lutheran high school. In the late eighteenth century, the great musician Haydn published many of his scores here. The town's theater dates from 1769 and was renowned for its productions; Hungarian composer Karl Goldmark gave some of his first performances there. Today the town maintains its musical tradition with an annual festival of ancient music, for which it is well known throughout Central Europe.

Sopron is a magical place at night. Gas lamps cast their mysterious light over the old town, and the mist that hovers over the river Ikva adds to the atmosphere of the scene. Floodlights outline the solid structure of the old watchtower, known locally as the Fire Watchtower (Tûztorony), with its balcony with an Italian-style loggia and a Baroque lantern on the top. Most of the houses in the town were built of wood, so watchers in the tower had the important role of warning of imminent fires. Every style of architecture seems to be represented on the nearby main square (Fõ tér). The Trinity Column, dating from 1701, is in ornate Baroque style, and the Town Hall, its balconies ablaze with geraniums, is in Eclectic style. The buildings known as Gambrinus House and the Angel Pharmacy House are medieval; Fabricius House has Roman foundations and an eighteenth-century façade. Storno House was built in the fifteenth century and renovated in the eighteenth century. It is now home to a magnificent collection of art formed by a middle-class family of Italian origin who shared in the town's restoration in the nineteenth century.

Several musicians lived on Church Street (*Templom utca*), in houses that are still standing. Joseph Haydn occupied number four from 1766 to 1791, while he was Prince Ezsterházy's *Kappelmeister*

Wander through the Baroque streets of Sopron, and you feel as if you've stepped back to the time of Maria Theresa's reign. The old houses are faced with large stone blocks, and are painted in the K & K color of yellow. Architectural decorations range from the amusing, such as a fox dangling his tail over the edge of the lintel, to the spiritual, with numerous statues of saints.

The streets of Sopron empty early in the evening. The paving stones reflect the bluish light of the gas lamps, and the lengthening shadows create an eerie atmosphere. German directors Fritz Lang and Karl Friedrich Murnau could easily have filmed their prewar, spine-chilling movies here. Pretty Orsolya Square, which slopes toward the fountain in the middle, seems less threatening when you come across it in the light of day.

(chapel master, or court musician). A plaque on the façade of the lovely Baroque-style house at number six informs visitors that Franz Liszt—whose father was steward on the neighboring Eszterházy estate—gave a memorable concert there in February 1840. As you walk along the street, there is many a detail to admire: a magnificent wrought-iron balcony, a corbeled room with Rococo windows, the statue of a saint in a corner niche. The whole street is a pageant of color, the light blue of one façade contrasting with the ochers and reds of another. In the old Castle Gate tearoom (Várkapu Kávéház), elements of the decor date from the time of Maria Theresa. The town is more than a film set, however, and as you pass an elegant house the movement of a heavy damask curtain catches your eye: someone is home.

The atmosphere is different in the daytime. On a clear fall day every façade is bathed in light. Winters are often cold in this part of the world, so the townspeople store little woodpiles in cellars that open onto the street. A young girl is helping her mother saw logs outside their house, to get ready for winter. Take the trouble to greet them in a few words of Hungarian and you will be rewarded with smiles. Through half-open doors you glance down long, vaulted passageways to courtyards full of late flowers or overrun with greenery. These glimpses into a still-living past give some idea of the history of this aristocratic town.

Recent history has stitched together the borders of Austria and Hungary in such a way that the quickest route from Sopron to Kőszeg runs far from straight. Kőszeg is a little town that played a major role in the struggle against the Turks. Legend has it that in 1532 Captain Jurisics and a garrison of fifty men held out for twenty-five days against an Ottoman army a thousand times larger. The castle defended by the intrepid captain is now open to the public, and in summer theatrical performances are held in the courtyard where armed Hungarian soldiers used to parade. Viewed from the little bridge over the moat, the remains of the fifteenth-century building with its massive square rampart towers are still impressive. There is an admirable view of the whole town from the tops of the towers.

At dusk, this tourist spot falls silent again and the evening shadows create a rather eerie atmosphere; on every corner you half expect to encounter a saber-wielding ruffian. The slender, fairy-tale profile of the neo-Gothic church of the Sacred Heart acquires a disturbing kind of mystery that dissolves in the light of day. Evening is the best time to stroll around the town—to admire the vista of old tiled roofs near the Vienna Gate (Bécsi kapu) restaurant, or to pay your respects at the popular statue of Saint John in the bluish light of the street lamps. And if that charm doesn't work, the Wizard's Tearoom (Garabonciás) in Grafitos ház will surely work its magic. The ornate and colorful Baroque façades themselves seem to diffuse an atmosphere of strangeness. Kőszeg too has its old pharmacy, where many a love philter or potion must have been dispensed to treat the secret passions of the town.

The impressive Celtic *oppidum* (fortified town) of Velem lies hidden among beechwoods in the Kőszeg mountains, at the foothills of the Alps on the Austrian border. These Iron Age remains give some idea of the remarkable culture of the Celtic tribes, who originated in the upper Danube region about 700 B.C.E. and migrated east and west through Europe during the next hundreds of years. In the neighboring hamlet of Cák, little craftsmen's tiny cottages with thatched roofs (*cáki pincesor*) and white-

washed walls have been carefully restored. These simple dwellings reflect a rural lifestyle, in harmony with the natural environment.

The overriding influence in Transdanubia, however, was aristocratic rather than rural or bourgeois. Most of the towns in the western provinces of Hungary still boast a château that once belonged to a great local family. Körmend, one of the finest examples, was the property of the Batthyány; Nagycenk was once the Széchenyi residence; and Fertõd, the "Hungarian Versailles," was built by the Eszterházy family. These splendid homes were confiscated after 1945 and their former owners have never been reinstated. But the Hungarian state has endeavored to keep these historic monuments alive by restoring them and encouraging their use as cultural or residential centers.

Körmend, the seat of the Batthyány family, lies south of Szombathely (the Roman town of Savaria). The château dates mainly from the later Baroque period, although part of the construction is medieval in origin. A gate flanked with elegant pavilions stands at the entrance to the grounds. The stone pillars are crowned with two groups of mythological sculptures, one of which represents *Hercules Slaying the Lernaean Hydra*, a many-headed creature. The grand front of the château faces you at the end of the garden; running its entire length is a projecting balcony supported by six massive columns. The building is due for renovation work. One wing houses a shoe museum, and in the central part there is a small local history museum with a rather eclectic collection of stuffed and mounted animals (examples of the wildlife of the nearby forests), historic weaponry, and memorabilia concerning personalities linked to the town's past.

One of several historical residences in Sopron County, Nagycenk is among the most interesting. From the main road, a long neoclassical façade is just visible in the middle of a well-kept park. This is the mansion that was home to the Széchenyi family. It has recently been converted into a pleasant hotel and conference center. The mansion itself, which was enlarged in 1838, is interesting to visit for its evocation of the daily life of a great aristocrat who left his mark on the history of Hungary. Count István Széchenyi was born in 1791 and lived and worked in Nagycenk for much of his life. He was a political reformer who made it his lifelong ambition to modernize the administration and economy of Hungary. He planned the building of the first permanent bridge across the Danube—the Chain Bridge in Budapest—and he donated a whole year's income from his estate to the construction of the imposing Academy of Sciences in the capital. Energetic and enterprising, he volunteered at age eighteen to serve in the Habsburg army during the Napoleonic Wars, and some forty years later joined Lajos Kossuth's Hungarian party at the outbreak of the 1848 Revolution. Bitterly disappointed by the outcome of the Revolution, he published a pamphlet in which he denounced the authoritarian and repressive Habsburg occupation of Hungary and was subsequently persecuted. In 1860, at age sixty-nine, he committed suicide.

This remarkable man packed many lives into one—passionate horse breeder and racing aficionado, he was also an engineer whose projects included regulating the Danube and the Tisza Rivers, paving the

You will find plenty of places to explore along the minor roads of Transdanubia. Among the attractions of the small town of Koszeg (left) is the old fortress (left, bottom) that witnessed Captain Jurisics' fierce resistance to the Ottoman invaders, and the neo-Gothic Church of the Sacred Heart (left, top). The latter is undeniably kitsch in style, but is lovely when lit at night. Körmend perpetuates the memory of the Batthyány family, who played a role in Hungary's modernization. Its great point of interest is the Batthyány château (right), with its imposing gateway and neo-classical façade. It now houses a local history museum.

The celebrated Hungarian magnate, Count István Széchenyi, enlarged the Nagycenk family mansion (facing page and above) when he decided to spend most of his time there in 1838. The original building dated from the late-eighteenth century. The mansion burned down during World War II, but has since been restored as a conference center. Part of it now houses a hotel; with its elegant façade and charming gardens, it is a perfect place to stay. Another famous family, the Inkeys, built the mortuary chapel of Nagykanizsa (top), in the southwest region of Hungary; it is a magnificent example of Baroque architecture.

roads of Hungary (something he had seen on his travels to England), and developing steam shipping on Lake Balaton. Count Széchenyi was also an inventive banker whose book *Hitel* (*Credit*) proposed a reorganization of the Hungarian banking system according to modern principles. Most of all, he was a humane man who spent his whole life fighting the prejudices of his class and his times.

Now that Nagycenk is a hotel, it is possible to spend a night in the mansion that was once home to the man who, in his own lifetime, was known as "the greatest Hungarian." There is a charming vaulted breakfast room, and the large banquet hall has a beautiful French-style parquet floor. But the garden, where the Count must often have strolled in the shade of the great plane trees, is perhaps the most striking feature of Nagycenk. From the grounds, which are an elegant combination of classical French-style park and English-style landscape garden, there is a particularly fine view of the façade of the classical two-story building. The pediment of the central block bears the Széchenyi coat of arms. The box trees and banks of flowers contribute to the pleasant atmosphere of Nagycenk, which seems to have come back to life and rediscovered a role for itself at the heart of Hungary's economic revival—something that would have delighted Count Széchenyi.

The Eszterházy family came originally from the eastern part of Hungary. They enriched themselves through their support for the Habsburg dynasty during the political struggles of the seventeenth century, and their late-Baroque palace at Fertõd, with its 126 rooms, has often been compared to the Habsburgs' summer palace at Schönbrunn, just outside Vienna. On the main front, a horseshoe-shaped staircase sweeps up to a magnificent balcony leading to the entrance on the first floor. The gardens were designed to give vistas onto the château and the fountains in front of each wing.

Fertõd, the "Hungarian Versailles," a monument to music

If you leave the expressway between Nagycenk and Fertõd, you will pass through the little village of Fertõszéplak, where several traditional houses have recently been restored. With their roofs of thatch or old tiles, vine-covered bowers, and white façades that often show the date of construction, they make a chocolate-box scene. Sometimes a farmer, sheltered from the sun by a canopy of straw, rattles past in a horse-drawn cart. This country idyll soon gives way to the splendor of Fertõd, the "Hungarian Versailles." The elaborate entrance gate anticipates the majestic proportions of the château. In 1762, Prince Miklós Esterházy ("the Magnificent" or "the Lavish") decided, with the assistance of an Italian architect, to embellish the building begun by his grandfather in 1720, so earning himself his nickname. His aim was to show that an Eszterházy could rival the Habsburgs in Vienna. The enlightened prince's dream was realized, but when he died in 1790 the château proved too remote and costly to maintain as a residence. The Esterházy family preferred to live in their neighboring property of Eisenstadt (now in Austria), and Fertõd became a mere monument, emptied of all its treasures.

The palace extends in a semicircle from the central building to the two side wings. This classic design features a two-story façade and a majestic balcony reached from a dual staircase supported by double columns. A magnificent wrought-iron gate stretches from one side of the horseshoe-shaped courtyard to the other. Each of the wings has a smaller, charming balcony; beneath one a fountain splashes water onto a statue group portraying Perseus's rescue of Andromeda. The garden offers a splendid view of the main façade along the avenue of large, carefully manicured yew trees. A caretaker's modest house is hidden among the trees and seems to be watching over the fate of this aristocratic dwelling.

Within the palace, some chinoiseries and floral motifs, a legacy from Miklós the Magnificent, remain on the ground floor. Large white-and-green ceramic stoves form a lovely counterpoint to the pink marble of the floor and the black Chinese lacquers reflected in the large mirrors. Walk through the concert hall with its vaulted ceilings, the pillars of which support the banquet room above, and admire the

craftsmanship of the frescoes created by artists from Italy, France, and Austria. The concert hall gleams with ornate gilded molding, an effect accentuated by the large crystal chandelier, which reflects light back onto the ceiling fresco of Apollo in his chariot. It exemplifies the sumptuous style that Miklós introduced at Esterháza, as the palace was formerly known.

The pleasing balance of the architecture immediately strikes visitors, while the recently refurbished rooms offer a nostalgic vision of the past. Many have been refurnished with borrowed pieces from the collections held in the Museum of Applied Arts in Budapest. The palace was laid to waste and all the furnishings plundered during World War II.

Miklós was also an excellent musician, performer, and composer who organized dazzling parties for his guests. In 1760, his father had hired a musician in Vienna, a man who was becoming well known in the music world, Joseph Haydn. Miklós wanted to transform Esterháza into a musical center in the heart of the Empire, and in 1766 he named Haydn as his Kappellmeister. In just a few years, Haydn's style and talent became a major influence throughout this region of Europe. The musician had an apartment in the palace—which was in the midst of never-ending construction—where he composed at a prolific rate. He made sure his scores were published and played in other major European courts. Haydn created new musical forms such as the sonata, the string quartet, and the symphony, and his inventive operas were the precursors to those of Mozart. Most of these fine operas were written for the Esterháza theater. Thirteen survive, although they are not all well known.

Let's stop for a moment and try to imagine life at the Esterháza Palace when the cream of European aristocracy came here to attend the musical performances. As well as a magnificent concert hall, Miklós built a French-style garden, an opera theater, and a puppet theater. The opera theater was located at the entrance to the gardens, which stretched over some 1,000 acres (400 hectares) and contained a sacred forest, grottoes, fountains, waterfalls, temples, and ruins. Inaugurated in 1768 with Haydn's opera *Lo speziale,* the theater burned down once and was immediately rebuilt, and was then destroyed in the late nineteenth century. Contemporary accounts describe the theater as being perfectly designed, complete with all the latest innovations of the time. Haydn had access to the most sophisticated theater machinery, which he used to manipulate the sets and backdrops during performances of his operas. He could even open the walls of the theater and use the natural setting of the palace gardens as a backdrop. The puppet theater, built in 1772 just opposite the opera at the entrance to the garden, was inaugurated the following year, with the Empress Maria Theresa in attendance. Like the opera theater, it too has disappeared.

Haydn lived at the palace for thirty years. He felt that its setting was essential to his music. Several of his operas include scenes set in whimsical gardens and forests that resemble those of Esterháza. But the dazzling festivities signaled the end of an era—not only of Esterháza's splendor but also of the sophisticated and luxurious lifestyle of the Age of Enlightenment, brought to a close by the upheavals of the French Revolution and the Napoleonic Wars.

You can still sense this history in Fertõd, the name given to the town in 1945 to lay the area's aristocratic past to rest. The ups and downs of Hungarian history, however, have not totally eliminated a desire to honor this glorious era of Fertõd's past, to which the Hungarian authorities pay tribute through a brilliant musical program. Memories of the historical palace and of one of the most ostentatious families in Europe linger. Liszt's father managed Esterházy estates and also influenced the career of Schubert, who was an unsuccessful suitor to one of the young women in the family. One of the most respected contemporary Hungarian authors, Péter Esterházy, is a descendant of the family.

Pécs, known as the gateway to the Mediterranean, has a charm all of its own. Over the years, the city has felt the influence of the Middle East; its large open spaces reflect the Ottoman past. The Baroque tradition is alive and well here—as, indeed, it is throughout Transdanubia. The Franciscan Church (facing page) is a lovely example of this style.

The "Turkish town" of Pécs, gateway to the Mediterranean

Arriving from the north, you'll see a sprawling, hastily built city, Hungary's third largest town, nestled in the valley at the base of the Mecsek Hills. But there's a whiff of the Mediterranean breeze here. Fig trees grow alongside chestnuts and evergreen oaks, and the scent of the pine forests seems ever so close. The French scholar Fernand Braudel regularly visited friends in Hungary and knew the country very well. He defined this area as Mediterranean—its Romanism, geography, and language, give it more of a southern European character than Slavic or Germanic.

After spending a few days in Pécs, you'll better appreciate the viewpoint of this great geographer and historian, author of the definitive work on the history of the Mediterranean. In the fifteenth and sixteenth centuries, the Ottomans made Pécs their leading administrative and cultural center. At the time, many churches were transformed into mosques. The *djámi*—the mosque reserved for Friday night prayers—built by Pasha Gazi Kasim and now a parish church, is the most imposing example of Turkish architecture in all of Hungary.

One of the features of this city is its large number of museums. In a single stretch of Chapel Street (Káptalan utca), only a few hundred yards long, there are no fewer than five museums. The most surprising is the Zsolnay Museum, situated in a former private residence. Monumental pieces of ceramic art such as large urns and jars shaped like elephants or deer are displayed in the museum's garden. The museum houses a magnificent selection of pieces produced by the Zsolnay ceramics factory since the nineteenth century. Most buildings built in Hungary in the 1900s were covered with colored glazed tiles from the Zsolnay factory. The Hungarian pavilion designed for the 1900 Universal Exhibition in Paris was entirely faced with these tiles. The dismantled pavilion is currently in crates in the basement of the Budapest Museum of Applied Arts, awaiting a generous sponsor to bring it back to life.

Among the rare works in the museum is a blue Zsolnay table service from 1928; the flatware with matching ceramic handles is magnificent. Crystal glasses made by this same company around 1920–1925 are also intriguing; the museum catalog notes that production of this crystal ended fairly quickly as it was insufficiently profitable. The museum has other noteworthy objects, including large Oriental-style jars and a pair of ceramic gas lamps from the Millennium period, and a series of Art Deco vases with Egyptian motifs. These works illustrate the innovative talents of members of the Zsolnay family, many of whose drawings were later used for the company's most beautiful designs. Unfortunately, the production of decorative objects was discontinued in 1925, and the Zsolnay firm survived by supplying ceramics to the building sector. It was only in the 1960s that it started once again to produce items for the retail market. The company's newfound success can be explained by its attention to detail, the quality of its designs, and a sales policy that aims to meet the demands of a clientele drawn to the factory's somewhat offbeat pieces.

A complete tour of Pécs's artistic wealth must include the Vasarely Museum, which offers an overview of the work of Vasarely, born in the region in 1908, and ranges from his early drawings to his famous paintings and tapestries dating from the Op Art period. Don't leave Pécs without visiting the Modern Art Gallery (Modern Magyar Képtár), which houses a vast collection exhibited in two buildings. It covers the entire history of modern art in Hungary, from the late-nineteenth century to the

The spacious public buildings and tree-lined streets of Pécs contribute to the charm of the city. Chapel Street is very characteristic of the old city: most of the opulent homes have been transformed into museums, for which Pécs is justly famous. The bishop's palace is surrounded by greenery and occupies a large section of Cathedral Square; don't miss the old woodwork, which was carved from oaks cut down in the nearby Mecsek Mountains. The Klara Leuwey High School, also on the square, is much more austere in style; its symmetrical neo-classical design is an effective counterpoint to the ebullience of the bishop's palace.

Pécs cathedral is a remarkable medieval monument, but it owes its present appearance to restoration work carried out between 1882 and 1891. Its four corner towers rise proudly above the city gardens.

present day, with works by major artists. Pierre Székely, one of the most interesting Franco-Hungarian sculptors of our time, bequeathed several monumental sculptures to the museum. They are arranged in the courtyard of the charming villa that houses works by artists prior to 1945.

Farther on is a tribute to a brilliant but little-known nineteenth-century Hungarian painter, Tivador Csontváry. This assistant pharmacist divided his time between family life at home and trips abroad, from which he returned with magnificent canvases depicting scenes such as Baalbek, Jerusalem, and the immense rocky landscapes of Transylvania. Nature, historical settings, and landscapes are omnipresent in his work. He often distorted his viewpoints and used bright colors to create violent contrasts, composing a singular and disturbing vision of a world in which man occupies a very subordinate position. His work has been compared to that of the French primitive artist Henri (Le Douanier) Rousseau as well as to Vincent van Gogh—he was born the same year as the Dutch artist, in 1853. Picasso admired him. His unique brilliance has not yet been fully recognized, and anyone visiting Pécs should take advantage of a visit here to discover Csontváry's major works.

After exploring these museums, you may want to stroll by the cathedral, built in neo-Romanesque historicist style, and contemplate the magnificent bishop's palace, a harmonious building of brick, stucco, and stone all in shades of red. A metal statue of Franz Liszt by contemporary sculptor Imre Varge leans out over the balcony. A craft market takes place from time to time on St. Stephen's Square (Szent István tér), a large, gently sloping open area bordered by great trees. The neoclassical Klara Leöwey high school and small Baroque cafés are also on this square.

Continue through the old streets of the town, where you'll find charming antique shops, such as Parti Szépségtár on Mary Street (Mária utca). Indeed, Pécs is famous for its antiques market, held the first Sunday of every month. It's a great place to visit in summer, when the market has a wide selection of objects arrayed in a picturesque setting.

Before leaving Pécs, take a walk to admire the impressive town walls, a reminder of the town's turbulent past; along the way, go down a street named Janus Pannonius utca. At one point, there is a grating covered with locks; short-term or lifelong lovers have clamped the locks around the metal bars as symbols of the strength of the links uniting them and the solidity of their hopes.

Pécs is therefore an obligatory stop. The best place to stay in town is the Palatinus Hotel, a recently renovated, magnificent Art Nouveau building. A double staircase leads up from the majestic lobby to a verandah framed with stained-glass windows; the central alcove is decorated with a large piece of Zsolnay ceramics. The dining room looks like a theater, with a small balcony with a wrought-iron handrail. The chandeliers in the coffered ceiling echo the tulip-shaped lamps in the main lobby below. The main façade is tightly framed by two buildings arranged around a large wrought-iron passageway, modeled after the traditional architectural style of Budapest. The hotel restaurant is of only average quality; the Golden Duck Restaurant (Arany Kacsa Étterem), which boasts a large wine cellar, may be a better place for a meal.

The Villány vineyards, situated a dozen miles from Pécs, are reputed to produce the best Hungarian red wines. Road signs, mark the wine route, which winds through the prettiest towns in this

The architectural details you see as you stroll through the streets of Pécs are best understood within the larger context of the city's historical and artistic past. A Baroque statue of the Virgin and a veil showing the face of Christ reflect the strong Catholic tradition of the city after it was recaptured from the Turks. Decorative elements on homes and fountains demonstrate the importance of the craftsmen who helped beautify this city of museums and Zsolnay ceramics, while the porch roof at the entrance to a puppet theater (facing page, bottom left) and the metal sculpture of Franz Liszt leaning over the balcony of the bishop's palace (bottom, middle) underscore the status of artists in this southern capital. Short-term or lifelong lovers place locks on a metal gate, for the residents of this fascinating city are also dreamers.

Bábszínház

HOTEL

Visitors to Pécs can sample its artistic vitality by choosing from among fifteen museums. Several of them are side by side on Chapel Street, including one devoted to the Zsolnay ceramics factory (facing page, top left). One particularly evocative room contains objects that belonged to the company's founding family. The designer Vilmos Zsolnay was also a talented painter, as a number of his works on show here illustrate. Not far from Pécs, in Decs in the Sárköz region, a small museum of rural traditions offers a charming contrast to the Mediterranean style of the city (facing page, top, right). Farther on, in the courtyard of the Modern Art Gallery, the monumental sculptures by Pierre Szekely are placed in a countrified setting (right, bottom). The city also has a number of lovely buildings, including the famous Palatinus Hotel (facing page). The entrance lobby features a grand corridor on the upper floor, while the dining room and colorful skylight are remarkable examples of the Art Nouveau style.

appellation. A brochure in many languages has been published with the support of the European Union; you can obtain it from one of the Tourinform information centers.

The village of Pálkonya symbolizes the wealth of this region's traditions. It is certainly one of the most beautiful villages in Hungary. In recent years, residents have worked hard to restore the vine growers' homes. They are tastefully decorated with flowers, and wooden tools related to the winemakers' trade are used as decorative touches. The mayor, Ms. Eleonora Becker, is a professional photographer. She is deeply committed to promoting this small village. Her white house with archways is a good example of a successful restoration project; many newcomers to the village have followed her example. A descendant of a family that arrived from Württemberg in Germany in the seventeenth century, she is an extremely energetic and enterprising figure in the town. Villány and the surrounding area owe her a great deal.

This southwest area of Hungary became depopulated during the Ottoman occupation, and so the Empress Maria Theresa encouraged German settlers, often of Swabian origin, to move here to revive the economy of this devastated region. The expression "Swabian Turkey" is still used to designate the districts, or *comitats*, of Tolna, Barany, and Somogy, which have a strong minority of people of German descent. The German immigrants were successful farmers and vine growers, and their villages have a distinct style characterized by well-maintained streets, abundant flower beds, bilingual street signs, and well-built homes. Pálkonya is one such town. The Batthyány family, large landowners in this region with holdings stretching from Siklós to Villánykövesd, built the round church in 1826, as well as other buildings. A stork's nest sits atop the roof; every year, the large migrating birds pass through and nest here; villagers believe this brings luck to their town. A series of small wine cellars at the edge of town (Pincefalu) is devoted to the region's wine-making activities.

The villages in the wine-producing region of Villány, particularly Pálkaonya, are famous for their traditional homes, many of which have been beautifully restored by a few well-known locals. The Hungarian community of German descent is very active in the preservation of their village heritage. When leaving the village, the harmonious alignment of the lime-bleached vineyard houses with their old tiled rooftops are striking examples of this proud heritage.

If you would like to taste some of the local wines, stop by one of the many restaurant/wine cellars of Villány. Polgár Pincészet is one of the best in the area. You'll take away a long-lasting memory of a dinner served in an immense cellar, remodeled in the last few years by the enterprising owner, Zoltán Polgár. The food is simple but delicious. Try the wild mushroom soup, confit of duck with garlic potatoes and bacon, and to top it off, a few *rétes* (strudels) with apples and cherries. The wines served with dinner are characteristic of the diverse vintages produced in Villány, and many foreigners make a special trip to the Polgár cellars to try out their variety. The sommeliers are young and usually women; they often speak a foreign language and will pass on their knowledge of the fascinating world of Hungarian wine.

As you leave behind the hills and valleys around Pécs, it's impossible not to reflect on Hungary's exceptional ability to preserve and promote the natural beauty of this region, which has suffered so much over the course of its history.

From the nearby villages and Mount Villányi there are splendid views over the Villány vineyards, which grow grapes ranging from Cabernet Franc, Merlot, and Cabernet Sauvignon to such traditional varieties as Kékfrankos and Kékoportó. These domains are perfectly kept up. If you pluck one of the sweet grapes from the rows of vines, you'll find it will melt in your mouth. And if you travel through here during the harvest season (usually the last two weeks of September), you may see young villagers decked out in traditional costumes. The atmosphere is festive and colorful, and everyone joins in. Decorated carts drawn by ribbon-bedecked horses carry the dancers and musicians from one place to another. If you stop to watch and listen to the gypsy music, you may even be invited to join in the celebrations and dancing.

ESSENTIAL HUNGARY

Hungary possesses extraordinarily rich, living folk traditions, yet modern-day craftsmanship is also flourishing, its art treasures are tastefully presented, and its natural resources are exploited to best advantage. Anyone eager to penetrate to the heart of Hungarian life can do so in a number of ways: by exploring its culture of bathing, its creative gastronomy, its high-quality craftsmanship, and its attractive, accessible museums. All these things make up the essential Hungary and can be enjoyed both in the capital city and in the heart of the provinces.

The Hungarian art of living goes hand in hand with the traditional bathing culture that visitors learn to appreciate more each time they come to the country. The Széchenyi and Gellért baths (facing page and left), both built at the turn of the nineteenth century and recently renovated, are undoubtedly the most spectacular. Their size, the originality of their architecture, and the perfection of their every detail make them a must for first-time visitors to Budapest.

The culture of bathing

In many parts of Hungary, warm water enriched with various mineral (sometimes radioactive) salts lies close beneath the soil or bubbles to the surface. These waters are believed to possess rich healing properties. It is possible to swim at about a hundred thermal springs in Hungary, more than thirty of which are in Budapest—a record for a European capital. The bathing tradition dates back to Roman times, when Hungary was called Pannonia. Its capital, Aquincum (whose well-preserved ruins can be visited in the northern district of Buda), was supplied with water from thermal springs, which were already being exploited when the Romans conquered the region in the first century C.E. The public baths were greatly frequented in those days, as they have been ever since: even today, bathing culture is an essential component of the Hungarian urban lifestyle.

Travelers from other parts of Europe who visited Budapest in the fifteenth and sixteenth centuries left admiring accounts of the baths. The incurably sick sought relief for their ills at the baths on Margaret Island. King Matthias Corvinus had new pools constructed during the Renaissance, and still more were added during the hundred and fifty years of Turkish occupation, some of which are still in use today, such as the Rudas, Rác, and Király baths in Budapest. During the late-nineteenth century, when the newly unified city of Budapest underwent remarkable expansion, the two-thousand-year-old bathing tradition was given a new lease on life with the construction of the huge Széchényi baths in City Park (Városliget), the Lukács medical and thermal complex near the Margaret Bridge (Margit hid) in Buda, and the baths at the Gellért Hotel at the foot of Gellért Hill (Gellért hegy).

Before setting out to explore any of these baths, first check their opening times, as these vary according to the season, and find out whether particular days are reserved for men and women; mixed bathing is not always the general rule. You should be aware that nude bathing is the practice in certain establishments, and that codes of behavior are sometimes a little hazy.

A list of bathing options is usually exhibited at the entrance to the baths, but if no translation is given, the foreign visitor has to deal yet again with the language barrier. Hungarian is one of the Finno-Ugric group of languages, dear to linguists and to the composer Berlioz who exclaimed in his *Mémoires*:

The baths from the Turkish period, built during the latter half of the sixteenth century, are like a world of their own. The capital's underground springs supply the water for these baths, where swirls of sulfurous steam rise upward to escape through openings in the vast cupola that encloses the pool, creating a dreamlike, intimate atmosphere. The impressive structure of the Rudás baths features large basalt columns in the *hammam* (facing page). In the Király baths, blue streaks of copper sulfate flow from the openings in the cupola, creating an oriental fairy-tale atmosphere (right). You feel you are in a magician's cave, gazing up at the star-spangled vault.

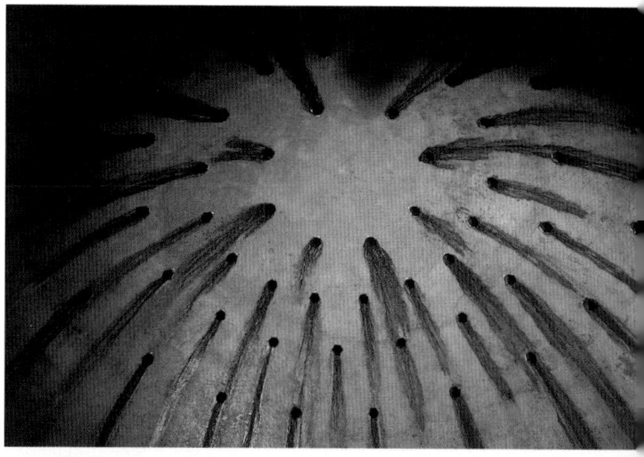

"Now there's a real language! One that nobody understands...without having learned it." A kindly local will usually step in to act as guide and interpret for you in another language (usually English or German). There are several choices to make: whether to change in a private cabin or communal locker room, what kind of pool to bathe in, and what kind of massage to have (these may be wet or dry, partial or total, but remain within the bounds of decency). Probably the best way to approach the bewildering culture of bathing is to be initiated in it by a regular user.

The time of year will affect the choice of baths. In winter, the medium-sized indoor baths are ideal: one large pool and several smaller ones, paved with red marble or volcanic tuff, under a great dome supported by ribbed vaults and pierced with openings to let the steam out. Bathing releases toxins in the skin, and the water is changed every night. The temperature varies between 77° F (25° C) and 122° F (50° C). From spring through fall, when the days are longer and the weather milder, baths such as the Gellért, the Széchényi, and the Lukács may be preferred for their combination of indoor baths and outdoor pools, which allow bathers to enjoy the contrast between the heat of the water and the cool of early morning or dusk.

A few years ago, Hungary's public baths underwent major renovation, and you can now spend a morning at any of them without worrying about their cleanliness or state of repair. In almost every establishment, the magnificent architectural structure has been restored, the locker rooms renovated, and the water-filtering systems overhauled. During a short stay it is impossible to explore the whole range of baths, but no visit to Budapest is complete without experiencing the unique atmosphere of some of these truly astonishing places.

The Rudas baths, on the banks of the Danube, were built between 1566 and 1578, during the Ottoman occupation of Buda. The edifice has eight basalt columns supporting a cupola surrounded by a vaulted corridor. The hexagonal pool is of the red marble from Upper Hungary that is used in so many public buildings. It contrasts well with the green volcanic tuff of the walls and the brick paving of the walkways between pools. Two ornamental doors open onto the steam room in the central niche, and four triangular corner pools add a pleasing touch of symmetry to the whole. Moderate in size, the Rudas baths have a regular clientele of users. They are an ideal venue for a first encounter with the ancient tradition of the baths.

From Fõ utca, the main street in the Viziváros neighborhood on the right bank of the river, you will reach the Kiraly baths, the city's oldest, dating from 1546. The building was restored to its original state after the terrible bombing raids of the winter of 1944–45, renovated in 1968, and has recently been repainted and smartened up. It combines traditional Turkish heated baths (*hammam*) with an adjoining medical complex housed in elegant classical buildings. The cupola is pierced with openings on the outside, through which the steam escapes; high in copper sulfates, it leaves streaky, dark blue metallic deposits. The hot water is piped from springs located under the Lukács baths five hundred yards away. Until replaced during recent renovation work, some of the pipework dated from the bath's

The Lukács is one of the capital's loveliest baths. The recently renovated main pool, part of a thermal establishment, looks like a theater décor, especially at night when the lighting of the façades and the water makes every surface sparkle.

original construction. The Kiraly is the smallest of the Budapest baths, and replicates most closely the atmosphere of a *hammam* of the Ottoman era. Visiting these baths, and watching the swirls of sulfurous steam rising to escape from the central cupola, is an experience you are unlikely ever to forget.

The nearby Lukács baths give an impression of comfort and space. The building housing the *hammam* and medical complex opens onto a large courtyard shaded by ancient plane trees and bordered by beautiful residential buildings. Over the entrance to the baths is a bas-relief of Venus emerging from her bath (unless it shows a bathing regular, chosen for her lovely figure!). The large rectangular outdoor pool has been totally renovated. The water, which reflects the surrounding trees, has a temperature of 90° F (30° C): it bubbles and splashes, adding to the pleasure of the experience. Nearby, two cooler pools—70° F (22° C) and 78° F (26° C) respectively—face each other across traditional late nineteenth-century walkways and a particularly inspired metallic architecture from the 1930s. In the *hammam*, there are many different pools of all sizes; temperatures range from 75° F (24° C) to 102° F (70° C) in the steam room. The water supply gushes forth at temperatures of more than 100° F (70° C) from four artesian wells dug under the building to a depth of 300 feet (100 meters). The Lukács baths are a favorite with families, and with intellectuals who come here to get into shape before starting their morning's work. Moreover, the combination of bathing and medical treatment is much appreciated by patients who come to have their backs fixed by a team of first-class specialists.

The only bathing establishment in Pest is the neo-Baroque Széchenyi spa, built in 1913. Its monumental domes are as high as the treetops in the neighboring City Park and, with its well-tended flower beds, in spring and summer the establishment looks rather like a stately home. The area reserved for thermal medical treatment is light and spacious. The Széchenyi baths are very popular, with a friendly family atmosphere all year round. There is something for everyone: older people play chess on giant floating boards, their heads seeming to float in a cloud of steam, while children have great fun in the bubbles and waves of a shallow pool specially designed for them. The best time to appreciate the Széchenyi baths is on a lovely winter's morning, when the outdoor pools are edged with snow. It is a truly pleasurable experience to immerse your body in the water's luxuriant warmth while cold, invigorating outdoor air refreshes your face. This remarkable place, with its domes, vast porticoes, and ivy-covered walls, is as beautiful as it is functional. The thermal area is fed by water that emerges from the ground at a temperature of 168° F (76° C), and the various facilities, such as massage salons, private changing rooms, and beauty parlors, make Széchenyi one of Europe's loveliest thermal spas.

The perspectives of the Széchenyi baths are quite remarkable. The harmonious curve of the row of changing rooms reflects the architectural finesse of this mythic place, which is also apparent in the proportions of the baths and the thermal buildings.

A sense of décor is an integral part of the Hungarian bathing culture. The bas-relief on the outer wall of the Lukács baths—which portrays Venus, or perhaps a shapely bather—adds a charming decorative touch (above). The grand lobby of the Gellért baths is adorned with female statues in white marble, in a neoclassical style reminiscent of the Italian sculptor Canova (pages 178–179).

On the opposite bank of the Danube is the Gellért Hotel, a grandiose example of Secessionist style, the Hungarian version of Art Nouveau. To appreciate its architecture fully, you should approach it across the remarkable metal structure of Freedom Bridge (Szabadság hid). Although the rooms themselves do not live up to the hotel's reputation, the Gellért houses a splendid spa complex whose interior décor is among the most sumptuous in Budapest, indeed Central Europe. Here hotel guests in white bathrobes and (unattractive but compulsory) blue plastic caps mingle with the baths' regular clientele: however, since the establishment raised its admission prices following recent renovation work, many locals have been put off from coming. The glass dome and multicolored mosaic flooring of the lobby are a masterpiece of Art Nouveau. In the hall housing the main pool, barley-sugar columns decorated with floral motifs support a pillared gallery covered in tiles made at the Pécs pottery started by Vilmós Zsolnay in 1855.

The magical atmosphere in the *hammam* itself is sustained by the deep turquoise ceramics, ribbed vaults, colored paving and flooring, and recesses for cold, warm, or hot pools. There are separate sessions for men and women, so swimsuits are not necessary: bathers can rent a sarong at the entrance. The full ritual of the bath has several stages, and its length depends on the bather's experience and stamina. It's important that you pass through a series of pools, each slightly warmer than the one before, before entering the hot pool and steam room and, finally, plunging into a cold water pool. In fine weather, the outside pools on the terraces at the back of the hotel are much appreciated: some people sunbathe on the tidy lawns, while others enjoy the swimming or wave pools.

Margaret Island (Margit-sziget) is both a part of Budapest, and, at the same time, a world of its own. It has long been a favorite recreation area for city dwellers, and in summer the island is a must for visitors, who can explore it on rented bikes (singles, tandems, or family bikes). The island is a particularly attractive place with many interesting features, including the ruins of a medieval convent (a reminder of how long the island has been occupied), all kinds of gardens (rose garden, Japanese garden, zoological garden), an outdoor theater, elaborate water tower, and a musical fountain. Margaret Island has the largest complex of outdoor swimming pools and baths in Budapest, including thermal springs and an Olympic-sized swimming pool (designed in 1937 by an architect who was also a champion swimmer).

There are therefore many different ways of "taking the waters" in Budapest. Swimming in the Danube is no longer recommended, but Lake Velence (Velencei Tó) is only half an hour's drive from downtown Budapest, and Lake Balaton just over an hour's drive away. These both provide a pleasant alternative for swimmers who want to get away from the hustle and bustle of the city.

Every aspect of the Gellért baths is a feast for the eyes. The large indoor pool is set in highly decorative surroundings, framed by a colonnade that creates a lovely symmetry, so you can enjoy your swim while admiring the splendor all around you (facing page). The fabulous thermal baths are covered in bright turquoise mosaics and ceramics (above). Finally, the outside area has popular attractions such as wave pools.

One of the joys of a Saturday morning in Budapest is an early-morning visit to the large central market. Beneath a huge metal-ribbed nave, a wide variety of stalls offer their wares: fruit and vegetable stands (with displays worthy of still-life paintings), fish dealers, delicatessens, poultry and tripe butchers, and many stalls selling spices, handicrafts, or fabrics embroidered with traditional motifs—all coexist peaceably here in the heart of Budapest.

Creative cuisine

Hungarian cuisine is a subtle combination of spicy dishes and country flavors, and is justly renowned for the freshness and variety of the traditional ingredients that go into its preparation. George Lang's classic recipe book, *The Cuisine of Hungary*, published in 1990, gives a good idea of the range of dishes.

One of the greatest pleasures of a Saturday morning in Budapest is going to one of the city markets to choose the ingredients you will need for Sunday lunch. The large central market (Vásárcsarnok) is an extraordinarily convivial place crowded with stalls selling a variety of produce. It is a huge structure of metal and wood, built in 1897, and recent renovation work has brought out all the beauty of its metal-ribbed framework. By contrast, the Lehel market (Lehel piac) is in a new, brightly colored postmodernist building designed by architect László Rajk. Every neighborhood of Budapest has its own permanent covered market, usually built along the same lines as the central market. A visit to one of these places is a fascinating experience.

The profusion of seasonal vegetables reflects the richness of the Hungarian soil, and housewives and cooks are spoiled for choice. There are many kinds of root vegetables and cabbages; to accompany a meat dish, Hungarians often make a purée of celeriac, kohlrabi, radishes, white or red carrots, potatoes of various flavors and textures, or fresh peas. Peppers (paprikas) come in all shapes and varieties—yellow, red, mild or strong—and hang everywhere from the market stalls, adding a splash of bright color among the strings of garlic. There are countless ways of preparing them: steamed or roasted, dried and ground to make paprika seasoning, or marinated in oil and served as a condiment. Hungarians are fond of serving gourds such as squashes, pumpkins, zucchini, and watermelons to add a decorative touch to a meal.

On some stalls, huge salamis hang above piles of sliced bacon, smoked spicy sausages, small pork and beef sausages, and smoked duck or goose fat. Elsewhere, shoppers who are tempted by the fresh goose foie gras on offer may spare a thought for the huge flocks of noisy geese that wander across the Hungarian plain, destined for the tables of gourmets all over Europe. Hungary is among the top European producers of foie gras. Fillets of Muscovy duck breast are reasonably priced and delicious.

Lamb and mutton are not very common in Hungary, but pork is extremely popular and is prepared in a number of ways. A filet mignon with paprika and onions makes an elegant dish; a simple pork chop (*sertés borda*) or shin of roast pork (*sertés csülök*) is a gourmet's delight when carefully prepared in a traditional *csárda* (small country inn). Beef (*marha*), especially from the great herds of gray cattle bred on the *puszta*, is famously firm and juicy, with a subtle spicy flavor. A well-spiced fillet steak cooked on a little bed of onions and shallots can be memorably delicious. In Hungary, however, real food lovers will particularly appreciate the great variety and abundance of game, including venison, mouflon (wild sheep), wild boar, hare, partridge, pheasant, duck, and woodcock. In season, every *csárda* has a variety of game dishes on its menu: venison fillet with cranberries, braised leg of wild boar with apple or quince, saddle of hare with Szekszárd wine, or saddle of mouflon with Aszú berries. Every chef has his secrets, but the quality and variety of game dishes makes a tour of Hungary a wonderful culinary experience for those who relish strong, spicy food.

Hungarian Paprika
mester
FŰSZERPAPRIKA ŐRLEMÉNY ÉDESNEMES
ÉDESNEMES
CSÍPŐS

Hungarian PAPRIKA
PAPRIKA

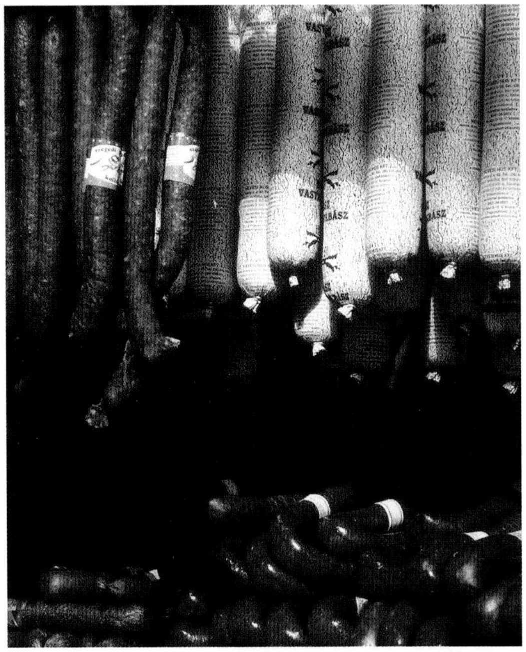

Balatoni
kg 350.-

Hízott
Libamáj
4500

HERZ
CSEMEGE SZALÁMI

Finally, no good Hungarian meal is complete without fruit or a dessert. Every orchard has its red fruits: cherries, strawberries, raspberries, red currants, blackcurrants, and cranberries. Bitter cherry trees line the village streets. The fruits on sale are usually of a good size and well ripened, as the markets are never very far from the small farms and orchards where they are grown. Pesticides are not used, so it is safe to eat fruit straight from the tree. Large quantities of apples—appreciated for their sugar and vitamin content, plus the fact that they can be kept in storerooms over winter—are grown. The region of Kecskemét, in the center of Hungary, is famous for its very sweet apricots, mainly grown to make an apricot brandy called *barack pálinka*. Unlike in supermarkets in most of Europe and the United States, peaches are not sold graded for size, and are as juicy and full of flavor as they were in your grandmother's time. Red plums are delicious too, and are often used in homemade cakes and pastries, or to make an excellent plum brandy (*silva pálinka*). People often distill their own fruits at home for private consumption. A particularly remarkable home distiller was an old pastor who lived in Zala County, in southwest Hungary; he knew better than anyone how to bring out all the flavor of pears or greengages through slow distillation in large copper stills. Unfortunately when he died, his secrets died with him.

The stores in the great central market are a great advertisement for the abundance and diversity of Hungarian-grown produce. Customers are enticed by the many tempting displays: alternating strings of red paprika and white garlic, dry sausages, hams and salami, dried fish, goose livers, piles of spices and powders, and biscuits for every day or special occasions.

In fall, city dwellers visit the country at weekends to gather walnuts. Every little garden boasts at least one walnut tree, and large plantations exist to meet the demand for walnut pastries at Christmas time. All Hungarians respect the Christmas tradition of making sugar-crust pastries stuffed with a creamy preparation of nuts (*diós beigli*) or poppy seeds (*mákos beigli*)—although they may worry that theirs are not as good as their neighbor's or cousin's, because the custom is to exchange these delicacies with friends or among relatives. Quinces are grown against house walls to protect them from frost, and when the bright yellow fruits are harvested in fall, they are crystallized or made into preserves in large copper pans as soon as the first cold weather arrives. They make a delicious dessert, which should be accompanied by an old Tokay Aszú (five or six *puttonyos*).

Sweet chestnuts grow well in Hungary, and chestnuts (marrons) are commonly used in pastries. The traditional *gesztenyepüré* is a delicious dessert: the chestnuts are cooked in syrup, pounded into a fine purée flavored with rum or *pálinka*, then heaped into little mounds, which are covered in whipped cream and served with a glacé cherry on top.

Gourmets with a sweet tooth who want to try the many delicious varieties of Hungarian cakes and pastries should visit the tearooms of Budapest (these are rarer in the provinces). The great Budapest cafés—especially Gerbeaud, Rusztwurm, or Mõvész—justify an exploration of the city both from an architectural and gastronomic point of view, as already mentioned in chapter 1. Nowhere is the Budapest art of living better illustrated. In each of these cafés you can try the famous *dobos torta*: six alternating layers of sponge cake and a thick butter and chocolate cream, glazed with caramel and coated with biscuit crumbs (those from the Mõvész deserve a special mention).

The great variety of Hungarian museums

On Andrássy Avenue in Pest, a beautiful neo-Renaissance building dating from 1875 is home to the Academy of Fine Arts, which can be visited on request. Particularly splendid features are the ceilings, adorned with lovely medallion portraits of women, and the colored marble on the upper-floor grand gallery.

One of the most surprising things about a tour of Hungary is the great number and diversity of its museums, many of them devoted to illustrating a single aspect of the country's history or heritage. The great Budapest museums house the national collections. The Museum of Fine Arts (Szépmûvészeti Múzeum) has magnificent Italian and Spanish collections, which were added to by aristocratic patrons during the golden age of the capital. The Hungarian National Museum (Magyar Nemzeti Múzeum), in a neoclassical palace, contains the Hungarian crown jewels, and has collections illustrating the most significant periods in the country's history. The Museum of Ethnography (Néprajzi Múzeum) is a neo-Renaissance palace of monumental proportions, with a particularly fine central staircase, where visitors are introduced to Hungarian peasant life of the eighteenth and nineteenth centuries.

The most extraordinary of these temples of learning, however, is the Museum of Decorative Arts (Iparmûvészeti Múzeum), designed by architect Ödön Lechner and inaugurated in 1896 during the Millennium celebrations. The oriental features of the building are in Secessionist style: in the entrance hall, multi-lobed arches with complex arabesques reach up to the second floor, and the central atrium is covered by a huge metal-framed glass roof supported by twenty flying buttresses. The collections of ceramics and porcelain, textiles and tapestries, furniture and so on are so rich and varied that the objects are regularly rearranged; indeed, visitors returning after an interval of several years may feel they are visiting a whole new museum.

Throughout the country, you will find charming museums devoted to foodstuffs such as paprika (in Kalocsa, for example), to crafts such as lace or pottery, and to traditional occupations—many former pharmacies have been converted into little museums. Hungary produced a large number of artists in the last century, many of whom emigrated to places throughout the world. The lives and work of native Hungarians are frequently remembered in local museums set up in their honor. There are several at Pécs, for example, but the award for the most attractive must go to the little town of Kaposvár.

Kaposvár is located south of Lake Balaton, 37 miles (60 km) northwest of Pécs. It is historically significant as the birthplace of three men who left their mark, in different ways, on modern Hungary. First and foremost, it was the hometown of politician Imre Nagy (1895–1958), who as premier of Hungary played a leading role in the anti-Soviet uprising of 1956. It was also home to two great early-twentieth-century Hungarian painters: József Rippl-Rónai (1861–1927) and János Vaszary (1867–1939). The latter is famous for his sense of color, and for helping to import a succession of artistic movements into Hungary: Secessionism, neo-Impressionism, Expressionism, and Fauvism. Rippl-Rónai was a member of the Paris group of painters called the Nabis, (prophets), which included Pierre Bonnard, Edouard Vuillard, and Maurice Denis.

The Rippl-Rónai Museum, in the main street of the town, presents a broad retrospective of modern Hungarian painting, with a few minor works by Vaszary and Rippl-Rónai. The villa where Rippl-Rónai spent part of his life is situated on a hill in a very rural setting away from the town center. A long path bordered with pretty chestnut trees leads to this early

Jószef Rippl-Rónai was one of the major figures of the Nabis movement, then of Hungarian decorative art. The villa in which he spent much of his life is on the outskirts of the town of Kaposvár, in a charming garden dotted with sculptures here and there (below). Several of Rippl-Rónai's remarkable works are on display in the house, together with some fine antique furniture. You should also visit the garden studio, where the artist's presence can still be felt.

The many museums in Pest are often as interesting for their architecture as for their collections. The Museum of Decorative Arts, designed by Ödön Lechner in Secessionist style, is a masterpiece by one of the greatest architects of his age. The atmosphere is unique in this lovely building; its galleries are adorned with complex arabesques (right), and the light that enters through the stained-glass roof (above) adds tinges of color to the pure white walls. The eclectic-style Museum of Ethnography also dates from the late nineteenth century; it is impressive for its grandeur and the richness of its decoration (page 187).

nineteenth-century residence, painted a beautiful Baroque shade of yellow. The villa is now a museum, and is a charming place in which to admire many of the artist's paintings and a few of his sculptures, which are dotted around the grounds. Rippl-Rónai's spirit still seems to inhabit the house; the three large ground-floor rooms contain some of his furniture. Rippl-Rónai's father had intended him to be a teacher, but after a few years at the College of Pharmacy (an experience he had in common with another painter—Tivadar Csontváry, the solitary genius from Pécs) he went to study art in Munich. He produced his first great painting, *Woman in a White Spotted Dress*, after joining the Nabis in 1888. This painting is exhibited in the villa, as is *My Grandmother*, a painting much admired by Gauguin.

In 1895, Rippl-Rónai had a small solo exhibition in Budapest, and on this occasion met Count Tivadar Andrássy, who asked him to paint a number of portraits for one of his castles, and to design the interior of his palace in Buda. This commission was a turning point in the artist's career. From now on he devoted all his energy to combining painting with the decorative arts. One of the paintings in his villa, of a large vase by Vilmós Zsolnay, illustrates this ambition, which was Rippl-Rónai's way of linking Hungarian national identity to its artistic life. The general public, however, showed little appreciation of his avant-garde designs for the Andrássy palace (which opened in 1900), and in 1902 he returned to live in Kaposvár.

This marked the beginning of Rippl-Rónai's second period in which color predominated. He often used pastel in his portraits of local worthies, several of which can be seen in his villa. His years in Kaposvár were happy ones, but on the eve of World War I he returned to Paris. He spent the war years in France, then left for Switzerland where the portraits he painted of writers and actors, with exaggerated features and very little color, betray a certain disillusion with the world. In this last period, just before his death in 1927 in a spa town on Lake Balaton, he painted large stained-glass windows and works that are almost Expressionist such as *The Woman with Glasses*. Everything about the comfortable interior of his villa with its Biedermeier furniture reflects Rippl-Rónai's desire for an ordered world, in which he could express his genius. In the first-floor bedroom, a self-portrait of the artist turning towards the spectator gives an idea of the power of his character. He seems to be willing the onlooker to acknowledge his work—and his talent. A lock of hair falls over the eyes. Their penetrating gaze is that of a man convinced of the power of the seduction of his art, but doubting the readiness of society to receive his message of modernism. The background suggests a rather bourgeois lifestyle, and the artist's heavy frame is reminiscent of portraits of worthy Victorian gentlemen. The garden leads to his lovely studio, which adds to this impression of calm and controlled use of space. Rippl-Rónai stored his homemade wine in part of this studio. His palette and wide-brimmed hat are still in a corner of the room, as if he had just gone out for a moment. A 1911 painting, *The Kaposvár Studio*, adds to this impression: Rippl-Rónai portrays himself in the middle of the room, busy painting a mother and daughter who are relegated to a corner. The whole scene is a profusion of color with bright yellows, reds, and whites framing the large window that opens onto the greens and blues of the garden.

One thing that strikes those on a tour of Hungary is the respect for traditional architecture. All over the country, the vernacular styles of each Hungarian province can be admired at countryside museums (*tájház*) or open-air folk museums (such as the Szabadadtéri Néprajzi Múzeum). One of the most spectacular is in Zala County, in southern Transdanubia (the western part of Hungary). This is the Göcsej village-museum (Göcseji Falumúzeum) in Zalaegerszeg, the first outdoor museum to open to the public (in the 1960s). A visit to this place is a very moving experience. A branch of

Traditional homes are often featured in open-air museums. The Göcsej museum in the Zala region is among the best known. Here, the past really comes alive. The wooden gateway opening onto the churchyard is loved by all the villagers, who come to worship at the foot of the charmingly naïve sculpture of Christ on the cross.

The Göcsej village-museum in Zalaegerszeg in southwestern Hungary is a particularly fine example of the national open-air museums, designed to make Hungarians realize the importance of preserving their traditional habitat. Various constructions such as houses, farms, country churches or Calvaries were dismantled and reconstructed in this rural setting on the banks of a little tributary of the river Zala. Authentic touches are added by a water mill and ducks that dabble in the stream.

the river Zala runs through it, and ducks and geese waddle around, accompanied by the refreshing sound of water trickling from a mill. There are about thirty buildings, including a little wooden belfry complete with old bell, and a Calvary decorated with pieces of painted metal, a testament to Hungary's deep-rooted, popular piety. Each house is furnished to look as if it were still lived in; the table is set for dinner, crockery and bedding are arranged in the old dressers and cupboards, and wood is piled in readiness for winter. The half-timber barns are full of freshly-mown hay, and there are live rabbits in the hutches. A donkey wanders noisily around hoping for tasty tidbits from the visitors. Every detail looks authentic: an old well, twisted wooden fences, houses with archways and reed-thatched roofs, and plowing implements in working order. As you wander through this fascinating museum, you tend to forget that traditional dwellings have almost disappeared in many villages, replaced by more comfortable modern homes. Nevertheless, in recent years there has been a growing trend throughout Transdanubia—especially among nostalgic city dwellers who want to get back to their roots, to preserve authentic details of the rural past—and this has given the villages a new lease of life. The open-air museums play a vital role in this respect, enabling the younger generation to rediscover the joys of country life.

Groups of people in many rural areas work hard to keep their local heritage alive. The little village of Hollókõ is a fine example of this. Until the 1960s, the village women used to meet in a place called a *fonóház* to wind wool or hemp and sing old songs. A few old ladies still observe the tradition, anxious to ensure the survival of these melodies. They wear the regional costumes of this Palóc area, and often welcome inquiring visitors with a piece of cheesecake (*túróslepény*) and a small glass of apricot brandy (*barack pálinka*).

The traditional costume consists of a black dress hemmed with colored embroidery worn over a minimum of six petticoats (*alsószoknya*). On special occasions, there can be as many as sixteen of these silk, flannel, or cashmere underskirts, worn as a sign of wealth or to indicate pregnancy. The headdress is also significant, as there are variations in each village, but it always consists of three parts: a cleverly folded scarf, rows of glass beads on the forehead, and colored threads tied at the nape of the neck. Some girls wind artificial roses around their necks to conceal a small mirror or portrait, or add a few extra rows of beads; little girls just tie ribbons in their hair. This attractive costume is completed with thick white woolen stockings, a hand-embroidered handkerchief worn on a chain, and black boots or shoes. Of the three hundred and seventy people who live in the village today, only a dozen women still observe the tradition. During the traditional Easter celebration or at craft markets, the inhabitants of the surrounding villages (Buják, Kozárd, or Rimóc) go to Hollókõ wearing their family costumes.

In Hollóku and some of the nearby villages in this Palóc region, local women still wear traditional hand-made costumes on festive occasions. These outfits consist of black skirts with colorful hems worn over several layers of petticoat, with white woolen stockings and colored waistcoats and jackets. Each village has its own style of headdress, corresponding to a complex code in which fashion mingles with tradition. Special pastries are also made for these occasions, and in some stores you can buy charming gingerbread figures (*mézeskalács*) whose themes vary according to the baker's inspiration. Among these hills in central Hungary, a love of nature and respect for age-old customs live on, reflecting a deep desire to maintain the old folk traditions of the Magyar people in face of the forced and perilous march towards modernism.

Inventive arts and crafts

The situation of the craft industry in Hungary is not yet akin to that of Western Europe, where its very survival depends on a determination to preserve certain skills now threatened by standardization. Although many forms of Hungarian craftsmanship now conform to industrial norms, some folk traditions have proved strong enough to survive changes in the manufacturing process.

To discover the various forms of traditional craftsmanship, a morning visit to Budapest's Ecseri flea market (Ecseri piac) is a must. Saturday is the best day, but you have to get up early because there are few bargains to be found after eight o'clock. A whole range of treasures awaits you, including furniture and household utensils, black pottery decorated with animal motifs from Nádudvar, porcelain vases with floral motifs from Hollóháza, brightly colored Ajka crystal, and a multitude of embroidered fabrics—provided you know how to hunt them out in the back of a shop or from among a pile of insignificant trinkets.

Pieces of crystalware and porcelain biscuit in the store window of a Pest antique dealer illustrate Hungary's rich craft tradition. Many provincial firms still produce craft items for the domestic and foreign markets.

The capital's antique dealers, most of whom are located near the Parliament in Falk Miksa Street, have interesting pieces, but the prices are high nowadays. On Váci Street, the main pedestrian street in Pest, there are many shops that specialize in craftwork from the provinces, or in Herend porcelain from the Transdanubian factory, which produces a wide range of designs.

Moreover, the increase in living standards in Hungary has contributed to the reemergence of a number of traditional crafts that had died out during the last half-century. Jewelers, for example, have rediscovered the creativity of their predecessors from the nineteenth century or between the World Wars, who produced the kind of pieces now found in specialist antique shops in downtown Budapest. A fine example of a modern-day jeweler is the Wladis Galéria at 13, Falk Miksa Street (the shop sign has two elephants), near the two great auction rooms of Kieselbach Galéria and Nagyházi Galéria. Jeweler Péter Vladimir uses simple settings for big cabochon stones to create beautiful rings in original geometric shapes. Silverwork designs incorporate animal themes that owe much to the traditional art of the Scythian and Avar steppe peoples.

A treasure hunt in the Ecseri flea market will turn up all manner of curios, including decorative works by minor painters. If you're hoping to find a bargain however, you'll have to get up early and would do well to go with a Hungarian friend.

In another sphere altogether, the elegant shoemaker Lázló Vass—whose small showroom is on Haris köz, on the corner of Váci Street—is famous for the quality of his work. Vass takes his inspiration from the great Austro-Hungarian tradition with his "Wien," "Budapest," or "Theresianer" models, and from the English with his "London" and "Old English" series. He uses top-quality leather and has exploited his highly developed sense of color to create a discreetly elegant style all his own. He will custom-make and deliver a pair of shoes anywhere in Europe in one month. Vass is a shy man, but he will speak passionately and with great conviction about the grain or tone of a piece of leather, the shape of a shoe, or the inspiration for his designs.

The recent development of auction sales in Budapest and the provinces reflects a renewal of interest in artistic movements that were somewhat overlooked in recent years. Prosperous firms such as the Kieselbach or Nagyházi Galleries have been successful in finding and selling Hungarian works from the last century. Young city executives also appreciate the original jewelry designed by creators like Péter Vladimir, owner of the popular Wladis Galeria in the antique dealers' district. The items of jewelry he produces here (rings, necklaces, or silver pendants) are often inspired by the traditional art of the steppes with its animal themes.

As noted in an earlier chapter, Lázló Vass's other passion is the collection of modern and contemporary Hungarian art he has assembled at his home in Buda and at his house on Lake Balaton since the 1970s. This patron of the arts began to take an interest in painting under the leadership of Master Jenõ Barcsay, one of the most important artists in modern-day Hungary. Barcsay studied with János Vaszary before the war, took a particular interest in color, and spent his whole life seeking to give form to the precepts of Cézanne and the Hungarian Constructivists, of whom Lajos Kassák was the pioneer. It was Barcsay who taught Vass to appreciate painting—and now anyone who wishes to understand twentieth-century Hungarian art should visit Lázló Vass's private museum. The core of his collection are works by the main heirs of Constructivism, such as Imre Bak, Pál Deim, Tamás Hencze, Tamás Konok, Dezso Korniss, and István Nádler, who all strove to maintain a close link between strong national tradition and the main trends of contemporary art. For Vass, this collection is central to a reflection about his craft: that the manifest usefulness of an object should not override the esthetic or artistic aspect involved in its creation.

This reflection on creativity can also be applied to the craft potters who work clay to produce shapes inspired by age-old tradition, to the coopers whose barrels are masterpieces in their own right, or to the local craftsmen of Mohács who make the *busó* masks for the annual carnival procession. There has been a renewal of interest in these masks in recent years—part of a more general trend in Central Europe to revive carnival traditions. In Mohács today, the children learn to make masks at school under the guidance of a new generation of master craftsmen, eager to transmit a skill that nearly died out in the 1960s. They teach the children to polish the wood to make their masks, to add sheep or goat horns, and to color them with bright red paint instead of the wild boar's blood that was once used (Hungary's minority population of Croats was apparently responsible for introducing this custom in the eighteenth century).

Lost among some rather uninspired buildings in Mohács is an old one-story house, where one of these young craftsmen has his workshop. He is passionate about his art, although it is only a hobby. His house and garden are full of the various bits and pieces needed to make the masks; beards of corn, hair and horns hanging from a cable in the workshop, pieces of wood and tools of all kinds create a cheerful muddle. The future now looks bright for the Mohács carnival, which also contributes to the economic development of the town.

In Erdobénye, a lovely village in the Tokay region, is a cooper's workshop where wooden barrels have been produced for several generations. The specialty of the workshop is a little casket for *palinka*, the local brandy distilled from plums, pears, apricots, or grapes. The cooper makes visitors welcome; he is happy to talk about this family passion and explain how he makes his caskets by heating his special tools on a burner before using them to curve the oak planks. Finished caskets await their future owners on his workbench and in the little garden. The cooper's wife arrives with a glass of dry white wine and a fresh goat cheese served on a chunk of whole-wheat bread, proving that the traditional hospitality of these country areas is still very much alive.

The future of the dyer's craft also looks bright, judging from the variety of dyes and fabrics to be found all over Hungary. In the Middle Ages, fabrics with white and indigo blue patterns arrived in this part of Europe along the Silk Road from Asia, and ever since they have appealed to the imagination of villagers and city dwellers alike. They remain popular today, and constitute a tourist attraction in the towns of Szentendre, Gyor, Veszprém, Szeged, and Kecskemet. Each of these towns has a street called *Festo*, which means both painter and dyer, and indicates that the profession was carried

On Váci utca in the heart of Pest, the Philanthia florist's is worth a visit, both for its creative floral arrangements and for the Art Nouveau décor in the store itself (above). Shoemaker Laszló Vass is reputed worldwide for the quality of his leather, and his stylish designs are highly appreciated by aficionados.

In Karcság, the heir to master Kántor Sándor specializes in pottery pieces representing the traditional "Miska" character, with his distinctive mustache, and produces many others items of folk art too. The wide range of brandies in the Tokay region inspired the Erdubénye cooper to start producing palinka caskets (left).

out here in the past and (sometimes) continues to be in the present. The dyed fabrics are used for a whole range of purposes including clothing, household linen, and soft furnishings. Their variety and perfection reflect a high degree of specialized craftsmanship. The dyers' artistic creativity is realized in the charming motifs they choose, using wooden or metal templates made by expert craftsmen. Little by little, enterprising dyers from the younger generation are taking over from their elders, who managed to keep going throughout the difficult years and thereby ensured the survival of this traditional and much prized skill.

An important aspect of Hungarian culture is its ability to enrich deep-rooted national traditions by adapting to outside influences. Each region cultivates its age-old customs and typical crafts, and the resulting woodwork, pottery, embroidery, and fabrics make up a fascinating, ever-changing landscape: a reflection of Hungarian vitality.

Buso masks are an age-old tradition in Mohács. They are made for the carnival by a young generation of craftsmen, who also teach their skills in the local schools. The traditional materials used are willow wood, cornsilk, cow horns and sheep's wool.

A tour of Hungary is a fascinating introduction to the richness and diversity of embroidered fabrics and original regional outfits. A whole range of styles and colors can be admired at tourist sites such as Tihany on Lake Balaton and Szentendre on the banks of the Danube, or in the secondhand stores in Pécs or downtown Pest. Clothes for everyday wear or for special occasions reflect a typically Magyar sense of harmony.

On Váci utca in Budapest, in a courtyard with a lovely wrought-iron balcony, the famous Tango store sells ceremonial outfits (*Diszmagyar*), antique wedding dresses, brocaded or frogged jackets, and also fabrics which can add a colorful touch to a city apartment.

The Hungarian art of living is closely linked to the glorious past of Greater Hungary and to folk traditions that are still deeply rooted in everyday life. This beautiful marquetry table (right, bottom) is a fine example of the Biedermeier style from the first half of the nineteenth century, which emerged to satisfy the bourgeois desire for comfort. The Herend porcelain pieces and ornaments in a Buda store are well suited to this style of furniture. A wedding bench dated 1874 and a horn mirror from 1897 were once the property of Transylvanian families, and a collection of painted eggs from all over Hungary illustrates the vitality of ancient traditions. The wine growers of Tokay produce tangible proof of their respect for their region, with syrupy wines which can be enjoyed at the Opera bar in Budapest (pages 200–201).

TOKAJI
SZAMORODNI
500,-Ft

USEFUL INFORMATION

This address book is intended for visitors to Hungary who want to know the addresses of Budapest's most elegant baths, visit interesting museums, find a room with a view of Lake Balaton, explore antique dealers, discover art galleries or admire the work of craftsmen who still respect tradition. It also offers a choice of restaurants and tearooms that best represent Hungarian gastronomy, where gourmets and wine lovers will be able to appreciate all the abundance and diversity of Hungarian produce and cuisine. Music lovers will also find the information they need to attend the concerts of their choice. In short, this address book is for travelers who want their exploration of Hungary to be as rich and varied as possible.

TRAVELS IN HUNGARY

Traveling in Hungary is no longer the adventure it used to be. Since the fall of the Berlin Wall, the restrictive notion of the Eastern European Bloc as represented by the Comecon (the former Communist economic grouping), with its strongly interventionist connotations, has gradually been replaced by that of Central and Eastern Europe. A visa is no longer necessary to enter the country; visitors need only a valid identity card to cross the Hungarian border and head for Budapest.

This city with its two million inhabitants no longer has cause to be jealous of other European capitals as regards hotel or banking facilities, restaurants or museums; there are elegant well-stocked stores too, although it seems a shame that Hungarian products and craftsmanship have progressively been replaced by ubiquitous western brands.

You will best perceive the charm of old Hungary with its many ancient traditions in the provinces, however. Moreover, distances from Budapest are not too great as the capital is never more than three hours' drive away from any point on the Hungarian border. The highway network has recently been developed, and the secondary roads are also excellent. It is therefore no problem to rent a car and set out to explore the entire country, preferably in spring or fall, bearing in mind the various stopping places and recommendations you will find in this book.

Nowadays it is increasingly common to meet Hungarians, especially of the younger generation, who speak foreign languages (English, German, and occasionally French). You will find them to be particularly friendly and helpful, as hospitality and a sense of welcome are among the many fine qualities of the Magyar people. You will come to appreciate their immense kindness and helpfulness throughout your travels.

Budapest

HOTELS

Whatever your tastes and budget, you will find a hotel to suit you in Budapest. Many new establishments have opened in recent years—some in converted historic monuments, others in new buildings—and many are of international standard. The following is a selection of three, four, and five-star hotels with plenty of atmosphere.

ANDRÁSSY

1063 Budapest Andrássy út 111
Tel.: + 36 1 462 2100
Fax: + 36 1 462 2195
E-mail: reservation@andrassyhotel.com
Website: www.andrassyhotel.com
There's a stylish atmosphere to this hotel, which recently opened on Andrássy Avenue in a building dating from the Bauhaus era. The rooms are well designed, and the deluxe rooms elegantly furnished. For a four-star hotel the prices are reasonable, and many rooms are available all year round. The terrace overlooking Andrássy Avenue is very pleasant for dinner in spring or summer, and the cuisine is of a high quality.

ART'OTEL

1011 Budapest, Bem rakpart 16-19
Tel.: + 36 1 487 9487
Fax: + 36 1 487 9488
E-mail: budapest@artotel.hu
Website: www.parkplazaww.com
This four-star establishment on the right bank of the river is both hotel and contemporary art gallery. It is bright and airy with good-sized rooms, an attractive dining room, and good food. At the back of the building there are several rooms in what was once a Baroque-style convent, where calm and authenticity compensate for the lack of river views.

ASTORIA

1053 Budapest, Kossuth L. U. 19-21
Tel.: + 36 1 484 3200
Fax: + 36 1 318 6798
E-mail: astoria@hungary.net
The Astoria, at the intersection of Kiskorut (Little Boulevard) and Rákóczi Avenues, is one of the most prestigious establishments in Budapest. The building itself is steeped in history: the proclamation of the Republic of Councils was signed here in 1919. It has a splendid Secessionist-style lobby and dining room. Most of the rooms have been refurbished and now have double glazing, which is indispensable in this lively neighborhood. You would be wise to book a room at the back of the building, such as room 609. The tearoom is a good place to take a break while exploring this district of the city.

DANUBIUS GRAND HOTEL MARGITSZIGET

1138 Budapest, Margitsziget
Tel.: + 36 1 452 6200
Fax: + 36 1 452 6264
E-mail: margotel@hungary.net
www.danubiusgroup.com
This recently renovated palace on peaceful, scenic Margaret Island is one of the most remarkable addresses in town. The rooms are spacious and tastefully decorated, with views of either the gardens or the river; some have attractive private balconies where you can enjoy the view as you breakfast (room 276, for example, has a vast balcony). Parking is in front of the hotel. Guests at the Margitsziget have free access via an underground corridor to the neighboring Thermal Hotel, where they can enjoy exceptional spa and fitness facilities in a completely renovated setting.

GELLÉRT

1111 Budapest, Szent Gellért tér 1
Tel.: + 36 1 385 2200
Fax: + 36 1 466 6631
E-mail: gellert@gellert.hu
www.danubiusgroup.com/gellert
The Gellért Hotel on the banks of the Danube has one of the loveliest Art Nouveau façades in the capital. It is famous for its spa, recommended all year round. Many of the rooms at the front of the hotel have been renovated; you would be wise to check if this is the case for the room you reserve. Your stay here may turn out to be one of the most unforgettable experiences of your vacation, but you should avoid the restaurant, which is not up to the standard of the rest of the establishment. The décor in the Viennese café is beautiful, however, and the pastries are delicious.

HILTON BUDAPEST

1011 Budapest, Hess András Hess tér 1-3
Tel.: + 36 1 488 6600
Fax: + 36 1 488 6644
E-mail: hiltonhu@hungary.net
Website: www.hilton.com
The Hilton hotel in the heart of the historic Castle district is a blend of modernity and cultural heritage. In the 1970s, the hotel took over the ruins of a medieval cloister and monastery in Buda, causing debate about the conversion of historic monuments for modern-day purposes. You should ask for a room overlooking the Danube—it's worth the extra charge.

KEMPINSKI CORVINUS

1051 Budapest, Erzsébet tér 7-8
Tel.: + 36 1 429 3777
Fax: + 36 1 429 4777
E-mail: hotel@kempinski.hu
Website: www.kempinski-budapest.com
A reputed address in downtown Pest, particularly recommended for the quality of its Sunday brunch. The rooms are worthy of the reputation of this hotel and restaurant chain. A great place for families.

MERIDIAN BUDAPEST

1051 Budapest, Erzsébet tér 9-10
Tel.: + 36 1 429 5500
Fax: + 36 1 429 5555
E-mail: reservation@le-meridien.hu
Website: www.lemeridien-budapest.com
The Meridian is the latest luxury hotel to open in Budapest. It occupies a magnificent neoclassical building, dating from 1911, which used to serve as police headquarters (and prior to that was home to an insurance company). The lobby sets the tone for the rest of this stylish hotel, whose rooms are particularly elegant.

MERCURE NEMZETI BUDAPEST

1088 Budapest, József kórút 4
Tel.: + 36 1 477 2000
E-mail: h1686@accor-hotels.com
Website: www.hungary.com/pannonia/nemzeti
This is a four-star Art Nouveau hotel in the shopping district of Budapest. It boasts 76 comfortable, air-conditioned rooms, furnished in a range of pastel tones. There is an impressive dining room in which you can enjoy quality cuisine. For a hotel of this standing, the prices are particularly attractive.

NOVOTEL BUDAPEST CENTRUM

1088 Budapest, Rákóczi út 43-45
Tel.: + 36 1 477 5300
Fax: + 36 1 477 5353
E-mail: h3560@accor-hotels.com
Website: www.novotel-bud-centrum.hu
This Secessionist-style hotel, near Blaha Lujza tér in downtown Budapest, originally opened in 1911 and has recently been renovated by the Accor chain. It has attractive reception areas and quiet rooms, and makes an excellent base for visitors who want to explore the city on foot.

RESTAURANTS

There are plenty of good restaurants in Budapest and the new generation of chefs endeavors to blend typical Hungarian savors and products with international influences. In the fall, delicious game dishes are available in many restaurants. The restaurant sector is an unstable one, however, and any selection of restaurants is necessarily subject to change. Booking a table is a way of checking that the restaurant still exists!

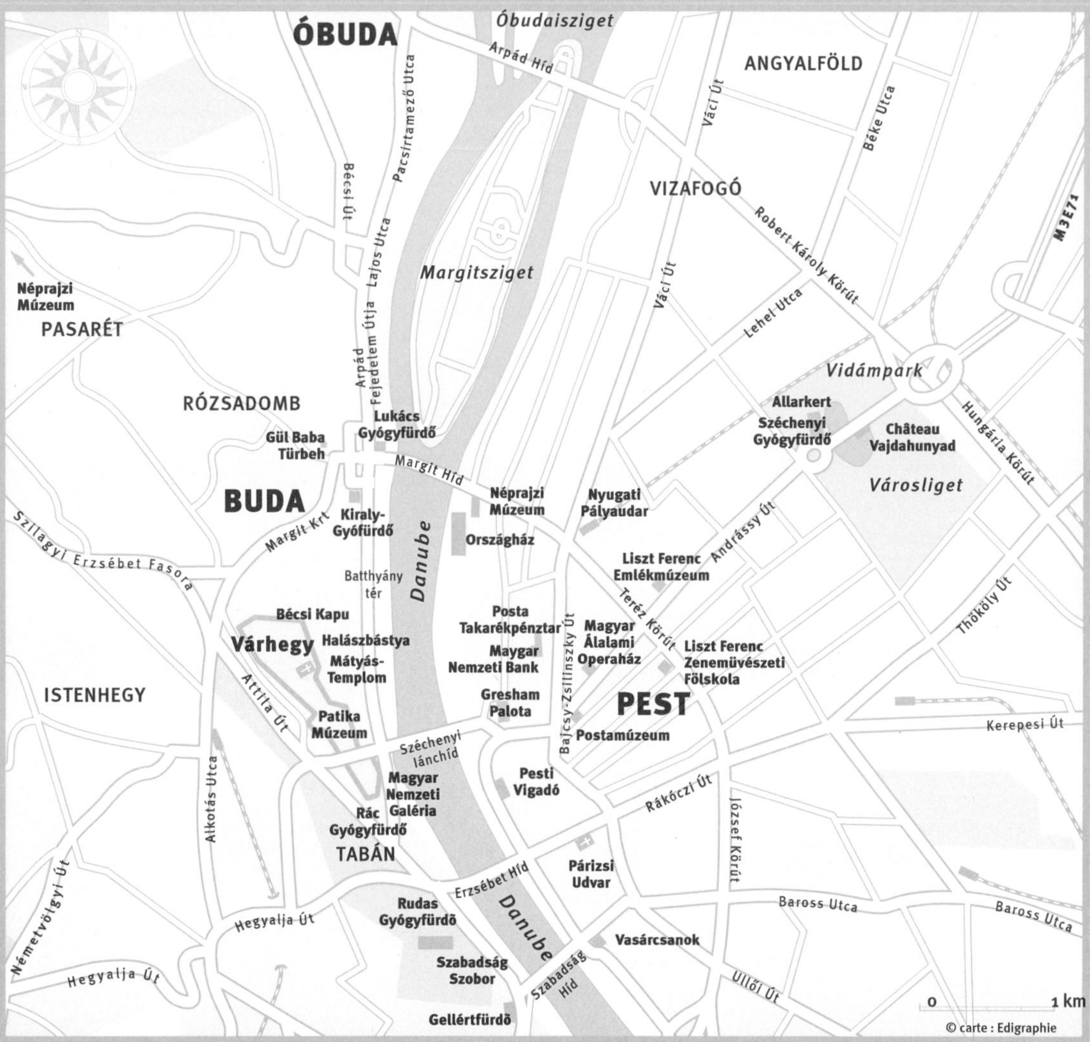

ARTICSOKA

1066 Budapest, Zichy J utca 17
Tel./Fax: + 36 1 302 7758
Website: www.articsoka.hu
A new upmarket restaurant where the young Budapest jet set enjoy inventive cuisine served in a vast friendly room. Recommended if you want to be in with the in-crowd!

BAGOLYVÁR

1146 Budapest, Állatkerti út 2
Tel.: + 36 1 468 0217 or + 36 363 7495
This tastefully appointed restaurant, not far from the famous Gundel Restaurant and run by the same team, is staffed entirely by women. The hard-working waitresses serve an intelligent selection of traditional dishes. The terrace is very pleasant for a meal in summer.

BELCANTO

1061 Budapest, Dalszínház u 8
Tel.: + 36 1 269 2786
Website: www.belcanto.hu
After an evening at the Opera you can hear some of your favorite arias again, sung by the Belcanto waiters who are often professional singers from the nearby opera school. This hit formula has been copied in other European capitals—but Budapest was the first! What's more, the music in no way detracts from the quality of the food.

CHEZ DANIEL

1063 Budapest, Szív u 32
Tel.: + 36 1 302 4039
E-mail: lecoq@matavnet.hu
Undoubtedly the best French restaurant in the city, opened several years ago by a French chef who is also a connoisseur of Hungary. Culinary skills and top-quality Hungarian produce make a great combination here, but it is essential to book, as there are not many tables in this increasingly popular restaurant.

FATÁL

Budapest 5th district., Váci utca 67
Tel.: + 36 1 266 26 07
This restaurant, a legend for a generation who sometimes went hungry, is famed for its huge portions, served on wooden platters. Quantity does not necessarily mean quality, but the atmosphere in this old cellar is a satisfaction in itself.

FAUSTO'S

1072 Budapest, Dohány utca 5
Tel.: + 36 1 269 6806
One of the city's finest Italian restaurants, with light, inventive dishes inspired by the best Tuscan traditions. The service is attentive and there is a good selection of wines, but the prices match the high-quality cuisine.

GUNDEL

1146 Budapest Allatkerti út 2
Tel.: + 36 1 468 4040
The Gundel Restaurant, amid the greenery of City Park, is still the most prestigious in Budapest. It opened in the late nineteenth century, and has recently been renovated by owner George Lang. The latter also owns a vineyard in Tokaj, so the wine list is excellent. The cuisine is refined (sometimes in the extreme), and includes some remarkable game dishes. Sunday brunch is an institution here, and the terrace is very pleasant in fine weather.

HEMINGWAY

1113 Budapest, Kosztolányi D. tér 2
(on the edge of Lake Feneketlen)
Tel./Fax: + 36 1 381 0523
E-mail: hemingway.club@axelero.hu
Website: www.miwo.hu/hemingway
Not far from the Gellért Hotel, the charming Hemingway Restaurant overlooks the Bottomless Lake (Feneketlen-tó), bordered with lovely Secessionist-style buildings. There is live music on the terrace, and the simple country fare is well suited to the natural setting.

KÁROLYI

1053 Budapest, Károlyi Mihály utca 16
Tel.: + 36 1 328 0240
Fax: + 36 1 328 0241
E-mail: karolyi.Étterem@axelero.hu
This is a new restaurant in the garden of the Károlyi Palace, which opens onto one of the most elegant squares in Pest. Large trees shade the quiet terrace, where good quality traditional cuisine is served (ask to try the *langos*, a sort of crispy bread stuffed with veal ragout).

KÁRPÁTIA

1053 Budapest, Ferenciek tere 7-8
Tel.: + 36 1 317 3596
Fax: + 36 1 318 0591
E-mail: restaurant@karpatia.hu
Website: www.karpatia.hu
The medieval decor in this restaurant is grandiose, with frescoes and furniture reminiscent of the time when Greater Hungary included the province of Transylvania; the menu is largely inspired by the traditional gastronomy of this region where Hungarian is still widely spoken. The sommelier will help you choose from the impressive wine list.

KÉPÍRÓ

1053 Budapest, Képíró utca 3
Tel.: + 36 1 266 0430
Fax: + 36 1 266 0425
E-mail: kepiro@hotmail.com
Website: www.kepirorestaurant.hu
A cozy, tastefully decorated little restaurant, with a central mahogany bar. The chef is influenced by French cuisine, which he adapts to suit Hungarian specialties. There is a prix fixe menu that includes an assortment of dishes and wines.

KISBUDA GYÖNGYE

1034 Budapest, Kenyeres utca 34
Tel.: + 36 1 368 6402
Fax: + 36 1 368 9227
Away from downtown Budapest, not far from the lovely Kiscelli Museum, the interior of this excellent restaurant evokes the atmosphere of a nineteenth-century salon. The light wood trim, frescoes, and beautiful paved floor enhance the overall impression of being in a private home. The chef excels at creating dishes that harmonize with this intimate setting.

KRIZIA

1065 Budapest, Moszár utca 12
Very probably the best Italian restaurant in Budapest. The setting—a sparely decorated cellar—is nothing special, but the creative cuisine uses quality ingredients and there is a superb selection of Hungarian wines. Recommended after a concert at the nearby Academy of Music.

LADIK CSÁRDA

1036 Budapest 3rd district, Obudai-Hajógyári Sziget 403
Tel.: + 36 1 457 1193
Obuda Island (on the Danube north of Budapest) is getting to be a fashionable place. Its unspoiled environment appeals to city dwellers, as they can play various sports in a country setting (you can have golf lessons at Golf Tanya; Tel.: + 36 302 694 995; E-mail: golfiskola@freemail.hu, website: www.golfcourses.hu. The restaurant has a festive atmosphere with its large riverbank terrace in the shade of an old willow tree, where fish and goulash dishes are served at wooden tables.

LA FONTAINE

1051 Budapest, Merleg u1 10
Tel.: + 36 317 3715
Fax: + 36 1 318 8562
Website: www.lafontaine.hu
This friendly restaurant in the business quarter has a Parisian brasserie atmosphere and is perfect for a quick meal. The menu varies from day to day according to the fresh produce available at the market—and the chef's inspiration! The wine list is short but well chosen.

LE JARDIN DE PARIS

1011 Budapest, Fö utca 20
Tel./Fax: + 36 1 201 0047
This restaurant is in the Vïziváros district of Buda on the right bank of the Danube, in a pretty yellow house with a corner turret that dates from the early nineteenth century. Gabriel Meunier, a familiar figure to Budapest foodies, has owned it for many years. His inventive cuisine attracts customers from the nearby French Institute and from the business world.

LOULOU

1051 Budapest, Vigyázó Ferenc utca 4
Tel./Fax: + 36 1 312 4505
With its Parisian bistro atmosphere, intimate interior, and well-spaced tables, this is a great place for a romantic dinner. The cuisine is tasty, though not wildly original.

MARGITKERT

1021 Budapest, Margit utca 15
Tel.: + 36 1 326 0860 or + 36 1 326 0862
A traditional old house in Buda is home to this restaurant, which is famous for its charming courtyard, virtuoso gypsy musicians, and tasty country dishes from the *puszta*—such as turkey breast stuffed with cheese, or Hungarian pancakes *(palacsinta)*. Many famous people have frequented the pleasant summer garden.

MOKKA

1051 Budapest, Sas utca 4
Tel.: + 36 1 328 0081
Fax: + 36 1 328 0082
The interior decoration here is a blend of Hungarian and North African traditions, with a minimalist touch. The impressive wine list includes comments to guide your choice. The menu is based on the "progressive cuisine" concept, with results that are sometimes surprising but usually delicious.

MÚZEUM

1081 Budapest, Múzeum körút 12
Tel.: + 36 1 267 0375
This old restaurant near the National Museum will delight gourmets who appreciate their surroundings. It has one of the most beautiful dining rooms in the city attentive service, and an original menu. Tokay wines are served with the foies gras in this top-class establishment; its foie gras "à la Lucullus " served warm with fruit, is a classic.

NÁNCSI NÉNI

1025 Budapest, Ördögárok út 80
Tel.: + 36 1 397 2742
This friendly restaurant in the hills of northern Buda is perfect for gourmets in search of authenticity, who will enjoy the family cooking. As in all self-respecting country inns, wood prevails. Booking is recommended.

NOSZTALGÍA

1051 Budapest, Október 6 utca 5
Tel.: + 36 1 317 2987 or + 36 1 318 9000
Fax: + 36 1 266 3310
This is an exquisitely stylish little restaurant in the heart of Pest, where a chamber music ensemble plays in the evening. The chef's culinary skills are reflected in the imaginative menu.

RÉGI SIPOS HALÁSZKERT

1036 Budapest, Lajos utca 46
Tel.: + 36 1 250 8082
Fax: + 36 1 368 6480
In the Obuda district (currently changing fast) this friendly restaurant is a great place for families. The tables are covered with checkered cloths, and the food is the traditional kind with excellent fish soups and freshwater-fish dishes. In the evening, gypsy musicians play good music with feeling.

REMIZ

1021 Budapest, Budakeszi út 5
Tel.: + 36 1 275 1396
Tel./Fax: + 36 1 394 1896
This restaurant on the hills of Buda near the tram station has a wonderful outdoor terrace. It has many regular customers, and is a favorite with the media crowd. The prices have not changed for years, and there are classic dishes such as venison ham with walnuts and quince cheese, or fillet of pike perch with almonds.

RIVALDA

1011 Budapest, Színház u 5-9
Tel.: + 36 1 489 0236
Website: www.rivalda.net
After a visit to the National Gallery or the Ludwig Museum of Contemporary Art, make your next stop the Rivalda restaurant. This eighteenth-century building has recently been renovated, and the ambience is one of luxury and elegance. A large open-air courtyard is a great place for receptions. The cuisine is a mix of traditional Hungarian dishes and international flavors.

ROBINSON

1146 Budapest, Városligeti tó
Tel.: + 36 1 422 0222, + 36 1 422 0224
Fax: + 36 1 422 0072
This restaurant on an island in the lake in City Park is housed in an attractive glass and metal structure, partially covered by climbing plants; eating here feels rather like taking a cruise! There is a warm welcome in the bar and restaurant, which are on several levels. The menu offers plenty of choice but no real surprises; there is a good selection of wines, however.

RONDELLA

1052 Budapest, Régi posta st. 4.
Tel.: + 36 1 483 08 29
Fax: + 36 1 483 08 31
E-mail: rondella@matavnet.hu
Website: www.restaurantguide.hu/rondella
The Rondella, in a historic cellar near the river, serves generous portions of good traditional food and has a wide selection of wines. In the evening, the great atmosphere and live gypsy music will make you reluctant to leave!

VÖRÖS ÉS FEHÉR

1065 Budapest, Andrássy út 41
Tel.: + 36 1 413 1545
E-mail: vorosesfeher@vorosesfeher.com
Website: www.vorosesfeher.com
The wine-bar atmosphere in this New York-style interior appeals to a young and friendly crowd. Wines are served by the glass here, and the food is good but unoriginal. On a lovely summer night, the terrace on the avenue is a great place for people watching.

ZAZIE

Budapest 1072, Klauzál tér 2
Tel.: + 36 1 321 2405
Fax: + 36 1 479 0423
E-mail: zazie@mail.alba.hu
Website: www.restaurantguide.hu/zazie
The Zazie Restaurant in the heart of the Jewish quarter gives onto an elegant square; nearby is the spectacular metal structure of one of the

local Budapest markets. The restaurant has a light-hearted atmosphere, and a bright modern interior with original contemporary furniture and plenty of color. There is a great selection of wines, and the menu must be one of the most original in town.

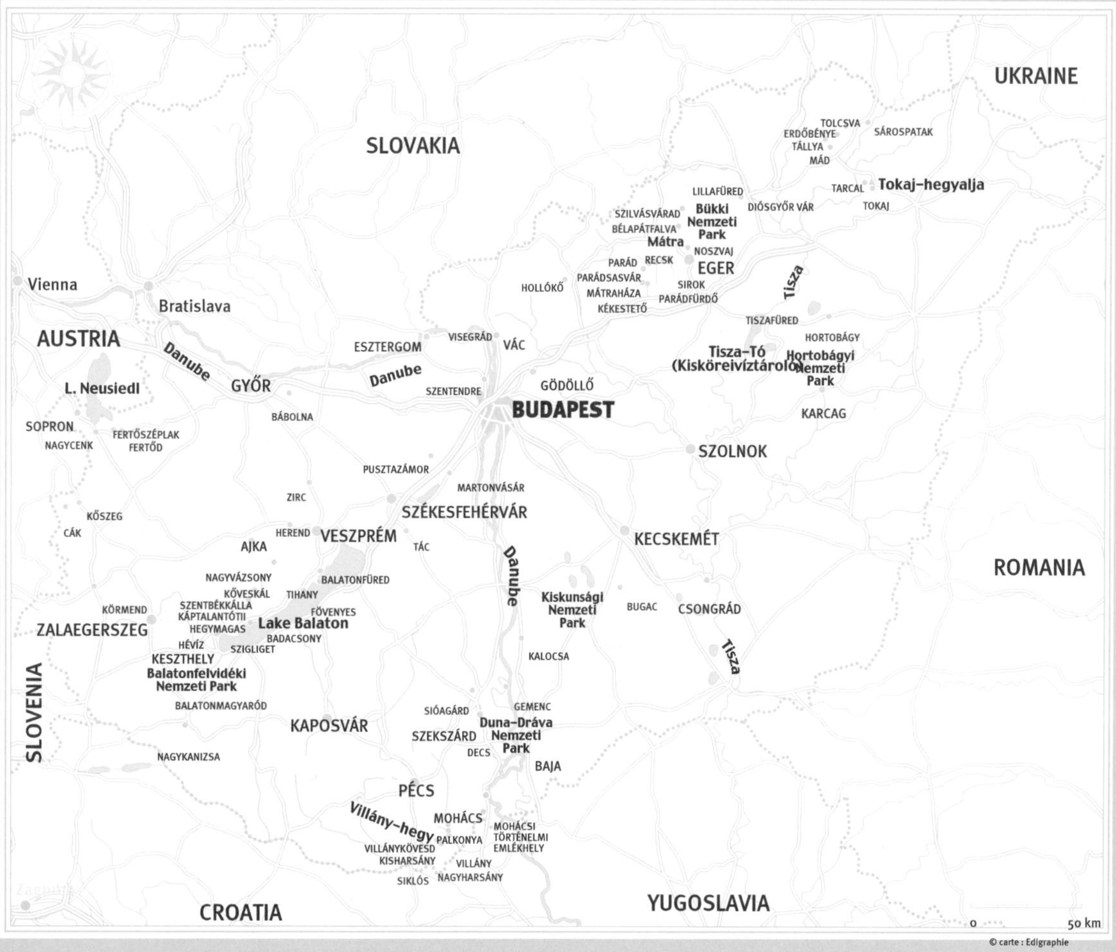

© carte : Edigraphie

CAFÉS

The café (*kávéház* in Hungarian) is a veritable institution in Budapest, and part of an age-old lifestyle tradition. The city's cafés lost something of their charm during the post war decades, but many historic places have now been renovated to offer a discerning clientele the kind of modern comfort they expect, while preserving tradition as far as possible. Authenticity may sometimes suffer in the process, however, so the following selection proposes establishments with a historic (or at least traditional) setting, a wide range of pastries, and a friendly atmosphere conducive to conversation. You should note that one of the capital's most prestigious places, the New York Café (Erzsébet körút 9-11), is currently closed for restoration work. Hopefully when it reopens "the world's most beautiful café" will still be worthy of its historic and literary reputation.

ANGELIKA

1011 Budapest, Batthyány tér 7
Tel.: + 36 201 4847
A quiet café on the riverbank in Buda, in a former convent with lovely Baroque vaults. This venerable institution is a perfect place to enjoy conversation . . . and mouthwatering pastries!

AUGUSZT CUKRAZCA

1053 Budapest, Kossuth Lajos utca 14-16
Tel./Fax: + 36 1 337 6379
Don't miss this patisserie/tearoom in a courtyard on a lively Pest boulevard. It's a modest-sized, attractively furnished place with a nostalgic atmosphere. Try the E-80 pastry, made with chocolate mousse, marzipan, and coffee-flavored whipped cream.

CAFÉ CENTRAL

1053 Budapest, Károlyi Mihály utca 9
Tel.: + 36 1 266 4572
Fax: + 36 1 266 4570
E-mail: centralkavehaz@matavnet.hu
The Café Central is a completely renovated establishment in downtown Budapest. It first opened its doors in 1887, and ever since has been a favorite daytime or night-time haunt for artists and intellectuals. Nowadays it functions as a restaurant too.

CAFÉ PIERROT

1011 Budapest, Fortuna utca 14
Tel.: + 36 1 375 6971
Fax: + 36 1 356 9973
The first privately owned café to open in the early 1980s, with a delightfully retro atmo sphere. In the evening, you can stop by after a show to enjoy a substantial salad and a glass of Tokay, while a pianist plays classic tunes.

ECKERMANN

1051 Budapest, Andrássy út 24
Tel.: +36 1 269 2542
The Goethe Institute has successfully revived the literary café tradition, and German-speaking students and intellectuals like to get together in this studious atmosphere to read the many German-language newspapers over a large cup of coffee. There is a limited range of pastries, but they are of good quality.

GERBEAUD

1051 Budapest Vörösmarty tér 7
Tel.: + 36 1 429 9000
Fax: + 36 1 429 9009
No trip to Budapest is complete without a visit to the Gerbeaud! After major renovation work over the last few years it has lost something of its rather outdated charm, but the setting and the pastries are still worthy of the reputation of this legendary café. Specialties include the gerbeaud and the *flódni* (an apple, walnut, and poppy-seed cake).

CAFÉ KÖR

1051 Budapest, Sas u 17
Tel.: + 36 1 311 0053
This upmarket café is frequented by journalists from the television studios on nearby Szabadság Square, plus a crowd of yuppies and habitués of this now trendy district. The food is basic and the pastries are nothing special, but it's an "in" place to be. Booking recommended.

CAFÉ DE L'INSTITUT FRANÇAIS

1011 Budapest, Fô utca 17
Tel.: + 36 1 489 4200
On the riverbank in Buda, near Chain Bridge, you can't miss the attractive postmodern structure of the French Institute, designed by Georges Maurios. Its French classes and varied cultural programs attract a regular clientele of artists, teachers, and students who also frequent the Institute's café, where they can enjoy an excellent breakfast of croissants and coffee.

LUKÁCS

1062 Budapest, Andrássy út 70
Tel./Fax: + 36 1 302 8747
The Lukács on Andrássy Avenue is one of Budapest's older establishments. It has recently undergone costly renovation and has lost something of its soul in the process, but the gilding and stucco still create a delightful setting for tired tourists, and the service is helpful and

attentive. Try the dobos torta (a caramel-glazed buttercream and chocolate layer cake), or the gesztzenye sziv with chestnut purée.

MUVÉSZ

1065 Budapest, Andrássy út 29
Tel.: + 36 1 267 0689
This café, right across from the Opera House, is frequented by people of all ages who enjoy its outside terrace and the cozy, quiet atmosphere in its two rather old-fashioned rooms. The pastry selection must be one of the widest in town; try the *francia kremes* (a sort of caramel-coated mille-feuille) or the *almás* torta (an excellent apple torte). A peaceful and calm place that makes a welcome break in this lively quarter.

RUSZWURM

1011 Budapest, Szentháromság utca 7
Tel.: + 36 1 375 52 84
This delightful little café with its old-world charm and slightly sagging armchairs gets very crowded during the day, but after a visit to the Castle District it's worth fighting for a table! A tip: arrive when it opens at 10 a.m., when wonderful pastries like the *retes* (strudels filled with apple, cherry, or fromage blanc) are still warm from the oven.

INTERESTING MUSEUMS

Budapest rivals any city in Europe in its rich variety of museums; many extraordinary collections are housed in mansions or Art Nouveau buildings constructed or converted for that specific purpose. The following selection includes the places you shouldn't miss during your stay in the capital.

BÉLA BARTÓK MEMORIAL HOUSE

Budapest 2nd district, Csalán út 29
Tel.: + 36 1 394 2100
The composer's former house on the Buda hills is open to visitors. It contains memorabilia related to the musician's life and times (1881–1945), including furniture from his years of exile in America. Chamber music concerts are often held in the little auditorium, and the garden is a haven of peace.

LUDWIG MUSEUM BUDAPEST–MUSEUM OF CONTEMPORARY ART

Budapest 1st district, Royal Palace of Buda (building A)
Tel.: + 36 1 375 9175
This beautiful museum caters to contemporary-art enthusiasts. Its permanent collections and temporary exhibitions reflect the major international artistic movements (American, German, French, and Hungarian visual artists are well represented).

MUSEUM OF DECORATIVE ARTS

Budapest 9th district, Üllôi út 33-37
Tel.: + 36 1 217 52 22 or +36 1 217 5171
This museum is housed in a building designed by Ödön Lechner and was inaugurated in 1896 during the millennium celebrations. The building is worth a visit in itself for its profusion of floral and animal motifs, multilobed arches in the exhibition galleries, and huge glass roof over the atrium. The extremely rich collections are frequently reorganized.

LISZT FERENC MEMORIAL MUSEUM

Budapest 6th district, Vörösmarty utca 35
Tel.: + 36 1 322 9804
Franz (Ferenc) Liszt (1811–1886) once lived here. Now a charming little museum, it still contains his instruments and the desk at which he composed many of his works.

ZOLTÁN KODÁLY MEMORIAL MUSEUM

Budapest 6th district , Kodály körönd 1
Tel.: + 36 1 352 7106
This museum is still haunted by the presence of the great musician himself (1882–1967). His apartment has been restored to its original state and contains many photos, manuscripts, and documents from the collections of folk music that he and his friend Béla Bartók gathered all over Hungary.

MUSEUM OF ETHNOGRAPHY

Budapest 5th district, Kossuth tér 12
Tel.: + 36 1 312 4878
The history of Hungarian folk culture is retraced in this splendid neo-Renaissance palace, with displays of traditional village costumes, furniture, and customs, together with many photographs.

HUNGARIAN AGRICULTURAL MUSEUM

Budapest 14th district, Vajdahunyad Castle
Tel.: + 36 1 343 0573
This is Europe's largest museum dedicated to agriculture. The hunting trophies are absolutely remarkable, and the building is interesting in itself.

HUNGARIAN GEOLOGICAL INSTITUTE MUSEUM

Budapest 14th district, Stefánia út 14
Tel./Fax: + 36 1 267 1427
The Hungarian mineralogical collections are exceptional, as are the dinosaur fossils on display here. The building, an Art Nouveau masterpiece by the great architect Ödön Lechner, is worth a visit in itself.

PETÕFI LITERARY MUSEUM

Budapest 5th district, Károlyi Mihály utca 16
Tel.: + 36 1 317 3611
This museum in the lovely Károlyi Palace is dedicated to the literary life of Hungary in the nineteenth and twentieth centuries. The collections feature many manuscripts and objets d'art, and there are often interesting temporary exhibitions.

POST MUSEUM

Budapest 5th district, Andrássy út 3
Tel.: + 36 1 269 6838
This museum is in one of Budapest's finest mansions, typical of aristocratic life in the late nineteenth century. It retraces the history of the postal service through a variety of everyday objects, and presents the successive inventions that have contributed to the art of communication.

STATUE PARK MUSEUM

Budapest 22nd district, at the corner of Balatoni út and de Szabadkai út
Tel.: + 36 1 227 7446
This museum, on the outskirts of Budapest on the road to the Balaton, is one of a kind: an open-air exhibition of the gigantic monuments to socialist realism that adorned public places during the Communist era.

TOMB OF GÜL BABA

Budapest 2nd district, Mecset utca 14
Tel.: + 36 1 355 8764
The burial vault of venerated Turkish dervish Gül Baba was built between 1543 and 1548. It has been converted into a museum and is now a place of pilgrimage. From the terrace there is a superb view of the old district of Buda.

ANTIQUE DEALERS AND BOOKSELLERS, ART GALLERIES AND AUCTION HOUSES

The Budapest art market has boomed over the last decade. Contemporary artists and gallery owners still struggle to make a living from their professions, but firms that specialize in direct or auction sales of modern Hungarian art have profited from the growing numbers of business people with money to spend on decorating their homes with traditional Hungarian artwork. Antique dealers who recently sold traditional Hungarian furniture at modest prices have also adapted to this new clientele. So it's not so easy to find a bargain in Budapest these days, unless you spot an old Transylvanian chest or painted wardrobe in the window of a state-owned BÁV (a kind of pawn shop) and are quick to react! As for the Ecseri flea market, even getting up early is no guarantee that you'll unearth a treasure: you need to be familiar with the place—and with the stallholders, who are used to negotiating in their own language.

ART DU MONDE GALLERY

1075 Budapest, Madách Imre út 5
Tel.: + 36 1 413 1899
Fax: + 36 1 413 1898
E-mail: artdumonde@freemail.hu
Young contemporary French and Hungarian artists are exhibited in this friendly little gallery run by a young entrepreneur who divides his time between the two countries.

BÁV

1055 Budapest, Szent István körút 3
Tel.: + 36 1 473 0666
Fax: + 36 1 331 0106
Budapest has several BÁV stores that act like pawn shops. The one on Szent István Boulevard has a wide range of furniture, paintings, and curios. The store at Bécsi utca 1-3, behind the Kempinsky Hotel in the fifth district, is also interesting. For rugs, the best places are Ferenciek tere 12 and Kossuth Lajos utca 1-3, both in the fifth district too. There is also an auction room in the ninth district (Lónyai utca 30-32 ; Tel.: + 36 1 455 7700) where bargains are to be had.

DARIUS ANTIQUES

1055 Budapest, Falk Miksa út 24-26
Tel.: + 36 1 332 8488
Fax: + 36 1 311 2603
E-mail: darius@csorge.net
Many rare and well-restored pieces of furniture are displayed in this pretty antique store run by Csaba and Elisabeth Csörge. Biedermeier and late eighteenth-century pieces can be acquired here in good condition.

KIESELBACH GALLERY

1055 Budapest, Szent István krt 5

Tel.: + 36 1 269 3148
Fax: + 36 1 269 2219
E-mail: gallery@kieselbach.hu
Website: www.kieselbach.hu
In only a few years, Tamás Kieselbach and his wife have established an auction house whose reputation extends throughout Hungary and Europe. Their excellent knowledge of the collectors' market has enabled them to acquire works by the greatest modern Hungarian artists (including Rippl-Rónai, Vaszary, Kadar, Scheiber, Ferenczy, Korniss, and others) and to arrange prestigious sales.

MAI MANÓ HÁZ

1065 Budapest, Nagymez utca 20
Tel.: + 36 1 302 4496
Fax: + 36 1 302 5847
E-mail: maimano@matavnet.hu
The Hungarian House of Photography is neither a museum nor, strictly speaking, a gallery. It is housed in a beautiful Pest mansion which was originally built for Mai Manó, the imperial and royal court photographer. The palace itself had various subsequent owners, and was even used as a brothel during the interwar period. It now provides an exhibition space for past and present Hungarian photographers, and sometimes for foreign photographers too. Visitors can come and work in the library, and books on photography can be purchased in the bookstore. Sales of photographs by reputed artists are occasionally held here, and the profits help finance the development of Mai Manó House.

MÉO-COLLECTION OF CONTEMPORARY ART

1047 Budapest, József Attila utca 4-6
Tel.: + 36 1 272 0876
Fax: + 36 1 272 0877
E-mail: info@meo.org.hu
In the industrial district of Újpest, which is currently being transformed, a magnificent former factory building from the early 1900s has recently been rehabilitated, thanks to private funds, and is now home to one of Hungary's fine collections of contemporary art. There is also space for temporary exhibitions, and the previews that are held here attract many of the capital's artists and contemporary-art aficionados.

MILLENNIUM ANTIQUES

1056 Budapest, Váci utca 6
Tel.: + 36 1 318 1478
This store in downtown Pest has a wide selection of Herend porcelain and Zsolnay ceramics; there are paintings too, and many pieces of furniture and silverware.

MORO ANTIK

1055 Budapest, Falk Miksa utca 13
Tel.: + 36 1 111 0814
An original store with a great variety of antiques and a marked preference for oriental objects, helmets, and armor at very reasonable prices.

MÚZEUM ANTIQUARIAN

1051 Budapest, Múzeum körút 35
Tel.: + 36 1 317 5023
Most of Budapest's antiquarian booksellers are grouped together on the same boulevard as the National Museum. You will find books in Hungarian and in various other languages too, and old maps or prints. Maybe as you browse the shelves you'll be lucky enough to spot the rare edition you've been hoping to find for so long! Further down the same street you can also explore the Honterus and Központi Antiquarian bookstores.

NAGYHÁZI GALÉRIA

1051 Budapest, Balaton utca 8
Tel.: + 36 1 331 9908
The storerooms of this auction house are like an Aladdin's cave. Rugs, silverware, jewelry, curios, folk art objects, furniture, paintings, drawings, and sculptures can be viewed all year round before the auctions are held. If you are patient, persistent, and interested in Hungarian art, regular visits to this gallery will enable you to build up a quality collection.

PREMIER ANTIQUES

1071 Budapest, Rákóczi út 30
Tel.: + 36 1 342 9415, + 36 1 269 6634
Fax: + 36 1 342 4593
E-mail: premier1@matavnet.hu
The largest antiques store in Budapest, on the main boulevard leading to Erzsébet Bridge. There are plenty of items to tempt you—paintings, sculptures, furniture, rugs, or jewelry—and provided you know how to bargain you're sure to find something of interest.

VÁRFOK GALÉRIA

1011 Budapest, Várfok utca 14
Tel.: + 36 1 213 5155, + 36 1 489 39 20/21
E-mail: galeria@varfok-galeria.hu
Not far from Moscow Square on the hill that leads up to the castle is the Várfok contem porary art gallery, which was quick to become one of the capital's most dynamic art venues. It annexed a series of other spaces in the same street and can now exhibit several artists at the same time in its different exhibition areas. It represents renowned artists such as Françoise Gilot, Endre Rozsda, István Nádler, Imre Bukta, László Fehér, and János Szirtes.

WLADIS GALÉRIA

1055 Budapest, Falk Miksa utca 13
Tel./Fax: + 36 1 354 0834
Péter Vladimir chose to set up his attractive jewelry store and workshop in the antique dealers' district of Budapest, which was a good decision because the models he designs himself are rooted in ancient tradition. Their motifs are often inspired by the art of the steppes . . . yet these pieces are also contemporary art works in their own right.

MUSIC

Budapest is one of the world's most musical cities, and every kind of music is represented. Traditional Hungarian music is an integral part of national culture, often learned at an early age, and it can be enjoyed at specific venues. Gypsy music ensembles play in many of the city's restaurants, and can also be heard in some of the city's many concert halls. Budapest boasts five permanent orchestras of national or international renown. There are also a great many festivals, two national operas, and a concert hall devoted to operetta. In addition, the Liszt Academy and various concert halls for young musicians contribute to the lively concert seasons. Jazz clubs are springing up all over Budapest too. The "Sziget" festival in August is Europe's largest amplified music festival. But in spite of all this, Hungarian musicians have the blues! Classical musicians tend to believe that things were more straightforward under the communist régime, when orchestras and music teaching were generously funded by the state. Other performers complain that the law of the market has destroyed all national specificity. Concert halls are ill-equipped and music teaching has fallen into neglect . . . But don't be discouraged! Plenty of concerts can still be enjoyed every day in Budapest.

Classical concerts and festivals

OLD MUSIC ACADEMY

Budapest 6th district, Vörösmarty utca 33
Tel.: + 36 1 322 9804
Liszt lived here at the end of his life. There is an attractive wooden concert hall, where the famous musician often played his organ. Nowadays many chamber music concerts are held here.

FRANZ LISZT MUSIC ACADEMY

Budapest 6th district, Liszt Ferenc tér 8
Tel.: + 36 1 342 0179
Surely one of Europe's most beautiful concert halls. The Secessionist style in all its splendor, a room with magnificent acoustics, and a concert season to attract music lovers from all over the world. The third cycle of the Franz Liszt conservatory is open to foreign students, many of whom flock to this mecca of music, where the price of seats is still very low.

DUNA PALOTA

Budapest 5th district, Zrinyi utca 5
This attractive concert hall near the Danube in Pest is a venue for jazz, traditional, or chamber music concerts, which attract appreciative audiences.

MATTHIAS CHURCH

Budapest 1st district, Szentháromság tér 2
Tel.: + 36 1 317 2754
Free organ recitals are held here on Sundays, as part of a program devised by the organist. During the season, early music concerts can also be attended in this lovely church, which is worth a visit in itself.

SPRING FESTIVAL, FALL FESTIVAL

Budapest Festival Center, 1055 Budapest, Egyetem tér 5
Tel.: + 36 1 486 3300, + 36 1 486 3311
Fax: + 36 1 486 3310
The Spring Festival takes place in Budapest in the last two weeks of March. About a hundred concerts are held all over the city, which becomes an undisputed capital of music. Many renowned musicians are keen to participate, and up-and-coming talents do their best to be featured on the program.
During the Fall Festival in late October–early November, the emphasis is on musical creation: many shows are created for the festival itself, and the various artistic disciplines are well represented. There are always many surprises in store, and quality performances are guaranteed.

BÉLA BARTÓK MEMORIAL HOUSE

Budapest 2nd district, Csalán út 29
Tel.: + 36 1 394 2100
The little auditorium with its 150 seats is ideal for chamber music; don't miss the Bartók string quartets that are regularly performed here.

KISCELLI MUSEUM

Budapest 3rd district, Kiscelli út 108
Tel.: + 36 1 388 8560
Performances of contemporary dance and music are held here in the unused chapel which provides an extraordinary setting and

remarkable reverberating acoustics. Perfect for early music too.

HUNGARIAN STATE OPERA

Opera House, Budapest 6th district,
Andrassy út 22
Tel.: + 36 1 353 0170
Erkel Theater, Budapest 8th district,
Köztársaság tér 30
Tel.: + 36 1 333 0540
There are two opera houses in Budapest, and they are rather different: the one on Andrássy Avenue is an exceptionally fine, eclectic building designed between 1875 and 1884 by the architect Miklós Ybl, whereas the more sober structure of the Erkel theater was inspired by the Art Nouveau movement. The former presents an extensive repertoire of opera and ballet; in the latter, the preference is for popular Hungarian works, or foreign works sung in Hungarian. You should therefore try to visit both, especially as the voices and dancers are often superb, although the staging occasionally leaves something to be desired.

PESTI VIGADÓ CONCERT HALL

Budapest 5th district, Vigadó tér 2
Tel.: + 36 1 318 9903
The Pest gala hall is considered a splendid example of Hungarian Romanticism. Its program is very varied and brilliant concerts are held all year round. There is also the occasional operetta.

OBUDA CONCERT HALL

Budapest 3rd district, Kiskorona utca 7
Tel.: + 36 1 250 0288
Music lovers from this popular district love this concert hall for its great acoustics and the quality of the small groups that perform here.

FESTIVAL ORCHESTRA HALL

Budapest 3rd district, Selmeci utca 14-16
Tel.: + 36 1 388 6538
The Budapest Festival Orchestra is one of the country's most successful musical ensembles, created as part of the Budapest Spring Festival about fifteen years ago. Attending one of the Orchestra's concerts in this remarkable rehearsal hall is an enthralling experience.

CONGRESS CENTER

Budapest 12th district, Jagelló út 1-3
Tel.: + 36 1209 1990
The Budapest Congress Center, in a park at the foot of the Buda hills, has a large hall with over two thousand seats and efficient acoustics. The major international orchestral ensembles perform here, and the program of concerts during the Budapest Spring Festival in March is particularly attractive: music lovers will find something to entice them every evening.

It would be impossible to list all the classical concert venues in Budapest (the Capuchin Church, the Church of Szent Anna, the synagogue on Dohány utca, etc.), but even the most demanding of music lovers will be overwhelmed by the number of performances that can be attended on a daily basis. Tickets are sold on the spot, but there are also several places around the city which centralize ticket sales and cater to last-minute requests: Music Mix (Váci utca 33 in the 5th district, Tel.: + 36 1 338 2237); Publika (Károly körút in the 7th district, Tel.: + 36 1 322 2010), Ticket Express (at various locations); and the Budapest Festival Center (Vörösmarty tér 1, Tel.: + 36 1 317 6222).

Traditional music and jazz

ALMÁSSY TÉRI SZABADIDO KÖZPONT

Budapest 7th district, Almássy tér 6
Tel.: + 36 1 342 0387
This popular recreation center (or "freetime center") is a great introduction to the atmosphere of the *táncház* (dance house). Everyone dances and sings along with the well-known refrains, in a charmless room that looks more like a gymnasium than anything else.
A very "foreign" experience!

BÁB SZÍNHÁZ

Budapest 6th district, Andrássy út 69
Tel.: + 36 1 342 2702, + 36 1 321 5200
The Budapest Puppet Theater is proof that the Hungarian puppet tradition is still flourishing. On certain days you can see a version of Mozart's Magic Flute as the composer imagined it. In the evenings, folk dance performances are sometimes on the program.

BELVÁROSI M VEL DÉSI HÁZ

Budapest 5th district, Molnár utca 9
Tel.: + 36 1 317 5928
If you want to take dance lessons and memorize the various Hungarian dance steps, this neighborhood cultural center in the heart of the old district of Pest has a certain charm.

BUDAI VIGADÓ

Budapest 1st district, Corvin tér 8
Tel.: + 36 1 317 27 54 or + 36 1 201 5928
E-mail: hunkonc@axelero.hu
This friendly concert hall in the Viziváros district is mostly devoted to performances by the Gypsy Orchestra with its extensive repertoire.

FAT MO'S

Budapest 5th district, Nyári Pál utca 11
Tel.: + 36 1 267 3199
The atmosphere in this popular nightspot is young and friendly, and you can listen to some good jazz rock while you enjoy a drink or a tasty meal. You will have to arrive early on concert evenings if you want to be sure of getting a place.

FONÓ

Budapest 11th district, Sztregova utca 3
Tel.: + 36 1 206 6296
A former aluminum foundry was converted into this venue for jazz or traditional music concerts. Exploring this little-known district and enjoying a session of Hungarian music here over a weekend is a good way of getting to know the city.

OPERETTA THEATER

Budapest 6th district, Nagymez utca 17
Tel.: + 36 1 269 3870
The people of Budapest are traditionally keen operetta fans and this beautiful theater, which has recently been renovated, offers a lively program all year round. During the Budapest Spring Festival, it stages a "fringe" festival featuring the great classics of Hungarian or Austro-Hungarian operetta.

TRAFÓ

Budapest 9th district, Liliom utca 41
Tel.: + 36 1 456 2040
This neighborhood has become very trendy in recent years, and Budapest yuppies come here to be seen in the restaurants and bars. The Trafó club anticipated the movement when it took over a one-time power plant, and for several years now aficionados have crowded into this venue to enjoy the many jazz concerts and contemporary music or dance performances.

Theater fans who are unable to follow performances in Hungarian may want to try some of the capital's theaters that offer performances of great classics (Shakespeare or Brecht), but also plays from the Hungarian repertory. Some of these places are beautifully restored, such as the Vigszínház (an Italianate theater that stages a wide range of productions, Budapest 13th district, Szent István körút 5, Tel.: + 36 1 311 1650) or the Új Színház (a theater dating from 1911, with a white façade and a blue interior blue, in the 6th district, Paulay Ede utca 35, behind the Dance Academy on Andrássy Avenue, Tel.: + 36 1 269 6021).

MARKETS

In Hungarian, *piac* means market and *csarnok* is the structure that houses it. The quality of local markets in Budapest is an indication of the importance of neighborhood life. The former insalubrious and smelly open-air markets were a nuisance to people living nearby, and were replaced in the late nineteenth century by these distinctive constructions that resemble upturned boats, with their metal framework and beautiful wrought-iron balustrades and gangways. Some of them have now been restored. A modern example is the new market on Lehel Square, whose construction caused a good deal of controversy.

CENTRAL MARKET OR VASÁRCSARNOK

Budapest 9th district, Vámház körút 1-3
Passersby could be forgiven for supposing this market to be a station, with its brick façade, roof covered in Zsolnay tiles, neo-Gothic towers, and large clock. Even the interior proportions of this central market hall, designed by Samu Pecz in 1896, are reminiscent of the West Station designed by French architect Gustave Eiffel and his team. There are several floors, with a multitude of stalls selling foodstuffs from all over the country. The first-story fabrics and embroideries are eye-catching, but the craftsmanship is not always entirely authentic.

HOLD UTCA MARKET

Budapest 5th district, Hold utca 13
Hold Street is in a downtown neighborhood behind elegant Szabadság Square. It is reputed for the quality of its architecture and the extraordinary building, designed by Ödön Lechner, that houses the Savings Bank. The metal frame of this well-stocked market encloses many a mouthwatering display. You will find top-quality poultry and foie gras here.

FÉNY UTCA MARKET

Budapest 2nd district, Fény utca
The area behind the Mammut on Moszkva tér has changed a great deal over the last few years. A little flower market has survived however, and on Sunday mornings hothouse and wild flowers are to be found here side by side. Make sure you see this market before it is swept away by the tidal wave of the consumer society.

LEHEL TÉR MARKET

Budapest 13th district, Dévai utca 23
Lehel piac was once an open-air market, famed for its hustle and bustle but also for its high prices. It has recently undergone a major

town-planning operation, and a postmodern building designed by architect László Rajk now houses the market. The structure is a medley of styles and vibrant colors, and the overall impression is one of power and dynamism. The stallholders now have more room, and shoppers have gained in light and salubrity what they may have lost in local color.

CHRISTMAS MARKET

Budapest 5th district, Vörösmarty tér

The tradition of the Christmas market is still flourishing in Hungary. As soon as Advent arrives, several squares in downtown Budapest are invaded by little stalls offering handicrafts, tasty delicacies such as poppy-seed and walnut rolls (*beigli*), crispy gingerbread (*mézeskalács*), mulled wine (*forrált bor*—much appreciated when the north wind is blowing), clothing, wooden toys, and a whole range of gifts. The market on Vörösmarty Square is particularly well stocked, but those on Jókai and Liszt Ferenc squares, on each side of Andrássy Avenue in the 6th district, are also well worth a visit.

FLEA MARKET OR ECSERI PIAC

Budapest 19th district, Nagykörösi út 156

This market is located in an unattractive area, and is rather difficult to get to. Saturday is the busiest day, and if you are a keen bargain hunter you should go very early in the morning—with a Hungarian friend if possible. You will find porcelain, furniture, paintings, toys, and traditional objects sold by secondhand goods dealers who are often of Gypsy origin. Beware of high prices, and don't hesitate to haggle if you know how! Another flea market is held every weekend in City Park, behind the Petőfi Csarnok concert hall; it is rather like an attic sale, and tends to attract families.

CRAFTS

ZSOLNAY CERAMICS AND AJKA CRYSTAL

Budapest 5th district, Kigyó utca 4

Earthenware from the Zsolnay factory in Pécs (southern Hungary) has now recovered its luster after a long period of purgatory. The designs have been adapted to suit present-day tastes in a subtle blend of tradition and modernity. The Ajka glassworks in Veszprèm County still uses traditional techniques such as glass-blowing by mouth for the finest pieces. Choose a decanter from one of the following places to do justice to a fine red wine from the Villány region.

FOLKART CENTRUM

Budapest 5th district, Váci utca 58

This store in the pedestrian area of downtown Pest offers clothes, embroidery, and traditional objects from all over Hungary. It proposes reasonable prices for good quality handicrafts.

BATHING ESTABLISHMENTS IN BUDAPEST

Bathing is an art in Budapest. The capital has a wide range of establishments on offer, ranging from historical baths to local swimming pools which are often very pleasant. Before you set out to try one, you should do some preliminary investigations to check on the opening times (which vary according to season) and to find out which days are reserved for which sex (as mixed bathing is not the case in every establishment). You should also be aware that nude bathing is the accepted practice in certain baths, where codes of behavior are sometimes a little hazy. Many establishments have been renovated in recent years, and you can now be reasonably confident of finding hygienic conditions, both in the changing rooms and in the pools. The following list indicates the specificities of each bath (or *fürd*), but a visit to just one establishment can provide no more than a glimpse into the extraordinary world of the Budapest baths.

HOTEL GELLÉRT

Budapest 11th district, Szent Gellért tér 1

When you practice the art of bathing in one of Europe's most beautiful palaces, the experience is bound to be extraordinary: the setting is majestic, and the variety of pools (hammam, thermal baths, water attractions of all kinds) ensures that there is something for everyone. A great place for a family outing on a Sunday. Men and women are separated in the thermal baths.

THERMAL HOTEL

Budapest 13th district, Margitsziget

Charming Margaret Island is a haven of peace to the north of the city, and is also home to one of the best thermal establishments in the country. This thermal hotel has been entirely renovated, and offers such a wide range of services (check on the details at reception) that it is worth making your stay an extended one and concentrating on getting into shape! Neighboring Grand Hotel Margitsziget is a wonderful place to stay, and guests have free access to the Thermal Hotel via an underground passage.

KIRÁLY

Budapest 2nd district, Fô utca 84

The capital's most mysterious bathing establishment, which dates from the Ottoman era, has recently been renovated but has lost nothing of its charm in the process. Its splendid green cupola, topped with a gold crescent, is streaked with blue copper sulfate. Bathing in this dimly lit, magical atmosphere in the warm, sulfur-yellow water makes for a wonderfully relaxing experience. Next to the baths, some fine Baroque buildings house a thermal establishment. The Király is open to men and women on alternate days.

LUKÁCS

Budapest 2nd district, Frankel Leó út 25-27

The Lukács, which was superbly renovated in 2000, is a particularly attractive combination of Art Deco thermal buildings and large open-air pools. The whole place is vast, as there is also a medical establishment adjoining the baths. A visit to the hammam is a very enjoyable experience. The Lukács is recommended for those with rheumatic afflictions, but is also great for family outings.

PALATINUS STRANDFÜRDÕ SWIMMING POOL

Budapest 13th district, Margitsziget

This open-air swimming pool on Margaret Island is very popular with families, especially on weekends. There are several pools at different temperatures, and attractions such as wave pools and slides make it a very enjoyable place to spend a hot summer's afternoon.

HAJÓS ALFRÉD

NATIONAL SPORTS SWIMMING POOL

Budapest 13th district, Margitsziget

The first Olympic swimming pool to open in Budapest during the interwar period was designed by architect Hajós Alfréd. The result is both functional and aesthetically pleasing. Recommended for real swimmers, who can do their morning lengths in the indoor or outdoor pool. The Hungarian National Women's Team do their training there on certain days.

RÁC

Budapest 1st district, Hadnagy utca 8-10

One of the capital's lesser-known bathing establishments, which also dates from the Ottoman occupation of the city. The waters have a high sodium content and are reputed for their medicinal qualities; indeed the Rác was once directly connected to the Royal Palace. The octagonal pool dates from the latter half of the sixteenth century. The thermal facilities are housed in a little rococo building (open on alternate days to men and women), and are currently being renovated.

RUDAS

Budapest 1st district, Döbrentei tér 9

The cupola of this Turkish bath can be admired from Erszébet Bridge. The interior is superb: the red marble surroundings blur with the green of the tuff walls in the semidarkness. The central octagonal pool contributes to the overall harmony of the place. This modest-sized establishment is frequented by habitués, and is probably the best introduction into the age-old bathing tradition—but not for everyone, as the Rudas is reserved for men only.

SZÉCHENYI

Budapest 14th district, Állatkerti körút 11

This bathing establishment, built between 1909 and 1913 and enlarged in 1926, is one of the attractions of the Budapest City Park. A medical wing heightens the grandiose character of the whole place. The thermal facilities are remarkable (men and women are separated here). Recent renovation work has done justice to the many architectural details of the establishment, such as the curving row of changing rooms and the harmony of structure between the pools and the building itself. The best time of year for a family outing to the Széchenyi baths is on the first cold fall days, and in winter when the open-air pools are rimmed with snow. Bathers can enjoy the warmth of the water, enveloped in a cloud of steam which protects them from the cold outside air.

NÉPM VÉSZETI KFT.

Budapest 5th district, Régiposta utca 12

This pretty store in a little street perpendicular to Váci utca specializes in folk art objects such as colorful pieces of Kalocsa embroidery. You will find, for example, charming photo albums bound in brightly colored fabric, beautiful tablecloths, and fabrics that you can buy by the yard.

PHILANTHIA

Budapest 5th district, Váci utca 9

This is the prettiest florist in Budapest. The plant and flower motifs on the walls of the Art Nouveau store provide a perfect backdrop for the flowers whose heady fragrances will entice you. There are many attractive flower arrang ements, and the hothouse atmosphere allows the store's beautiful orchids to thrive.

HEREND PORCELAIN

Budapest 5th district, Kígyó utca 5 and József Nádor tér 11

Many stores carry a whole range of Herend porcelain pieces straight from the factory north of Lake Balaton. These two addresses in the pedestrian area near the river have a particularly wide selection. You might hesitate between the Biedermeier-style dinner services with their sober decoration of traditional motifs (Golden Age and Young Forever), and the rather flashier (not to say overloaded) more recent collection (Majestic). The figurines are graceful, but their prices are in keeping with the reputation of this fine craft ware.

HOLLÓHÁZA PORCELAIN

Haas & Czjzek, Budapest 6th district, Bajcsy-Zsilinszky út 2

In this charmingly old-fashioned store that dates from before Hungary's economic liberalization, you will discover porcelain that is less famous—and less expensive—than that of Herend. Hollóháza, in the northeast of the country, produces lovely white porcelain with discreet floral motifs. There is a wide selection of dinner services.

TANGÓ

Budapest 5th district, Váci utca 8

Kati Hempel set up this pretty store at the back of a courtyard, complete with traditional balcony. It sells items of embroidery and party clothes, many of which are antique—the kind of magnificent outfits that seem to bring Old Hungary back to life.

VASS

Budapest 5th district, Haris köz 2

Tel.: + 36 1 318 2375

Lázsló Vass, the most elegant shoemaker in all of Hungary, has a discreet little store in the pedestrian area—yet many personalities find their way to this address! His models are inspired by various traditions, yet have a distinctive character all of their own. A pair of made-to-measure shoes can be produced and delivered anywhere in Europe in one month, and prices are still reasonable in view of the top-quality craftsmanship. Mr. Vass will gladly welcome you, provided you give prior notice of your visit—as when he is not in his workshop, he roams the whole country in search of contemporary art works to add to his exceptional collection.

FINE-WINE CELLARS AND WINE BARS

Hungary is justly renowned for the great wealth of its vineyards. From the north to the south of the country, original grape varieties manage to hold their own against competition from international vine stocks by emphasizing their diversity. As you travel through Hungary you will be able to taste a whole range of local wines; when you return to the capital, it can be fun to put your new knowledge to the test by comparing various wines in one place. You can do this in a number of wine cellars throughout the city, where you will also be able to discuss the wine with specialists.

BUDAPEST WINE SOCIETY

1011 Budapest, Batthyány utca 59

Tel.: + 36 1 212 2569

This store on a little street on Castle Hill, near Moscow Square, offers a very wide selection of Hungarian wines. The service in English is competent and friendly. There are free wine-tasting sessions on Saturdays. A monthly magazine entitled *Borbarát* (*Friends of Wine*, with texts in English) is available there; it publishes critical assessments and analyses of the major vineyards. Its founder and chief editor, László Alkonyi, is an excellent connoisseur of Tokay wines, and has published a remarkable book on the subject entitled "Tokaj, the Wine of Freedom".

PRÉSHÁZ

Váci utca, 10

Tel.: + 36 1 266 1100

In this lovely eighteenth-century cellar on Váci Street, you are sure to find one of the wines you have enjoyed during your tour of Hungary. Tokay wines are particularly well represented in the wine-tasting rooms; make the most of this opportunity to rediscover the exceptional flavor of a great Aszú wine.

THE HOUSE OF HUNGARIAN WINES

H-1014 Budapest, Szentháromság tér 6

Tel.: + 36 1 212 1030

Fax: + 36 1 212 1032

This vast cellar in the Castle district opposite the Hilton Hotel has been fitted out to ensure that every wine growing region in Hungary can be represented. On arrival you buy a tasting cup and a few savory biscuits, and can then wander the labyrinth as you please, tasting any wines that suit your fancy from the many bottles that are open to tempt you. Your little wicker basket will gradually fill up with the bottles you select!

ZWACK BORVILÁG

H-1053 Budapest Károlyi Mihály u 12. I. em

Tel.: + 36 1 486 3640

Fax: + 36 1 486 1845

E-mail: info@boresparlat.hu

In a magnificent mansion designed by Miklós Ybl in downtown Pest, the founder of the Zwack House (which produces the Unicum liqueur and various Hungarian wines) has recently opened a large area devoted to the world of wine. The windows showcase the great variety of Hungarian wines from the country's most prestigious domains. Numerous accessories—glasses, decanters, corkscrews, and books about wine—complete this fascinating visit.

From the Danube to the Tisza

HOTELS

KECSKEMÉT

CENTRAL HOTEL

Kisfaludy utca 10
6000 Kecskemét
Tel.: + 36 76 502 710/711/712
Fax: + 36 76 502 713

UDVARHAZ HOTEL

Csány utca 1-3
6000 Kecskemét
Tel./Fax: + 36 76 413 912/914

Both these modern hotels in the heart of the historic old town can be recommended. The rooms are bright and some are very large (check beforehand). A conference room seating sixty people is available in the Central Hotel. The Udvarház Hotel overlooks a courtyard and is very calm. Both hotels are run by the same group; they have twenty six and seventeen rooms, respectively.

SZEKSZÁRD

HOTEL ZODIACO

Szent László utca 19 7100 Szekszárd
Tel.:+ 36 74 511 150
Fax: + 36 74 511 140
E-mail: hotel.zodiaco@nextramail.hu

This relatively new, well-appointed hotel is built in the organic architectural style. The good-sized rooms are furnished in light wood, and the atmosphere is welcoming. This makes an excellent base for anyone who wants to explore the charms of the region (Szekszárd vineyards, Gemenc Forest, Sárköz and its folk traditions, etc.).

SZENTENDRE

HORVATH FOGADO

Daru Piac 2
2000 Szentendre
Tel./Fax: + 36 26 313 950

It is well worth spending more than one day in Szentendre. A comfortable little family hotel is the best place to stay—especially as there are no big hotels in this town. Mr. and Mrs. Horvath run a quality establishment, a stone's throw from the old town: the eight rooms are very spacious and the prices very reasonable. Breakfast is served by a hostess.

SZENT ANDREA FOGADO

Egres út 22
2000 Szentendre
Tel./Fax: + 36 26 311 989

This hotel can be recommended for its calm. It's only a five-minute drive from the center of the old town, but away from the main tourist zone. The rooms are comfortable and bright, and guests are given a kind and friendly welcome. There is a copious breakfast too, providing the perfect start to the day!

SZOLNOK

TISZA HOTEL AND THERMAL BATHS

Verseghy park 2
5000 Szolnok
Tel.: + 36 56 371 582 (hotel)
+ 36 56 422 104 (thermal bath)
Fax: + 36 56 421 520
E-mail: reserve@hoteltisza.hu

The town of Szolnok on the banks of the Tisza is worth a visit—if only for the Tisza Hotel and its riverbank bathing establishment. The hotel has a splendid old-fashioned interior and beautiful spacious rooms, and the thermal baths have been renovated and offer a wide range of services. The experience is so pleasant that you will be tempted to extend your stay, even though the cuisine is traditional and not very imaginative.

RESTAURANTS

BUGAC

BUGACI KARIKAS CSARDA

Nagybugac 135
6114 Bugac
Tel.: + 36 763 726 88
Fax: + 36 76 481 643

This traditional inn at the entrance to the Kiskunsag National Park is ideal for an outdoor meal in spring or fall after a walk through the vast territory of the Bugac *puszta*. The cuisine is traditional but of good quality. Coach parties often stop here for lunch on weekends, but there is plenty of room as the inn seats three hundred people.

SZEKSZÁRD

FOISPAN ÉTTEREM ES BORMÚZEUM (FOISPAN RESTAURANT AND WINE MUSEUM)

Béla tér 1
7100 Szekszárd
Tel.: + 36 74 312 139

Seventeenth-century vaulted cellars were converted to house this restaurant, where you can also admire instruments which were once used for wine growing and which symbolize the wine-producing tradition of this region. The cuisine is inventive, with typical local and regional specialties, and you can enjoy an informative wine-tasting session with wines produced in Szekszárd.

SZENTENDRE

ARANYSÁRKÁNY ÉTTEREM (GOLDEN DRAGON RESTAURANT)

Alkotmány u 1/A
2000 Szentendre
Tel.: + 36 26 301 479
Tel./fax: + 36 26 311 670
E-mail: aranysarkany@aranysarkany.hu

The Aranysárkány is in a pretty little street leading to the main square in Szentendre, and is probably the best restaurant in town. The menu is extremely varied, the dishes are delightfully presented, and the wine list is short but well selected (each wine is individually presented). Hungarian foodies have been flocking here for over a generation now. Writer Ferenc Karinthy, a well-known gourmet, was a regular diner in this, Hungary's first private restaurant, which has preserved its original atmosphere. The little room seats forty with its traditional benches and straw chairs. Booking indispensable.

VAROSHAZA SOROZO (TOWN HALL RESTAURANT)

Városház tér 3
2000 Szentendre
Tel.: + 36 26 312 700
Fax: + 36 26 312 524

During the summer, at the height of the town's cultural season, the large terrace of this restaurant is overrun with customers, as it gives straight on to the courtyard where the shows take place. The crowds are also drawn by the excellent and inventive cuisine and the charming Art Deco interior.

RAB RABY RESTAURANT

Péter Pál utca 1
2000 Szentendre
Tel.: + 36 26 310 819

Right in the heart of the old town, the Rab Raby has a tasteful interior decoration, mixing traditional musical instruments, folk art, and a few ancient engravings depicting the town in years gone by. It is very popular with visitors from Budapest, which means it is becoming more touristy, although the traditional dishes are still top quality.

SZOLNOK

GALÉRIA ÉTTEREM (THE GALLERY RESTAURANT)

Szapáry út 1
5000 Szolnok
Tel.: + 36 56 513 053
Fax: + 36 56 513 054

A mere stone's throw from the Tisza promenade, this charmingly decorated restaurant has an astonishingly wide-ranging menu and a most engaging atmosphere, making for a delightful evening all in all.

MUSEUMS

CSONGRAD

TARI LÁSZLO MÚZEUM

Iskola utca 2
6640 Csongrád
Tel.: + 36 63 483 103
Fax: + 36 63 481 052

The museum, named after its principal benefactor, is absolutely charming and utterly unpretentious. László Tari was a local worthy who spent years building up the archeological, historical, and ethnographical collections before donating them to the town. The museum thus reflects one man's interpretation of the history of his homeland: his love for the region shines through.

CSONGRÁDI TAJHAZ

Gyökér utca 1
6640 Csongrád-Belsöváros
Tel.: + 36 63 483 103

On the outskirts of town, on the banks of the Tisza, this old neighborhood, traditionally home to farmers and fishermen, has over time been skillfully and sensitively restored. One of the homes now houses a small but enchanting ethnographic collection, consisting of furniture and many rarities. The best time to visit is in the spring or perhaps the fall, when the very small garden glows with a quite magnificent range of hues.

KARCAG

ISTVÁN GYÖRFFY NAGYKUN MÚZEUM
Kálvin ut 4
5300 Karcag
Tel.: + 36 59 312 087
This museum devoted to the folk traditions of the Kiskunsag region was the brainchild of one of Hungary's greatest ethnologists, Professor István Györffy. It introduces visitors to the traditional way of life of the great plains—a way of life which is still very much alive in some parts of the region.

KECSKEMÉT

MAGYAR FOTOGRAFIAI MÚZEUM (THE MUSEUM OF HUNGARIAN PHOTOGRAPHY)

Katona József tér 12
6000 Kecskemét
Tel.: + 36 76 483 221
This small museum in a former synagogue houses the finest collection of Hungarian photography anywhere in the world, including works by such world-famous masters of their art as Brassaï, Kertész, and Capa. The museum director, Károly Kincses, has devoted his life to building up the collection, persuading people and institutions to donate photographs, and seeking out rare and precious books and other memorabilia relating to the history of photography. Some of these are occasionally put up for sale to fund the museum's work.

LESKOWSKY HANGSZERGYUJTEMENY (THE LESKOWSKY MUSICAL INSTRUMENT COLLECTION)

Zimai L. utca 6
6000 Kecskemét
Tel.: + 36 76 486 616
When visiting Zoltán Kodály's hometown, it would be a real shame to miss the superb collection of musical instruments donated by Albert Leskowsky. He runs the collection himself, acquiring instruments on his regular trips around the country. This must be one of the only museums in the world to remain open twenty-four hours a day!

FOLK CRAFTS MUSEUM

Seföző utca 19/A
6000 Kecskemét
Tel.: + 36 76 327 203
In this region which is famed for the quality of its folk art and craftsmanship, this little museum makes for an interesting visit. It presents the craft traditions of various regions of Hungary—woodcarving, pottery, embroidery, and so on—in a series of workshop settings.

ZOLTAN KODALY INTEZET (THE ZOLTAN KODALY INSTITUTE)

Kéttemplomköz 1
6000 Kecskemét
Tel.: + 36 76 481 518
The Zoltan Kodaly Institute is housed in a superb Franciscan monastery dating from the eighteenth century and recently restored. In one of the cloisters is a small yet interesting exhibition devoted to the works of the great composer. The rest of the institute is usually off-limits to ensure a studious atmosphere for the young musicians in residence, but it is possible to call ahead and book a visit—a real treat for music lovers. During the summer, the institute hosts regular concerts, in which case there is no need to book ahead.

MOHÁCS

MOHÁCSI TÖRTELNOLMI EMLEKELY (MEMORIAL OF THE BATTLE OF MOHÁCS)
Five miles (eight km) south of Mohács, follow road 56. After four miles (six km), follow the road signs. In 1960, a gruesome discovery was made in the heart of the plain here: the remains of the Hungarian army crushed by the Turks at the Battle of Mohács in 1526. The site is now commemorated with steles and wooden stakes carved in the local craft tradition to represent warriors and horses, rather like Indian totem poles. The absolute hush that cloaks the site gives it an eerie and majestic beauty and is well worth a visit.

THE MUSEUMS OF SZENTENDRE

The little town of Szentendre, twelve miles upriver from Budapest, is outstanding for the unspoiled charm of its old streets, its many churches of various denominations, and the variety of its museums, which reflect the important cultural role this town has played since the seventeenth century. The town's museums are dedicated to such wide-ranging themes as painting from the Szentendre School, ceramics, Serbian orthodox religious tradition, marzipan sculptures, and reconstructions of ethnic Hungarian architecture. Practical information about the museums is available from the **Directorate of Pest County Museums at the Ferenczy Múzeum** (Fö tér 6 2000 Szentendre; Tel.: + 36 26 310 244; Tel./Fax: + 36 26 310 790; website: www.pmmi.hu), a fine eighteenth-century building that houses works by neo-Impressionist artist Károly Ferenczy. What follows is a selection of the main museums of interest in Szentendre.

MARCIPÀN MÚZEUM CUKRASZDA

Dumtsa J. utca 12
2000 Szentendre
Tel./Fax: + 36 26 311 931
This delicious little museum offers a marzipan version of the history of Hungary, with figures representing famous historical characters made by an imaginative confectioner. It is worth a visit (especially for the sweet-toothed) and you can take away brightly colored little figures that will delight both children and adults.

MARGIT KOVÁCS MÚZEUM

Vastagh György utca 1
2000 Szentendre
Margit Kovács (1902–1977) was the greatest Hungarian ceramicist. She depicted the world around her in sensitive, expressive work: picturesque characters or street scenes, and large religious compositions. Visiting this well-appointed museum in an old Baroque Szentendre house is a genuinely moving experience.

JENO BARCSAY COLLECTION

Dumtsa Jenö utca 10
2000 Szentendre
This famous painter (1900-1988) and master of Hungarian Constructivism influenced several generations of Hungarian artists. Experienced artists and students alike used to flock to the lessons he gave in his studio or at the Academy of Fine Arts.

SERBIAN ORTHODOX MUSEUM

Pártiárka utca 5
2000 Szentendre
Tel.: + 36 26 312 399
The Serbian orthodox tradition is deep-rooted in Szentendre and the collection of religious objects from the seventeenth and eighteenth centuries in this museum presents a fascinating overview. A visit to the nearby Episcopal cathedral is also recommended.

HUNGARIAN OPEN-AIR MUSEUM (SZABADTÉRI NÉPRAJZI MÚZEUM)

Sztaravodai út
2001 Szentendre
This ethnographic museum or Skansen, from the name of the famous ethnographic museum in Stockholm, is a great place to learn about Hungarian architecture and folk traditions. It takes a long time to go around if you want to explore the many different kinds of houses and traditional churches reconstructed here over the museum's many acres of ground. An excellent way to discover the roots of Hungarian culture.

ARTS AND CRAFTS

DECS

SÁRKÖZI NEPI IPARMUVESZETI SZOVETKEZOT (ASSOCIATION OF SÁRKÖZ FOLK CRAFTSMEN)

Kossuth Lajos utca 36
7144 Decs
Tel./Fax: + 36 74 495 320/040
Decs, in the heart of the little region of Sárköz, is famed for the richness of its folk traditions. The Sárköz Ethnographical House (Tájház) regularly hosts demonstrations of folk customs such as dances, where the young men and women of the local village perform in traditional costume accompanied by local musicians playing old Hungarian instruments. One of the village houses is entirely decorated with local handicrafts, and its neighbor has a fine collection of dolls and hand-painted eggs (contact Mrs. László Farkas, Tel.: + 36 74 495 734, Kossuth Lajos utca 8), proof of the vibrant folk traditions that are still very much a part of life in Sárköz today. In nearby Szekszárd, Mrs. Eva Bogár (Tel.: + 36 74 413 177) also has a fine private collection of folk craftwork open to visitors who call ahead.

KARCAG

SÁNDOR KÁNTOR (THE POTTER'S HOUSE)

Erkel Ferenc utca 2
5300 Karcag
Tel.: + 36 59 312 087
Right next door to the museum founded by Sándor Kántor (1894-1989), a famous Hungarian potter, the master's studio is still turning out fine pieces, thanks to his sons and grandsons. The building itself is interesting, but the real highlight is the superb collection of naïve pottery in the Kiskunsag tradition. The most famous of these is doubtless the series of little figurines of a character called Miska Kancso, created by Sándor Kántor himself.

MOHÁCS

ENGLERT ANTAL

Craftsman specializing in *busó* masks
Kígyó utca 7/A
7700 Mohács
Tel.: + 36 69 302 548, + 36 70 215 4289
Making *busó* masks is an art that requires both a creative imagination and great skill with a range of materials, from sheep or goat horn to willow and corn silk. The finished articles are highly impressive masks that are a traditional feature of the Mohács carnival. Over the last few decades, the tradition had lost a lot of ground, but fortunately today a new generation of artists has brought new vigor to the art. Today, the masks are so popular that there are even classes in making them, given by artisans like Mr. Englert, who take great delight in their work. His pride shines through when he shows visitors around his studio—a real treat for anyone interested in folk art

WINE

SZEKSZÁRD

Szekszárd is reputed throughout Hungary and beyond for the quality of its wines, from light reds such as Kadarka to bolder vintages like Bull's Blood or Bikavér. The best moment to visit Szekszárd is, of course, in early fall, when the grape harvest is in full swing. A few miles from the town is the wine-growers' village of Sioagárd which has retained its age-old traditions. Several of the wine cellars are worth a visit, but we can especially recommend Bajnok Sándor's in Probus Borászati Kft.

THE WINE WELL IN THE PREFECTURE GARDENS

Béla tér, 1
7100 Szekszárd
Tel.:+ 36 74 412 828
To celebrate certain festivals, wine flows from the taps of the Wine Well to quench the thirst of bibulous passersby.

KORONA WINE MERCHANTS

Béri Balog Adám utca, 70
7100 Szekszárd
Tel.: + 36 74 311 817
This wine merchant has a vast range of wines from the Szekszárd region on offer for tastings, with an expert on hand to help you make the most of the experience—in English.

GARAY WINE CELLAR

Place Garay, 19
7100 Szekszárd
Tel.: + 36 74 412 828
One of the best addresses in Szekszárd, where you can taste the wine of one of the region's best producers.

PROBUS BORASZATI KFT.

Béri Balog Adám utca 107
7100 Szekszárd
Tel./Fax: + 36 74 413 199
E-mail: probus@terrasoft.hu
The wine on offer here comes from the delightful village of Sioagárd. Make a point of planning a visit here for a wine tasting in the traditional old cellar. When you call ahead to book a time, request that the owner's niece dress in her traditional brightly colored finery.

SZEKSZÁRD REGION WINE ROUTE

Dózsa György utca 1
7100 Szekszárd
Tel.: + 36 74 311 628
This association has brought out a remarkably informative leaflet on the various villages and vineyards scattered around the Szekszárd region. It is best to pick up the leaflet in Szekszárd itself, to be sure of not missing any of the numerous fascinating stopping points along the route.

HUNTING

TROFEA VADASZATSZERVEZO ES VADASZATELSZAMOLO KFT. (THE TROFEA HUNTING COMPANY)

Arany Janos utca 3
7100 Szekszárd
Tel./Fax: + 36 74 316 718
Trofea has been organizing highly professional hunts since 1989. It covers some of the loveliest landscapes in all Hungary, in the heart of the Gemenc forest hunting reserve. The conditions are ideal for bagging both furred and feathered game.

NATURAL PARKS

KISKUNSAGI NEMZETI PARK (KISKUNSAG NATIONAL PARK)

6114 Bugac
Tel.: + 36 76 312 583
Mobile: + 36 304 884 547
Before visiting this *puszta*, it is a particularly good idea to ask for the times of the spectacular demonstrations of horsemanship organized reguarly by the Shepherds' Museum (Pasztor Múzeum). The *csikós*, who look after the herds of horses, are a magnificent sight astride their mounts. Other animals of the *puszta* (sheep, cows, pigs, and dogs) live wild on the arid plains. A visit to the museum is a captivating way to find out about the ancestral lifestyle of the great plains.

HORTOBAGY

HORTOBÁGYI NEMZETI PARK (HORTOBÁGY NATIONAL PARK)

Sumen utca 2
4024 Derecen
Tel.: + 36 52 349 922
Fax: + 36 52 410 645
Hortobágy National Park, a reserve of nearly two hundred and fifty thousand acres (one hundred thousand hectares) of pristine countryside, has an ecosystem that is unique in Europe. Signs of human activity are few and far between, and there is an abundance of wildlife. To make the most of the park, it is indispensable to visit it in the company of one of the guides accredited by the parks service. A stop at the Shepherds' Museum (Hortobágyi Pásztormúzeum), which is devoted to the lifestyle of these workers, is highly recommended, as is a trip to the Round Museum (Körszinmúzeum), which has displays on the park's flora and fauna. Two miles (3 km) from the little town of Hortobágy, the village of Máta plays host to the International Horse Festival every summer. One of the main attractions is the *noniusz* breed of Hungarian draught horses, famed for their strength and endurance. The festival also features horse shows and competitions for decorated carts.

GEMENCI ERDO ES VADGAZDASAG RT. (GEMENC FOREST)

Szent Imre tér 2
6500 Baja
Tel.: + 36 79 324 144
Fax: + 36 79 324 181
The Gemenc forest, covering forty 49,000 acres (20,000 hectares) of flood plain between two reaches of the Danube, is the loveliest of Hungary's many woodlands. There is a small train line through the forest, but the best way to visit is without doubt on foot, at dawn or dusk, to get up close to the plant and animal life of this exceptional ecosystem. Hunters and anglers are also sure to find plenty to keep them occupied.

TISZAFÜRED

KORMORAN KIKOTO

5358 Tiszafüred-Orvény (Mr. Hegedüs Gábor)
Tel./Fax: + 36 59 305 305
E-mail: kormoran@mail.datanet.hu
Tiszafüred Lake is one of the most spectacular stretches of water in Hungary, and an outing in a flat-bottomed skiff is a great way to get a close-up look at the flora and fauna in this exceptional landscape where the earth and the lake seem to blend into the sky. Mr. Gábor organizes boat trips on the lake and can be prevailed upon to plan a memorable fishing trip, which will be appreciated by all the family.

FESTIVALS

MOHÁCS

MOHÁCSI BUSÓJARAS (MOHÁCS BUSÓ MASKS CARNIVAL)

Bartók Béla Müvelödési Központ
Tel.: + 36 69 511 120
Fax: + 36 69 511 122
E-mail: bbmk@hu.inter.net
The Mohács carnival takes place annually on the seventh Sunday before Easter. It provides dramatic evidence of the vibrancy of folk traditions whose origins are lost in the mists of time. The main attraction is the range of designs of *busó* masks. For three days, the locals parade in their masks, shaking rattles and ringing handbells to celebrate the death of winter and the arrival of a new spring. The climax of the festival is the huge bonfire on the third day, to which people flock from miles around..

SZEKSZÁRD

GRAPE HARVEST FESTIVAL (THIRD WEEKEND IN SEPTEMBER)

Festival office: Epreskert utca 10
7100 Szekszárd
Tel.: + 36 74 529 950
Fax: + 36 74 529 953
E-mail: sednyomda@axelero.hu
For a full taste of the joyous atmosphere that reigns in Szekszárd during the grape harvest, the best time to visit is towards the end of September, when the towns and villages all organize cultural and trade events, from a Central European Writer's Festival and well-known folk gala to sporting competitions and, of course, wine tastings.

DANUBE INTERNATIONAL FOLKLORE FESTIVAL (MID-JULY)

Tourist information: Garay tér 18
7100 Szekszárd
Tel.: + 36 74 511 263
The main Hungarian towns along the southern Danube—Baja, Kalocsa, and Szekszárd—have joined forces to plan a superb folklore festival that plays host to some of the finest folk music ensembles in the whole country.

THE CARPATHIANS AND TOKAJ

HOTELS

EGER

OFFI HAZ HOTEL

Dobó István tér. 5
3300 Eger
Tel.: + 36 36 311 005, + 36 36 311 330
Fax: + 36 36 417 247
E-mail: offihaz@mail.matav.hu
This recently renovated hotel in the heart of the old town has a warm atmosphere with a historic feel. Its five rooms are tastefully decorated in light wood. The dining room is particularly attractive, and the chef, Gábor Müncz, produces creative cuisine which is rooted in Hungarian tradition yet influenced by his international experience. Master confectioner Lajos Kopcsik has won several international awards for his pictures and sculptures in sugar, many of which are displayed in the hotel restaurant.

PANORAMA HOTEL

Dr. Hibay K. Utca 2
3300 Eger
Tel.: + 36 36 412 886
Fax: + 36 36 410 136
E-mail: panhotel@elender.hu
This is a modern hotel, located in a very quiet area on the outskirts of the old town. Its rooms are spacious, well equipped, and calm. The restaurant is rather lacking in character, but the cuisine is perfectly decent. All in all, this is a comfortable place to stay which offers good value for your money.

EGER & PARK HOTEL

Szálloda utca 1-3
3300 Eger
Tel.: + 36 36 522 222, +36 36 522 220
Fax: +36 36 413 114, +36 36 522 230
E-mail: sales.eger-park@danubius.group.com
This hotel belongs to the Danubius chain. It is well situated in the center of town, and boasts 165 rooms and many sporting facilities (swimming pool, tennis courts) and a fitness center (sauna, solarium). Conference rooms are also available. One of the specialties of this hotel is the organization of wine-tasting sessions in the wine cellars of the region.

FENYVES KASTELY

Szomolyai út
3325 Noszvaj
Tel.: + 36 36 463 041, + 36 36 463 371
Fax: + 36 36 563 059, + 36 36 563 039
After a wine-tasting session in the Vilmos Thummerer cellars you would be wise to take a break at Fenyves, a recently renovated manor house where you can choose from thirty one rooms and nine comfortable suites. It is near the pretty village of Noszvaj, where the neoclassical castle of Szepessy-De la Motte is worth a visit.

SENATOR HAZ HOTEL

Dobó tér 11
3300 Eger
Tel.: + 36 36 320 466
Fax: + 36 36 411 711
E-mail: hotelsen@axelero.hu
This charming eighteenth-century house at the foot of the fortress boasts eleven small but well-appointed rooms and quality cuisine. The prices are unbeatable, as is the hotel's location in the pedestrian area of downtown Eger. On warm summer evenings the terrace restaurant can sometimes get a little noisy, however.

TOKAJ

BORTO PANZIO

3931 Mezözombor-Dorgói Tó
Close to Highway 37
Tel.: + 36 47 369 475
Fax: + 36 47 569 015
This hotel in the Tokaj region is a very peaceful place in the heart of the vineyards on the edge of a little lake. It is highly recommended for the quality of its cuisine and its simple but comfortable rooms. This is a good place to stay during a tour of the Tokaj vineyards, especially as the managers of the hotel are well acquainted with the region's wine producers.

LILLAFÜRED

PALOTA HUNGUEST HOTEL

Lillafüred, Erzsébet sétány 1
3517 Miskolc
Tel.: + 36 46 331 411
Fax: + 36 46 533 203
E-mail: reserve@hotelpalota.hunguesthotels.hu
The Palota Hotel is one of the most spectacular establishments in Hungary, in a beautifully picturesque setting near a forest-covered mountain on the edge of a lake. It was built during the interwar period to symbolize the glory that was Greater Hungary prior to the Treaty of Trianon. It is a majestic neo-Renaissance structure with a hanging garden and a vast park planted with many fine tree species. It provides a perfect base from which to explore the Mátra and Bükk Mountains and the old town of Eger some 30 miles (50 km) away. The communal areas (dining rooms, lounges) are worthy of the reputation of this great hotel. The cuisine is good, although somewhat lacking in originality. The rooms are of various sizes, so you should check both the size of your room and its exact position: rooms with a view of the lake tend to be very popular.

TÓKERT ÉTTEREM-PANZIO

Erzsébet sétány 3
3500 Miskolc-Lillafüred
Tel./Fax: +36 46 531 202
E-mail: tokert@tokert.hu
The Tókert Inn on the edge of the charming little Hámori Lake has a number of peaceful rooms in pleasant surroundings. The cuisine is humble, but various kinds of excursions can be organized from the hotel, together with sporting activities such as hunting and fishing.

PARÁDFÜRDÖ

ERZSEBET KIRALYNE PARK HOTEL (QUEEN ELISABETH PARK HOTEL)

Kossuth út 372
3244 Parádfürdö
Tel.: + 36 36 444 044
Fax: + 36 36 544 170
E-mail: erzsebethotel@axelero.hu
Parádfürdö owes its reputation to the medicinal properties of its famous springs. The Queen Elisabeth Park Hotel was designed by the great architect Miklós Ybl and constructed in 1893. Nowadays it boasts thirty six rooms and six suites which have recently been renovated to offer spa visitors or mountain hikers all the comfort they could require. This hotel is highly recommended if you want a healthy holiday in a prestigious environment.

PARÁDSASVÁR

KASTELYHOTEL SASVAR

Kossuth utca 1
3242 Parádsasvár
Tel.: + 36 36 444 444
Fax: + 36 36 544 010
E-mail: sasvar@sasvar.hu
This luxury hotel has just opened in a historic property whose original owners were among

THE TOKAY WINE ROUTE, "THE KING OF WINES, THE WINE OF KINGS"

Tokay wine has been famous since the seventeenth century. It was a great favorite with the royal and imperial courts of Europe and was served at the best tables until World War I. However, international conflict and the collectivist régime were not favorable to the development of the Tokay vineyards, which only began to recover in the early 1990s thanks to the combined efforts of Hungarian winemakers and foreign investors. The main estates grouped together in 1995 and created an association intended to restore the reputation of Tokay and uphold the quality of Tokay wines: Tokay Renaissance (3910 Tokaj, Pf. 17. Tel./Fax: + 36 47 353 612). A leaflet about the Tokay wine route is available from various tourist sites(Tokaj/Hegyalja Wine Route Association / Tokaj-Hegyaljai Borút Egyesület: 3915 Tarcal, Fô u. 61. Tel./Fax: + 36 47 380 146; E-mail: tarcal@mail.matav.hu). For anyone who hopes to become a connoisseur of the region's white wines (dry wines, late harvest wines or wines from botrytised grapes) it is important to be familiar with the grape varieties from which they are made : Furmint, Hárslevelü, Sarga Muskotály (Yellow Muscat), Zeta and Kövérszolo. A top quality Aszú wine (made from botrytis cinerea, or "noble rot") depends on the maturity and plantation of these grape varieties. It is impossible to discover all the wealth of the Tokay vineyards on your first visit, but you should be sure to visit the main villages that belong to the appellation: Tokaj, Tarcal, Bodrogkeresztúr, Mád, Tállya, Erdobénye, Tolcsva and Sárospatak. When tasting the different wines, you should also be aware of the various techniques that are used to produce these syrupy wines: sometimes traditional oxidative methods are used, but sometimes other techniques are preferred, which are intended to emphasize the flavor of the fruit. The following producers are especially noteworthy for the fine quality of their wines and are worth paying a visit to:

ARVAY PINCE

3911 Tokaj
Rákóczi út 48
Tel.: + 36 47 552 156
János Arvay worked for a long time at Disznóko, one of the greatest Tokaj estates, before setting up his own winery. He produces some ambitious wines on his 150-acre (60-hectare) estate; his first Aszú 6 puttonyos (1996), is a remarkable success.

DISZNÓKO SZOLOBIRTOK ÉS PINCÉSZET

3919 Mezozombor
Disznóko Dolo
Tel.: + 36 47 569 410
This estate was classified a prime cultivation area in 1734 by royal decree. It now belongs to Axa Millésimes, a subsidiary of the French Insurance group AXA which also owns vineyards in the Bordeaux region and in Portugal. It is managed by a talented young Hungarian, Laszló Meszáros. The 320 acres (130 hectares) of this estate produce some remarkable wines. The dry Furmints are harmonious and well balanced; of the Aszú wines, the Aszú 5 puttonyos of 1993 is a marvel. The 1995 (6 puttonyos) and 1995 vintages are also impressive.

GRÓF DEGENFELD SZOLOBIRTOK ÉS PINCÉSZET

3915 Tarcal
Terézia Kert 9
Tel.: + 36 47 380 173
This estate of almost 250 acres (100 hectares) near Tokaj was created in 1995 by Countess Mária Degenfeld and her husband Thomas Lindner. The vineyard uses state-of-the-art technology and produced some magnificent Aszú wines in 1998 (5 puttonyos) and 1999, which are now available on the market. A semi sweet Muscat Lunel 2001 is also to be recommended.

GUNDEL PINCÉSZET

3909 Nád
Árpad út 37
Tel.: + 36 47 348 383
This 60-acre (25-hectare) estate produces the main wines that are served at the great Gundel restaurant in Budapest.

KIRÁLYUDVAR

3915 Tarcal,
Fô út 92
Tel.: + 36 47 380 111
This ancient estate has been renowned since the eighteenth century. It now belongs to an American businessman and is managed by István Szepsy, who is reputed to be one of the best winemakers in the region. The estate is being developed and will eventually cover over 200 acres (90 hectares). The first Aszú 6 puttonyos, 1998, is a top quality wine.

MEGYER

3950 Sárospatak
Nagy Lajos u 12
Tel.: + 36 47 312 310
This estate of almost 200 acres (80 hectares) was bought in 2000 by Jean-Louis Laborde, and its acid soil produces wines with great character. These are made using state-of-the-art technology and matured in optimal conditions in the Ráckóczi cellar in Sárospatak – a spectacular place which is steeped in history and is open to visitors. The very impressive Aszú 5 puttonyos of 1993 and 1998 are particularly commendable.

PAJZOS

3950 Sárospatak
Nagy Lajos u 12
Tel.: + 36 47 312 310
This vineyard of over 120 acres (50 hectares) is north of the hilly Tokajhegyalja region. It is the brother of the Megyer estate and also belongs to Jean-Louis Laborde. It is managed by Hajnalka Szabó and produces some of the finest Tokaj wines. The 1993 Aszú 5 puttonyos is a marvel; and although 1997 was not a good year for the appellation, the 1997 is also an unqualified success.

SZEPSY ISTVÁN

3909 Mád
Táncsics utca 57
Tel.: + 36 47 348 349
István Szepsy has his own vineyard of about 50 acres (20 hectares), selected both for its mineral richness and its low yield, which produces very generous, complex, and elegant wines. It has been said of István Szepsy that his estate was to Tokaj what Château Yquem was to Sauternes …
His greatest Aszú wines (such as the 6 puttonyos of 1995 and 1996) are particularly striking and should definitely be tasted.

TOKAJ HÉTSZOLO

3910 Tokaj
Kossuth tér 15
Tel.: + 36 47 952 009
This vineyard on the best slopes of the Tokaj hill was an estate which belonged to the emperor. It has been carefully replanted since 1991, when it was bought by the French insurance group GMF. Its 136 acres (55 hectares) of arid loess soil produce unique and highly original wines, thanks to the determination and inventiveness of estate manager Tibor Kovács. The Rákóczi cellars are an exceptional place to enjoy wine-tasting: you can try a very wide range of Furmint or Hárslevelü wines, and some very powerful Aszú wines (6 puttonyos 1995, 1996, and 1999).

TOKAJ KERESKEDOHÁZ

3980 Sátoraljaújhely
Mártírok utca 17
Tel.: + 36 47 322 133
The wines produced by the state-owned trading-house (which succeeded in 1993 to the Tokaj State Farm) are made with grapes that come from a number of small estates and also from the famous Szarvas vineyard in Tarcal. This enterprise defends the traditional style of Tokaj wines, but is also open to the idea of wines with a more clear-cut aroma. A fine Aszú 5 puttonyos from 1994 is recommended.

TOKAJ OREMUS

3934 Tolcsva
Bajcsy Zsilinsky utca 45
Tel.: + 36 47 384 504
One of the region's greatest properties, which now belongs to the Spanish group Vega Sicilia, covers nearly 370 acres (150 hectares) to the north of the Tokaj region. Talented manager András Bacscó uses splendid modern installations together with cellars that date from the thirteenth to the eighteenth century, where large quantities of old vintage Aszú wines are stored (the 1972 is especially remark able). Grape varieties such as Yellow Muscat or Zeta are very plentiful here, with the result that highly original wines are produced in which the fruit bouquet is strongly present. The 6 puttonyos of 1997 and 1999 are very concentrated wines.

ÚRI BOROK

3909 Mád
Kossuth Lajos utca 40/a
Tel.: + 36 47 348 601
The wines that are produced on this small, ideally-situated 37-acre (15 hectares) property are top class and perfectly vinified by the owner-winemaker, Vince Gergely. One of the most striking wines produced by this fast-developing estate is an impressive Muskotály Aszú 6 puttonyos 1998, which is made from Muscat grapes only.

the first Magyar conquerors. The clientele (essentially from Budapest) can enjoy the many fitness facilities provided in this five-star establishment, which still seems rather new but is genuinely comfortable. Horse-riding excursions in the nearby Mátra Mountains can be organized from the hotel.

RESTAURANTS

EGER

FEHER SZARVAS VADASZTANYA (WHITE STAG HUNTING INN)

Klapka György út 8
3300 Eger
Tel./Fax: + 36 36 411 129
E-mail: szarvas@mail.agria.hu
The atmosphere in this restaurant takes you straight to the heart of the Hungarian hunting world. The hunting trophies on the walls, the game dishes on the menu, and the furniture itself all contribute to creating a hunting-lodge decor. The cuisine is good-quality, traditional fare, and the region's best wines are served by an attentive and efficient sommelier.

TALIZMAN-TULIPANKERT VENDEGLO

Szépasszony-völgy utca 47
3300 Eger
Tel.: + 36 36 412 533
E-mail: marosfalvi@axelero.hu
This garden restaurant in the heart of the Valley of the Beautiful Woman (famous for its wine cellars) is one of the best addresses in town and is as pleasant in winter as in summer. The garden is planted with conifers and equipped with wooden tables, and the large indoor restaurant is attractively decorated. The wine list is very full, and the sommelier will gladly help you choose the best wines to accompany your meal. A Gypsy ensemble performs well but discreetly as you enjoy your dinner.

HOLLÓKÖ

MUSKATLI VENDEBGLO (GERANIUM INN)

Kossuth út 61
3176 Hollókö
Tel.: + 36 32 379 262
The delightful village of Hollókö features on Unesco's World Heritage List. A good place to stop for a meal is the simple but quality Geranium Inn, set in a garden full of colorful shrubs and geraniums. The local specialties are highly recommended—especially the *palóc leves* (a thick green bean and garden vegetable soup) and the *bab gulyas* (an invigorating goulash soup with meat and beans).

VAR ÉTTEREM

Kossuth út 93-95
3176 Hollókö
Tel./Fax: + 36 32 379 029
This unpretentious restaurant is ideally situated in the heart of the little town of Hollókö, surrounded by newly renovated rural houses. It is a good place for lunch on a fine day, when you can sit outside on a wooden bench in an alleyway of trees and enjoy the particularly flavorsome cuisine. Moreover, you may encounter some of the old ladies of the town who still wear the traditional outfits of this Palóc region.

TOKAJ

DEGENFELD RESTAURANT AND WINE CELLAR

Kossuth tér 1
3910 Tokaj
Tel.: + 36 47 553 050
Fax: +36 47 552 174
E-mail: contact@tokajtc.com
The splendidly restored Degenfeld Palace stands proudly on the main square in Tokaj. It was renovated by Count Degenfeld and his family, who have given the family property a new lease on life. Visitors can now discover the remarkable wines of the Degenfeld vineyard (which was recently replanted) as they enjoy some highly imaginative dishes such as grilled liver with figs, grilled pikeperch with walnuts and sunflower seeds, or chicken stuffed with dried apricots and served on dill-flavored fromage frais with a lemon sauce. Moreover, the wines produced on the Degenfeld estate can be purchased at the restaurant. There are a few rooms available on the first floor, but a luxury hotel is soon to open in the family castle in the nearby village of Tarcal. As the region is currently experiencing a tourist boom, this hotel will provide welcome additional accommodation.
The estate's wine store is also in Tarcal, and is worth a visit for the quality both of its architecture and of its wines.

TOLCSVA

OS KAJÁN RESTAURANT

Kossuth Lajos utca 16
3934 Tolcsva
Tel./fax: + 36 47 384 195
E-mail: oskajan.restaurant@matavnet.hu
The Os Kaján is a magical place in Tolcsva, in the heart of the Tokaj vineyards. This restaurant was opened by Anne and Paul, a French couple with a passion for the Tokaj region and its many treasures. The cuisine is particularly inspired, and makes good use of the best the region has to offer. The menu is the most extraordinary you will find in this part of Hungary, with pikeperch, trout, or catfish; deer, mouflon or mutton from the *puszta*; mountain mushrooms; fruit from the nearby orchards; and homemade desserts. The various rooms in the restaurant each have their own special atmosphere, and are also used to exhibit well-known artists. The medicinal plant garden, library, and wine cellar further contribute to the reputation of the Os Kaján. Moreover, Paul is a connoisseur whose wine-tasting sessions will enable you to discover the diversity of local wines.

GASTRONOMY AND WINES

EGER

SZÉPASSZONY VOLGY (THE VALLEY OF THE BEAUTIFUL WOMAN)

The best Eger wines are produced in this valley to the southwest of the old town. There are many legends concerning the origin of its name, which include references to Venus and tales of a beautiful cellar owner or a flighty aristocratic lady. However it may be, the valley has been exploited by wine growers since the late eighteenth century, and a multitude of cellars are hollowed out of the region's volcanic tuff. The wine is stored all year round at a temperature of between 42° F and 47° F (10° C and 15° C). The various mosses and molds that thrive in the cellars grow in symbiosis with the wines, helping them to mature and contributing to the composition of their bouquet. Nowadays, over two hundred cellars contribute to the reputation of the Eger wines. Some (cellars n°. 9, 15, and 24) are considered to be historic monuments; these include the cellar-museum (Istenes Pince) on Tulipánkert utca, which is the oldest cellar in town and was preserved intact after being used as a secret church during the Turkish occupation. Wine-tasting sessions, cheerful meals, and concerts by Gypsy or folk groups are regular occurrences in this very popular place. It can also be arranged for visitors to participate in the grape harvest, which is a great way of learning about the various grape varieties that produce the region's white wines (Egri Olaszrizling, Egri Leánkya, Egri Muskotály, Egri Chardonnay) or red wines (Egri Kékfrankos, Egri Cabernet Sauvignon, Egri Bikavér).

Among the region's best wine producers the following are of particular interest: **Vilmos Thummerer** (Szomolyai út 3325 Noszvaj, to the northeast of town, Tel.: + 36 36 463 385), whose wines are some of the finest in this region thanks to skillful production methods and carefully selected plots on a vineyard of 130 acres (52 hectares); **Tibor Gál** (Veröszala utca 22, 3300 Eger, Tel.: + 36 36 429 800), "Wine-grower of the Year" in 1989, who benefits from the know-how of the great Tuscan house of Ludovico Antinori; and **Béla Vincze**, a family business that produces fine red wines, matured in new barrels, in a 45-acre (18-hectare) vineyard (Váci M. utca 65, 3300 Eger, Tel.: + 36 36 427 515).`

MUSEUMS

EGER

LICEUM (LIBRARY AND OBSERVATORY)

Eszterházy tér 1
3300 Eger
Tel.: + 36 36 325 211, + 36 36 520 400
The majestic edifice that houses the Liceum, built in late Baroque style, is now a college which is home to the famous Episcopal library with its one hundred and thirty thousand volumes. Codices, incunabula, old manuscripts, and rare books constitute an exceptional collection which is stored in this library with its magnificent wood trim and famous frescoes. The observatory's museum of astronomy and the camera obscura with its periscope make it well worth climbing the Liceum tower, if you can find the energy!

DOBO ISTVAN VAR MÚZEUM (ISTVAN DOBO CASTLE MUSEUM)

Dózsa György tér
3300 Eger
Tel.: + 36 36 312 744
The Castle Museum is in the former Bishop's Palace, within the walls of the splendid fortress which put up such valiant resistance to the Turkish invaders. It presents an interesting overview of the history of Eger and its heroes, with its network of underground galleries and passageways (which can be visited on request and help clarify the history of the castle siege), and its dungeon.

GÖDÖLL

THE GÖDÖLL ROYAL CASTLE

Pf.406
2100 Gödöll
Tel.: + 36 28 410 124, + 36 28 420 588
Fax.: + 36 28 422 077
E-mail: informacio@kiralyikastely.hu
The Gödöll Royal Castle in its 70-acre (28-hectare) park is the largest Baroque castle in Hungary. It has been open to the public since 1996, and houses a permanent exhibition which commemorates the castle's glorious history and foundation in the eighteenth century by the Grassalkovich family. The royal apartments of Francis Joseph and Queen Elizabeth have been recreated with great authenticity, and are open to visitors. Festivals and classical concerts are organized in the great hall, or in the main court yard during the summer months. There is also a friendly cafeteria, with fine copies of Bieder meier furniture and a Herend porcelain service.

HOLLÓKÖ

FALU MÚZEUM

3176 Hollókö, Kossuth utca 82
Tel.: + 36 32 379 258
This little museum gives a refreshing view of traditional village life in Hollókö, a little town which features on Unesco's World Heritage List. All manner of everyday objects serve to illustrate the various aspects of local family life. Since the 1920s, several generations of villagers have added to the museum's collection of objects that are representative of this Palóc region.

RECSK

RECSK NATIONAL MEMORIAL PARK

Three miles (5 kilometers) from the town of Recsk a National Memorial commemorates the labor camp for political prisoners set up by Stalinist dictator Mátyás Rákosi between 1949 and 1953. The country setting makes it difficult to imagine the dreadful conditions endured by inmates in this camp, where the death rate was extremely high, especially during the harsh winters in this mountainous region. The groups of huts have been left as they stood, and a large sculpture by artist Adám Farkas pays a moving tribute to the victims.

TRADITIONAL AND CREATIVE CRAFTS

EGER

MEGYEHAZA (COUNTY HALL)

Kossuth Lajos utca 9
3300 Eger
The wrought-iron gates of the County Hall are undoubtedly the finest example of Hungarian craftsmanship in the field of iron work. They were made by Heinrik Fazola, a craftsman whom Bishop Eszterházy commissioned to create this masterpiece in the early nineteenth century.

ERD BÉNYE

COOPER

Attila Hotyek
3932 Erd bénye, Dombi út 2
Tel.: + 36 47 336 056
Mobile: + 36 302 284 000
In the charming village of Erd Bénye, this small producer of Tokay wines also specializes in the manufacture of casks for *palinka*, a local brandy, the finest variety of which (*barac palinka*) is made from apricots. You will find his picturesque workshop up a steep and narrow street.

HOLLÓKÖ

Many traditional crafts are still flourishing in Hollókö and the villages of the Palóc region. If you are interested in learning more about the craft industry and visiting the various workshops consult Ispán Dániel (Tel.: + 36 06 32 379-273; E-mail: idker@elender.hu) who can organize meetings with the various artists of this region.

PARÁD

GLASS ARTIST: JONAS BALINT'S WORKSHOP

Kékesi út 25
3240 Parád
Tel./Fax: +36 36 364 757
In this forest region, the traditional glass industry still employs some master glassworkers. Here the artist's creations are on sale.

FESTIVALS AND CULTURAL EVENTS

EGER

The town of Eger is reputed for its festive tradition, especially in summer and fall during the grape harvest. The famous "Valley of the Beautiful Woman" (Szépasszony Völgy) is particularly rich in festive events, such as the **Summer of Muses** (June 24–26, a friendly family festival involving all kinds of artistic disciplines) or the **Festival of the Valley of the Beautiful Woman**, which takes place from August 17 to 20 and is largely devoted to Bacchus. István Dobó Square, in the heart of the old town, is the site of musical events (**Military Band Festival**, June 25–27), medieval markets (**The Medieval Market Place**, early August), or a **vintage car rally** in mid-September. Information from the Eger Tourist Office/ Tourinform: Bajcsy-Zs út 9, 3300 Eger, Tel.: + 36 36 517 715, Fax: + 36 36 518 815,

HOLLÓKÖ

The little town of Hollókö is famous for its traditional lifestyle and respect for folk customs related to the Palóc ethnic group. The best time to visit is during Easter, when a variety of events take place in Hollókö and the surrounding villages. The gaily embroidered, festive costumes, painted eggs, and pastries will make your memor able. For information on the various festivities that take place throughout the year, contact Ispán Dániel. (Tel.: + 36 06 32 379-273, Website: www.hollokotourism.hu).

TOKAJ

In the months of May and June, many festivals are held in the Tokaj region. The town of Tokaj itself hosts the Wine Festival (Tokaji Borfesztivál) in late May, with wine tasting, enthronement of new members of the "Vinum Regum Rex Vinorum" Wine Brotherhood, as well as concerts, fish soup contests, sporting events, street balls, and majorette parades. Most of the events are free. In late June, open-air classical concerts are held in the main square in Tokaj. Information: Tokaj Cultural Center/M vél dési Ház, Rákóczy út 52, Tel.: + 36 47 352 003.

LE BALATON

HOTELS

HÉVÍZ

HUNGUEST HOTEL HELIOS

Vörösmarty u 91
8380 Hévìz
Tel.: + 36 83 342 895
Fax: + 36 83 340 525
E-mail: reserve@hotelhelios.hunguesthotels.hu
There are a number of thermal spas in Hévíz, all offering a similar range of services, based around the spectacular lake whose slightly radioactive water and mud have long been known to have health-giving properties. This top-flight hotel is a chateau with two modern annexes, standing on grounds of 15 acres (6 hectares) It specializes in top-of-the range fitness programs, and has its own large swimming pool, sauna, Jacuzzi, and a broad selection of treatments on offer. However, it must be said that the restaurant is not quite up to the high standards of the rest of the hotel.

WELLNESS HOTEL HÉVIZ

Sümegi utca 35
8372 Hévíz
Tel.: + 36 83 320 200
E-mail: heviz-pension@netropolis.hu
This three-star hotel is an excellent place to book a health cure, as it has a swimming pool, gym, and sauna, and also organizes a program of enter tainments. It is a popular summer destination for the bright young things of Budapest.

NAGYVÁZSONY

NAGYVÁZSONYI KESTELYSZALLO (NAGYVÁZSONYI CHÂTEAU HOTEL)

Kossuth L. utca 10-14
8291 Nagyvázsony
Tel./Fax: + 36 88 264 109
The village of Nagyvázsony is well known for its fifteenth-century fort, a gift from King Matthias to the Hungarian army captain Pál Kinizsi, in recognition for his military exploits against the Turks. Nearby is the baroque home of the Zichy family, which has been renovated and is now an eight-room hotel. The rooms are still a little rough and ready, but the charm of the site is such that any minor discomforts are swiftly forgotten. Located near the historical, Baroque town of Veszprém and Lake Balaton, the hotel is recommended to all those who appreciate a touch of authenticity. There are also numerous opportunities for horse riding in the area.

KÖVESKÁL

KÁLI ART INN

Fö utca 8
8274 Köveskál
Tel.: + 36 87 706 090
Fax: + 36 87 468 412
E-mail: mail@kali-art.com
Lying on the edge of the fertile Káli basin, one of

the most charming landscapes on the northern shores of Lake Balaton, the village of Köveskál is a popular stopping point for people who love the natural beauty of the hills here. In 1998, Kati Koller founded a private art school aimed at helping young artists discover the natural wonders of this region (E-mail: kali.art@budapest.blackbox.at, Tel./Fax: + 36 87 478 721). When Kati Koller is not running courses, the residence opens to paying guests. The rooms are tastefully decorated by the artists who have passed through. The food is wonderfully inventive and uses only the very freshest of ingredients. The local honey and homemade jams at breakfast are a real treat. The hotel is a little costlier than others in the region, but is extremely reasonable given the quality of the rooms and the facilities, which include a swimming pool, sauna, bicycle rental, library, and superb garden.

TIHÁNY

KASTELY ES PARK *HOTEL TIHÁNY*

Fürdötelepi utca, 1
8237 Tihány
Tel.: + 36 87 448 611
Fax: + 36 87 448 409
E-mail: hotel.fured@matavnet.hu

The Château and Park Hotels in the town of Tihány—a popular tourist destination—together offer a generous range of facilities just a few dozen miles from the lake. From April 15 through October 15, they even have their own private beach on the lakeshore, as well as sporting equipment. The Park Hotel is a graceless building dating from the 1960s, but the château more than makes up for its unattractive neighbor. Built in the early years of the twentieth century, it was designed to be the summer residence of Joseph, Archduke of Habsburg. The grand reception halls and large rooms look out onto the grounds that cover 15 acres (6 hec tares). Unfortunately, the service is not quite of the high standard the surroundings would lead you to expect. However, all in all, this is a pleasant departure point for walks round the Tihány peninsula, and other popular destinations are easily accessible by car.

SZÉKESFEHÉRVÁR

HOTEL SZÁRCSA CSARDA ES FOGADO

Szárcsa utca, 1
8000 Székesfehérvár
Tel.: + 36 22 325 700, + 36 22 506 820
Fax: + 36 22 506 818

This address, on the southern side of the town on road 63, is very familiar to the locals, who come here to enjoy tasty meals served in generous portions in one of the dining rooms decorated in the style of traditional country inns, with lots of wood paneling, brightly colored tablecloths, and fine carved furniture. The thirty one rooms, which look out over the inner courtyard, are likewise furnished in a charmingly old-fashioned style. As hotels in the old town center can be rather difficult to book, this is certainly a perfectly acceptable alternative.

VESZPRÉM

OLIVA ÉTTEREM GRILLKERT PANZIO

Buhim utca, 14-16
8200 Veszprém
Tel.: + 36 88 403 870 (restaurant)
Tel.: + 36 88 403 875 (hotel)
E-mail: oliva@oliva.hu

In the heart of the old town in Veszprém—one of the most harmonious groups of baroque buildings in all Hungary—this modest hostelry offers a decent menu based on grilled meats, and also has ten or so recently restored bedrooms. The superb vaulted ceilings create a warm and inviting atmosphere, which on summer evenings spills out into the garden, where jazz concerts are held regularly.

HOTEL VILLA MEDICI

Kittenberger K. utca 11
8200 Veszprém
Tel.: + 36 88 590 070

This relatively new hotel at the foot of the old town is hidden behind a traditional Baroque façade. The rooms are spacious and airy, and the food, while perhaps lacking a little in imaginative flair, is nonetheless perfectly acceptable. All in all, a comfortable hotel, if you can overlook the rather insipid interior design.

PUSZTAZÁMOR

ÖREG TÖLGY (THE OLD OAK)

Kastély
2039 Pusztazámor
Tel.: + 36 23 347 744, + 36 30 964 9533

Half an hour from Budapest, heading towards Lake Balaton, this superb manor house has been entirely renovated by its owner, a retired antiques dealer from Szentendre. Each bedroom is decorated with original, personal touches that make this a truly enchanting (and surprisingly reasonably priced) experience. The owner is happy to organize horse rides, hunts, or even concerts, and for the less adventurous, there are tennis courts and a swimming pool in the grounds. Breakfast is served in the large dining room, which houses an eclectic collection of objets d'art. Lunch and dinner are available on request.

RESTAURANTS

BADACSONY

SZENT ORBAN BORHAZ

8261 Badacsony
Tel.: + 36 87 431 382

This is without doubt one of the prettiest addresses in the northern Balaton region. Szeremley has 62 acres (25 hectares) of vines on the slopes of Badacsony hill. Great care is taken to marry the remarkable wines with the fine cuisine based on the very best local produce—foie gras, pike perch from the lake, and ham with acacia jam. The restaurant terrace has unparalleled views over the hills around the lake.

VESZPRÉM

MALOM CSARDA (THE MILL INN)

Veszprémi utca, 3
8229 Csopak,
Tel.: + 36 87 446 063, + 36 30 947 2291

Along the pretty road 73 that wends its way from Veszprém to the shores of Lake Balaton, this charming traditional inn makes for a refreshing break, as it is set on a stream that still powers the mill. The thatched roof, wood paneling, and tiny courtyard set with a few tables form an enchanting ensemble. The cooking is plain but decent, in particular the game and the various goulashes on offer.

MUSEUMS

KESZTHELY

FESTETICS KASTELY (FESTETICS CASTLE)

Kastély utca
8360 Keszthely
Tel.: + 36 83 312 190

This splendid neoclassical mansion on the shores of the lake was one of the few monuments in Hungary to survive the war unscathed—in fact, it still has most of its original furniture and fittings. The salons, the superb Helikon library of over fifty-two thousand volumes, and the magnificent English-style garden make this a wonderful place to visit.

BALATON MÚZEUM (THE BALATON MUSEUM)

Múzeum utca 2
8360 Keszthely
Tel.: + 36 83 312 351

The Balaton Museum, housed in a fine late-nineteenth-century house, provides a fascinating glimpse into the lake's unique ecosystem and the traditional way of life of the people who dwell on the shores here. There are lively exhibitions on the flora and fauna, the trades and crafts of the locals—fishermen, weavers, millers, and peasants—and folk costumes. Children in particular appreciate the section on the fish, birds, and mammals of the lake.

NAGYVÁZSONY

KINIZSIPÁL VARMÚZEUM (PÁL KINIZSI FORTRESS MUSEUM)

Vár út 9
8291 Nagyvázsony
Tel.: + 36 88 264 786

A visit to the fortress held by Captain Pál Kinizsi during Hungary's heroic struggles against the Turks gives an idea of the state of siege that this part of the country found itself in in the fifteenth and sixteenth centuries. The castle was spared by the Habsburgs when they reconquered this territory in the seventeenth century. The museum recreates the atmosphere of a medieval castle thanks to the impressive decor consisting of original furniture and fittings. The bold captain's tombstone can be seen in the restored chapel.

POSTAMÚZEUM (POSTAL MUSEUM)

Temetö utca 3
8291 Nagyvázsony
Tel.: + 36 88 264 300

This village lay at the junction of several important postal routes, and the mail coaches would stop here to change horses. The Postal Museum has an exhibition featuring the various methods of postal distribution through the ages. The most charming thing about it is its rather quaint, old-world feel.

SZÉKESFEHÉRVÁR

BABA MÚZEUM (DOLL MUSEUM)

Megyeház utca, 17
Tel.: + 36 22 329 504

TRADITIONAL HOUSES ON THE SHORES OF THE BALATON

The Lake Balaton region is an ideal place to visit if you are interested in the architectural traditions of this part of Hungary. Many homes here have been tastefully restored in keeping with the past, and once you have exhausted the delights of water sports or swimming in the lake, you can explore the beautiful surrounding area on foot, and may perhaps be invited to admire some of these renovated properties.

Most of the owners of the houses on the lake's northern shores leave Budapest at the beginning of summer and stay in their Balaton homes for long stretches, even if that means commuting back to the capital from time to time. They only return to the city in early September, harvest time. Incidentally, this is undoubtedly the best time to encounter the fortunate owners of the region's small vineyards—they are usually proud to let passing strangers taste their house wines, providing, of course, that they respect the local lifestyle and show interest in finding out about the regional wines.

Two addresses can be recommended: the **Pusztazámor Castle-Hotel** and the **Kali Art Inn**. Their owners like to encourage exchanges between their clientele and local artists, intellectuals, or business people interested in meeting foreign visitors, and for their part the inhabitants are extremely proud to share their research and discoveries with others. Here your stay is guar anteed to be stimulating.

City dwellers who want to rediscover the authentic Hungary of their childhood are especially fond of the **Kali Basin**, the **Tihany** peninsula, the village of **Szigliget**, and **Badacsony Hill**. Enchanting buildings in **Szigliget** and the nearby village of **Nemesvita**, with their thatch ed roofs, whitewashed walls, and sober interiors decorated with traditional regional household and agricultural objects, are particularly fine examples of the recent revival in rural architecture.

This delightful museum is a real treat for children, with its lively and colorful displays of dolls in miniature settings, perfect in every detail. Some of the most exceptional pieces date back to the eighteenth century.

FEKETE SAS PATIKA (THE BLACK EAGLE PHARMACY)

Fö utca, 5
Tel.: + 36 22 315 583
Hungary seems to specialize in beautiful old pharmacies. This is one of the loveliest. The building and its interior are worth a visit them selves, and there is also a fascinating collection of phials, ceramic pots, and flasks containing mysterious herbal preparations and unguents to cure all manner of ills. The apothecary also sells replicas of his collection of antiques.

VESZPRÉM

LACZKO DEZSÖ MÚZEUM

Tel.: + 36 88 426 081
A mere stone's throw from the fine late-nineteenth-century building that houses the regional council, this museum devoted to local traditional art and costumes is worth a visit. It gives an insight into the ancestral way of life of the inhabitants of the Bakony Mountains, starting in Roman times. On the way out of the museum there is a reconstitution of an traditional home, perfect in every detail, where a glass-blower now has his workshop—a reminder of the important role crystal ware once played in the local economy.

TAC-GORSIUM

SZABADTÉRI MÚZEUM (OPEN-AIR ROMAN MUSEUM)

Village 15 km south of Székesfehérvár
Tel.: + 36 22 362 243
Visitors should definitely plan to spend at least an afternoon at the ruins of the Roman town of Gorsium, in the heart of the countryside. Gorsium was once the largest Roman camp in what was then known as Lower Pannonia. The site is well thought out, and all in all it makes a most pleasant place for a country stroll on the way to Lake Balaton.

SPAS

HÉVÍZ

KEHIDA TERMÁL GYÓGY-ES ELMENY FURDO (KEHIDA THERMAL BATHS)

Kossuth utca, 60
8784 Kehidakustány
Tel.: + 36 83 534 500
Near the famous spa town of Hévíz, the village of Kehidakustány has become a popular destination for young vacationers visiting Lake Balaton. The various thermal springs and pools are a great way to while away the time, and there is also a plain but decent restaurant.

HUNTING

VADEX RT.

Tolnai utca, 1
8000 Székesfehérvár
Tel.:+ 36 22 329 420
Fax: + 36 22 327 525
E-mail: adravecze@vadex.hu
Hungary is the ideal vacation destination for hunters, and the region of Székesfehérvár has a wealth of both furred and feathered game. The hunt specialists Vadex have acquired several sizeable reserves where they organize hunts in line with their clients' wishes. The quality of the sport and the magnificent landscape make for an unforgettable experience..

ARTS AND CRAFTS

HEREND

PORCELANIUM

Kossuth L. utca, 140
8440 Herend
Tel.: + 36 88 523 100, + 36 88 523 190
Fax: + 36 88 260 566
Tel.:(Budapest office): + 36 1 267 4626
E-mail: porcelanium@herend.com
Herend porcelain has been unfailingly popular ever since the company was first founded in 1826. Nowadays, visitors can spend a day at the museum–inspecting the small factory, lunching at the restaurant or tearoom-and purchase samples at the factory shop. The museum takes a look at the story of how this local craft became a highly successful industry, including an interesting film on porcelain manufacturing techniques. Visitors also have the opportunity to watch the craftsmen at work.

WINE

SZENTORBAN WINERY-HUBA SZEREMLEY

Római út 93
8262 Badacsonylábdihegy
Tel/Fax: + 36 87 432 532, + 36 87 432 352
This family-owned property of 62 acres (25 hectares) on the flanks of Badacsony hill produces some of the best wines in the Balaton region. Most of the varieties of grapes grown in the region are represented, including some extremely ancient Hungarian varieties such as *kéknyelü* and *budai zöld*. The late-harvested 1997 and 2000 Szürkebarát, Olaszrizling, and Zeuzs vintages are highly recommended—especially the latter, which has a perfect balance of acidity and sweetness, with a marked note of "noble rot." These wines can be tasted along with an excellent meal at the Szent Orbán Borház restaurant, which offers a magnificent panorama over the Badacsony vineyards, the Kali basin, and Lake Balaton.

VULKÁN-ISTVAN INHAUSER

8483 Somlószölös
Tel.: + 36 30 562 741
The volcanic soil of the Somló hill produces wines of great quality, although the appellation only covers a few dozen miles of vineyards. The Juhfark (sheep's tail) grape variety in particular gives dry wines with a remarkable bouquet. Wines from Vulkán are notable for the balance and harmony of their nose. Furmints give a more classic wine to be drunk young; if the fall is blessed with sunshine, it develops fine notes of "noble rot."

Baroque Hungary

HOTELS

FERTÖD

ESTERHÁZY CASTLE HOTEL

Tel: + 36 99 537 640
Fax: + 36 99 537 642
If you are more interested in discovering an authentic relic of Hungarian history than in your own personal comfort, then you might like to book a stay in one of the wings of the Esterházy Castle. You will have to climb several flights of stairs—there is no elevator—but the sense of living history in the rooms, furnished with an assortment of oddities from different centuries, is truly special. Each room has several beds. The view over the park is superb and the ambience is one of refined calm—unless you happen to arrive when the hotel has been booked by a boisterous Hungarian wedding party! Information on prices and availability of rooms is available from the castle ticket office.

SZIDÓNIA MANOR HOUSE

Röjtöki út 37
9451 Röjtökmuzsaj
Tel.: + 36 99 544 810
Fax: + 36 99 380 013
Six miles (ten kilometers) southwest of Fertöd, Szidónia Manor House has recently undergone a thorough renovation to become a luxury hotel. The thirty-nine rooms and seven apartments are furnished with antiques, while the sporting facilities in the grounds are modern and well maintained. There is also a fine wine cellar, a private salon, a cozy café, and a superb restaurant seating one hundred guests. All in all, this is an excellent base for a stay in the region, although the prices are naturally commensurate with the quality of the facilities. Maybe that is why most of the guests seem to be wealthy Austrians.

HEGYKÖ THERMAL HOTEL

Nyárfa sor
9437 Hegykö
Tel.: + 36 99 376 917
Not far from Fertöd, the village of Hegykö has a good thermal hotel whose spa and restaurant are both equally popular with young Hungarians. While in the area, don't miss the superbly renovated rural houses in the nearby village of Fertöszéplak.

GYÖR

GRÓF CZIRÁKY PANZIÓ

Bécsi Kapu tér, 8
9021 Györ
Tel.: + 36 96 528 466, + 36 96 310 688
Fax: + 36 96 528 467
E-mail: grofczirakypanzio@matavnet.hu
Located in a pleasant spot on a knoll at the entrance to the old town, with a view over the little river Raba, a tributary of the Danube, this modest inn with just eleven rooms is worth knowing about. It is relatively inexpensive, and while the home comforts are rather basic (the building dates from the eighteenth century), it is perfectly adequate for a short stay—and above all, it is just a ten-minute stroll from the center of Györ.

KLASTROM HOTEL

Zechmeister utca, 1
9021 Györ
Tel.: + 36 96 516 910
Fax: + 36 96 327 030
This hotel was originally a Carmelite convent, founded in the seventeenth century. It was fully renovated and converted into a three-star hotel in 1987 by the Györ town council. As befits a former convent, the forty-two rooms are rather sparsely decorated, but very large, and the building itself is magnificent. An atmosphere of quiet reigns here, but guests can relax in the pub, sauna, and solarium. In summer, the tables of the courtyard restaurant are shaded by the mighty branches of a venerable three-hundred-year-old walnut tree. Concerts are also held there in the evenings. The library can be booked for functions with up to fifty guests. All this is just a stone's throw from the heart of the old town.

NAGYCENK

HUNGUEST HOTEL KASTÉLY

Kiscenki út 3
9485 Nagycenk
Tel./Fax: + 36 99 360 061
E-mail: reserve@hotelkastely.hunguesthotels.hu
The neoclassical castle of Count István Széchenyi has recently undergone a sensitive restoration and one wing is now open to guests. The 37 acre (15 hectare) grounds are magnificent, ensuring an atmosphere of perfect peace and quiet. The Esterházy castle in Fertöd is close by, making this a good base for visits to the region. When the wea ther is warm enough, guests can enjoy the restaur ant's delicious cooking on the castle's terrace. The hotel offers seventeen double rooms and two suites, as well as reception or concert halls and horse-riding lessons. Since the hotel recently re-opened, the decoration of the rooms is still a little basic, but this will surely improve over time.

PÉCS

HOTEL PALATINUS

Király utca 5
7621 Pécs
Tel.: + 36 72 514 260
Fax: + 36 72 514 738
E-mail: palatinuspatria@mail.matav.hu
This hotel is generally considered to be one of the finest in all of Hungary. It is housed in a superb Art Nouveau building; the façade, entrance lobby, and reception are masterpieces. The rooms have been renovated, and although small, are perfectly comfortable. The cooking is not astoundingly original, but the breakfasts are generous, and the lovely ground-floor dining room is fabulously decorated with a splendid mosaic peacock. Since it has such a central location, right in the heart of this ancient Turkish capital, it is an ideal base for exploring the charms and baroque splendors of the town on foot. It is also ideally situated for excursions into the surrounding countryside and the charming vineyards and villages of Villány.

ARANYHAJÓ FOGADÓ (THE GOLDEN SHIP HOTEL)

Király utca 3
7621 Pécs
Tel.: + 36 72 210 685, + 36 72 310 263
Fax: + 36 72 212 733
E-mail: aranyhajo.hotel@axelero.hu_
This modest hotel in an eighteenth-century building benefits from a central location in the old part of this charming town, next to the Palatinus Hotel. It has a pleasant family atmosphere and small rooms decorated with taste. It is in the lower price bracket, and is thus especially recommended for families traveling with children.

SOPRON

PANNONIA MED HOTEL SOPRON

Várkerulet, 75
9400 Sopron
Tel.: + 36 99 312 180
Fax: + 36 99 340 766
E-mail: sopron@pannoniahotel.com
Another hotel in a fine location just a stone's throw from the old town. While the decoration won't be to everyone's taste, the newly refurnished rooms are nonetheless comfortable and calm. The immense dining room, with its rows of columns and glass cupola, is striking. The food is good, and the short but thoughtful wine list does justice to the superb wines of the Sopron region, made from grape varieties not commonly found elsewhere. Since this region is relatively close to the Austrian border, prices are accordingly higher than in other parts of Hungary.

CAFÉS AND RESTAURANTS

GYÖR

SÖRPATIKA 2001

Baross G. utca, 3
9021 Györ
A pretty tearoom in the center of the old town makes an ideal place for a breather between two museums, or a visit to the exceptional Jesuit pharmacy on the central town square, Széchenyi tér.

PÉCS

ARANYKACSA (THE GOLDEN DUCK)

Teréz utca 4
7621 Pécs
Tel.: + 36 72 518 860
Fax: + 36 72 518 868
E-mail: aranykacsa@mail.datanet.hu
A good wine cellar, inviting bar, and reception rooms for all parties, from intimate gatherings to huge wedding parties—no wonder this hotel is so busy. The cooking is inventive, but occasionally suffers from its own over-ambition. Do make a point of asking the sommelier in charge of the cellar for his advice on Villány wines before going on a visit to the vineyards themselves.

SOPRON

VARKAPU KAVEHAZ-ÉTTEREM

Hátsókapu utca, 3
9400 Sopron
Tel.: + 36 99 340 095

THE VILLÁNY-SIKLÓS WINE ROAD

There are many surprises in store when you set out to explore the **Villány-Siklós** vineyards. This region of small hills and rivers southeast of Pécs is interesting from both a historical and an oenological point of view. You take highway 58 out of **Pécs** and head for the town of **Harkány**, a famous spa whose warm waters contain fluoride and sulfur. The mud baths are effective against rheumatism and various gynecological disorders—and will also restore you if you've overindulged in wine tasting in the surrounding villages! After Harkány you can further redeem yourself with a visit to **Máriagyüd**, the oldest place of pilgrimage in Hungary, then head for the little town of **Siklós**, famed for its castle, which has overlooked the vineyards since the fifteenth century. The Romans were the first to plant vines here for wine. An interesting place to visit in Siklós is the Bey Malkoch mosque, reconstructed from the remains of a sixteenth-century building. As you explore the southern slopes of the Villány Mountains (Villáni hegyek) you will pass through the little village of **Nagyharsány**. Marble from Nagyharsány is used on public buildings throughout Hungary, and every summer an international colony of sculptors comes together in a huge stone quarry in the hills to work in the open air. When you reach **Villány**, start your initiation into the art of wine making by visiting the brief history of local viticulture at the Wine Museum (Bormúzeum; Tel.: + 36 72 492 130). Hungarians consider the wines produced by this vineyard, with its Mediterranean atmosphere, comparable to some of the wines of Burgundy or the Rhône Valley. Wine tasting can be enjoyed at the museum and in the pretty cellars that line the main street, where the major producers attract many visitors. The **Polgár** cellar is a must (**Polgár Pince**, Rákóczi u. 32; Tel.: + 36 72 492 053; Fax : + 36 72 492 194); its famous wines can be enjoyed at dinner, after which you can spend the night at the simple but stylish Polgár Panzió. **József Bock**'s well-structured wines can also be tasted nearby (Batthyány utca 15; Tel.: + 36 72 492 919) and are greatly admired. He was elected winemaker of the year in 1998, and his red wines are outstanding. **Attila Gere** (Fáy utca 7; Tel.: + 36 72 492 401) is another remarkable Villány character whose winery owes its success to his careful selection of grapes and efficient marketing methods. Another major winery is **Vylyan Rt.** whose cellar is in the little village of **Kisharsány**. This great firm produces wines of authentic and regular quality, made to a highly professional standard. The region's five main grape varieties are *kékfrankos*, *kékoportó*, Merlot, Cabernet Franc, and Cabernet Sauvignon, and whether you try wines from small producers or known winemakers, the red wines of Villány will be a constant source of surprise and pleasure. The white wines are lesser known, but also score some wonderful successes; the many grape varieties result in a wide range of wines. Continue the Wine Road northward and go through the village of **Villánykövesd** with its picturesque double row of cellars built into the hillside—one of the finest examples of Hungarian rural architecture, accessible from Petőfi utca. Two miles further on, the pretty town of **Palkonya** has preserved the culture and traditions of the German-speaking community who settled there in the eighteenth century. The village is bright with floral displays, and an exceptional concentration of close-packed cellars gleams white on the hill. The Mayoress, Leonóra Beker (Fö utca 79; Tel.: + 36 72 492 325; E-mail: bekernora@dravanet.hu) devotes all her energy and artistic talents to her village, and when her busy schedule permits she enjoys showing visitors around. There is a splendid view of the vineyards from the little villages of **Kistótfalu** and **Nagytótfalu**, atop the Villány Mountains, where the inhabitants (who call themselves "hill people") have maintained their deep-rooted folk traditions. The best time to follow the Wine Road is harvest season, and during the Wine Festival in the last week of September. All the villagers take part in the many traditional events and wear gorgeous colored costumes for these occasions. For information: Villány-Siklós Wine Route Association, H-7800 Siklós, Kossuth tér 1. Pf. 29, Tel./fax : + 36 72 352 746, E-mail: borut@siklos.hu; website: www.borut.hu.

A sumptuous baroque interior dating from the days of Empress Maria Theresa (the chandeliers and tapestries are originals) makes this the prettiest place in Sopron for a cup of luscious, rich, creamy hot chocolate—a reminder that we are not far from Vienna—and a light meal. Come here after a long day spent exploring the narrow street of the old town or climbing the Fire Tower and enjoying the remarkable view.

MUSEUMS, SITES OF INTEREST, AND MONUMENTS

BÁBOLNA

NEMZETI MENESBIRTOK KFT. (BABOLNA STUD FARM)

Mészáros utca, 1
2943 Bábolna
Tel.: + 36 34 569 284,
or + 36 34 569 129
Fax: + 36 34 569 397
E-mail: turizmus@babolnamenes.hu
Horse lovers will not want to miss a visit to the Bábolna stud farm, which breeds the most handsome Arabian horses in all of Hungary, including the famous Shagya or Bábolna Arabian breed. The site itself is magnificent. Visitors can watch the horses being put through their paces if they call ahead (contact Valéria Kórósi, Tel.: + 36 34 469 360). Nearby there is an arboretum with over five hundred species of trees. The thirtyfive thousand acres (fourteen thousand hectares) of the Bábolna region mean there is plenty of scope for hunting as well as for nature walks. The Imperial Hotel, with eighteen comfortable rooms, and the Ötösfogat Étterem (Five in Hand) Restaurant offer every possible creature comfort.

FERTÖD

ESTERHÁZY CASTLE

Tel.: + 36 99 370 971
Hungary's answer to Versailles is an absolute must. The architecture, inspired by the classical French style, and the majestic horseshoe-shaped Rococo façade in the yellow ocher color that is so characteristic of this part of the world, are a real splendor. The castle's collections are gradually being put together again, drawing on the holdings of the Museum of Decorative Arts in Budapest. The prince's own collection of antiques in the Chinese style and the furniture in the ceremonial hall and concert room give an idea of the magnificence that reigned here in the days of Maria Theresa and Joseph II. Joseph Haydn spent much of his life in the service of the Esterházy family, and composed some of his best-loved symphonies here. A season of chamber and early music is held annually from June to August in some of the loveliest rooms in the castle; the chandeliers are all lit for the occasion. It is a most magnificent sight. Further information can be obtained from the castle itself or in ticket agencies in Budapest, or directly from the offices of the Philharmonia (Vörösmarty tér 1, Tel.: + 36 1 318 0441). Music lovers can also visit the Esterházy Palace in Eisenstadt, 9 miles (15 kilometers) from Sopron, just over the Austrian border—the Hungarians call it Kismarton. (Tel.: + 43 26 827 193 900, Fax: + 43 26 827 193 923, Website: www.haydn-zentrum.at)

KAPOSVÁR

RIPPL-RONAI JOZSEF EMLEKMÚZEUM (RIPPL-RONAI MEMORIAL MUSEUM)

Fôutca, 8 Kaposvár
Tel.: + 36 82 320 404
The Villa Rome, acquired by the artist József Rippl-Rónai in 1908, is now a museum in his memory. It displays more than one hundred of his works: paintings, pastels, charcoals, drawings, photographs, and objets d'art. Rippl-Rónai studied first in Munich and then joined the Nabi movement in France, before finding his own style on his return to Budapest, then to his home town of Kaposvár. He was one of the leading proponents of Art Nouveau in Hungary and played a major role in the development of Hungarian modernism at the dawn of the twentieth century. The museum is very moving, and the collection of this great artist's works is absolutely unique.

KÖSZEG

TABORNOKHAZ (THE GENERAL'S HOUSE)

Jurisics Miklós tér, 6
9731 Köszeg, Pf.47
Tel.: + 36 94 360 240, + 36 94 360 156
The General's House was built in the sixteenth century in a late Renaissance style. A loggia was added in the seventeenth century. Today, the building houses a museum representing several traditional crafts, such as blacksmithing, goldsmithing, bookbinding, and clock making.

JURISICS MIKLOS VARMÚZEUM (JURISICS MIKLOS MUSEUM)

Rájnis József utca, 9
9730 Köszeg
Tel.: + 36 94 360 240
The museum is in Köszeg castle, a marvel of thirteenth-century Gothic architecture. It underwent numerous renovations during the

Renaissance and the Baroque period. The displays recount the history of the town. While in Köszeg, try and catch one of the shows organized in the castle courtyard or in the knight's hall.

PÉCS

Pécs is home to a number of interesting museums—there are fifteen or so in the old town. The Board of Museums for the region (Káptalan utca 5, 7621 Pécs; tel.: + 36 72 310 172, Fax: + 36 72 315 694, E-mail: jpm@jpm.hu) has brought out an informative leaflet with all the relevant details. The largest is the **Csontváry Museum** (Janus Pannonius utca 11, Tel.: + 36 72 310 544), devoted to the major works of a much-underrated artist, Tivadar Csontváry, whose works were admired by Pablo Picasso. Káptalan Utca (Chapel Street) has no fewer than five museums. Numbers 5 (**Andre Nemes Múzeum**, Tel.: + 36 72 324 822) and 6 (**Martyn Ferenc Múzeum**, Tel.: + 36 72 324 822) are two charming museums with exhibitions on twentieth-century artists born in Pécs or the surrounding region. Number 3 is the **Vasarely Múzeum** (Tel.: + 36 72 324 822), devoted to the youth of the founder of Op Art, Victor Vasarely. The basement is rather surprisingly given over to a **Museum of Mining**. The Modern Art Gallery (**Modern Magyar Képtár**, Tel.: + 36 72 324 822), at number 4, has a wonderful collection of works by the best-known Hungarian artists from the late nineteenth and early twentieth centuries, including artists of the famous Nagybánya school. The gallery garden is a green oasis of calm. It is dotted with large-scale sculptures by Péter Székely, a major Hungarian artist who spent most of his life in France. An annex was recently opened in a beautiful eighteenth-century building nearby, at Papnövelde 5, for the contemporary collections that are a homage to the vigor and dynamism of Hungarian art, from the avant-garde classicism of Korniss, Bálint, and Lili Ország to Land Art, from hyper-realism to representatives of the Pécs school such as Ilona Keserü. The **Zsolnay Múzeum** (Káptalan Utca 2, Tel.: + 36 72 324 822) gives a fascinating in-sight into the rich artistic vocabulary of Zsolnay ceramics. From the founding of the factory in the early nineteenth century to the latest designs, every piece tells the story of one of Hungary's most successful ventures in applied art. The pieces are displayed in bright, summery rooms, and some of the largest works are in the garden. Fine ceramics can also be admired at **Szerecsen Patika** (the Saracen Pharmacy) on the main square, Szechényi tér, on the corner of Apáca utca. Before leaving Pécs, you must make time for a tour of the archeological displays at the **Regészeti Múzeum** (Szechènyi tér 12, Tel.: + 36 72 312 719), a lively presentation of the history of this part of Pannonia before the arrival of the earliest Magyars. The building was once the home of a Turkish dignitary—a reminder of the long period Pécs spent under Ottoman rule.

SOPRON

PEKMÚZEUM (THE BREAD MUSEUM)

Bécsi utca, 5
9400 Sopron
Tel.: + 36 99 311 327
The owners of this pretty seventeenth-century bakery have created a small museum presenting different baking methods and types of bread and pastries. An aroma of spicy gingerbread seems to waft through the air.

SOPRONI MÚZEUM-STORNO HAZ (THE SOPRON MUSEUM)

Fö tér, 8
9400 Sopron
Tel.: + 36 99 311 327
The Storno House, first built in the Gothic style in the fifteenth century and totally renovated on several occasions, is now a fine example of Baroque architecture. It houses the Sopron Museum, the centerpiece of which is the Storno collection. Ferenc Storno was an artist and picture restorer of Italian origin. The furniture collection he left on his death is a perfect illustration of the lifestyle enjoyed by the Hungarian bourgeoisie in the latter half of the nineteenth century.

FABRICIUS HAZ

Fö tér, 6
9400 Sopron
Tel.: + 36 99 311 327
This ancient building—far older than the Baroque façade would suggest—has a fine medieval cellar with Roman foundations. It houses an exhibition on the three-thousand-year history of the Amber Route, and a series of life-size tableaux depicting daily life in Sopron since the seventeenth century.

FESTIVALS

GYÖR

Györ seems always to have something to celebrate, all through spring and summer. The town is just an hour from Budapest on the highway. The Györ Spring Festival (last two weeks in March, Tel.: + 36 96 316 020) is a great occasion, with numerous traditional music concerts and a famous painted-egg market. In June and July, it is the turn of the Györ Summer Cultural Festival (tel.: + 36 96 500 100), the International Ballet Festival organized by the renowned Györ Ballet (Tel.: + 36 96 326 999), and the International Folk Dance Festival (Tel.: + 36 96 326 522). There is also a major Opera Festival at the Györ National Theatre (Tel.: + 36 96 312 044) and an international artist's colony at the Petöfi Cultural Center (tel.: + 36 96 327 466).

PÉCS

PÉCSI NAPOK

In Pécs, the last ten days in September are given over to the grape harvest festival: classical music and jazz concerts, folk songs and dances, exhibitions, conferences, and sports events are organized to celebrate this momentous occasion. Most of the events are free of charge, and the program for the days' events are easy to come by.

SOPRON

REGI ZENEI NAPOK (EARLY MUSIC FESTIVAL)

Interart Festival Center
Vörösmarty tér, 1
Tel.: + 36 1 317 9910
This series of concerts, held annually in late June and early July, is Hungary's foremost early music festival. For the last fifteen years, musicians and ensembles from all over Hungary and abroad have been invited to perform in various settings in the town and the surrounding area, in churches, the Fertörákos quarry, and Fertöd castle, for example. It is usually possible to meet the musicians after the performance.
Szombathely, a delightful small town south of Sopron, has acquired an enviable reputation for its groundbreaking contemporary music festival (International Bartók Seminary, Tel.: + 36 1 117 99 10) which follows the festival in Sopron.

BIBLIOGRAPHY

Hungary is a complex country with a rich and fascinating past. You are highly recommended to read one or two books before your visit to get a better understanding of its people, and their customs. Since the fall of the Soviet bloc, travel to Hungary has of course become much easier, and the number of recent works on the country reflects this. There has also been increasing interest in Hungarian literature in translation. The author Imre Kertesz was awarded the Nobel Prize for literature in 2002, putting his native literature firmly on the map.

GUIDES

HUNGARY

Ardo, Zsuzsanna. *Culture Shock! Hungary: A Guide to Customs and Etiquette*. Portland: Graphic Arts Center, 2000.
Baedeker's Hungary. New York: Fodor, 2000.
Fallon, Steve, and **Neal Bedford**. *Lonely Planet Hungary*. London: Lonely Planet, 2003.
Hebbert, Charles, ed. *The Rough Guide to Hungary*. London: Rough Guides, 2002.

BUDAPEST

Fallon, Steve. *Lonely Planet Budapest*. London: Lonely Planet, 2003.
Ferkai, Andras. *Budapest Architectural Guide*. Budapest: Art Data, 1997.
Lieber, Joseph, ed. *Frommer's Budapest and the Best of Hungary*. New York: Macmillan, 1998.
Olszanski, Tadeusz, ed. *Eyewitness Travel Guide to Budapest*. New York: Dorling Kindersley, 1999.
Time Out Budapest. London: Penguin, 2002.
Török, András. *Budapest: A Critical Guide*. Budapest: Corvina, 1999.
András Török is a writer and journalist, and was formerly secretary of state for culture in the Hungarian government. This guide is the most personal and funniest of all the guides to Budapest.

HISTORY

Köpeczi, Béla, Ed. and. Adrienne Chambers-Makkai, trans. *History of Transylvania*. Budapest: Akadémiai Kiadó, 1994.
Lendvai, Paul, *The Hungarians: A Thousand Years of Victory in Defeat*. Trans. Ann Major. Princeton: Princeton University Press, 2003.
Lettis, Richard. *The Hungarian Revolt*. La Vergne, Simon, 2001.
Lucaks, John. *Budapest 1900: A Historical Portrait of a City and Its Culture*. London: Weidenfeld & Nicolson, 1989.
A fascinating and scholarly account of the heyday

of a great European capital.

Molnár, Miklos, *A Concise History of Hungary*. Trans. Anna Magyar Cambridge: Cambridge University Press, 2001.
This well-known historian, has produced a clear and precise reference to the history of his home country.

Nemestkürty, István, *Word and Image: A History of Hungarian Cinema*. Trans. Zsuzsanna Horn and Fred Macnicol.Budapest. Corvina, 1974.

Polcz, Alaine. *One Woman in the War: Hungary 1944-1945*. New York: Central European University Press, 2001.

Sisa, Stephen. *The Spirit of Hungary: A Panorama of Hungarian History and Culture*. Morristown: Vista, 1995.

Teleky, Richard. *Hungarian Rhapsodies: Essays on Ethnicity, Identity, and Culture*. Seattle: University of Washington Press, 1997.

LITERATURE

Bánffy, Miklós, *The Transylvanian Trilogy: They Were Counted*. London: Arcadia, 1999.
They were found wanting. London: Arcadia, 2000.
They Were Divided. London: Arcadia, 2001. *The Phoenix Land*. London: Arcadia, 2003.
Trans. Patrick Thursfield and Katalin Bánffy-Jelen.
Bánffy's *Transylvanian Trilogy* is a neglected masterpiece. It has been compared by some critics to a Hungarian version of Giuseppe Tomasi di Lampedusa's *Leopard* for its portrayal of a decaying empire.

Csáth, Géza, *Opium and Other Stories*. Trans. Jascha Kessler and Charlotte Rogers. New York: Penguin, 1983.
A masterful writer whose work is characterized by a certain elegant cruelty.

Esterházy, Peter, *The Book of Hrabal*. Trans. Judith Sollosy. Evanston: Northwestern University Press, 1994.
Celestial Harmonies. Trans. Judith Sollosy. New York: ECCO, 2004.
She Loves Me. Trans. Judith Sollosy Evanston: Hydra, 2000.
A Little Hungarian Pornography. Trans. Judith Sollosy. Evanston: Northwestern University Press, 1997.
Helping Verbs of the Heart. Trans. Michael Henry Heim. New York: Grove Weidenfeld, 1991.
The Glance of Countess Hahn-Hahn (Down the Danube) Trans. Richard Aczel, Evanston: Northwestern University Press, 1999.
Peter Esterházy, a scion of one of Hungary's noblest families, is an immensely talented writer. His oeuvre is a derisive and yet compassionate study of Hungarian society.

Füst, Milán, *Twenty-Five Poems*. Trans. István TotfalusBudapest: Maecenas, 1990.
The Story of my Wife: Trans. Ivan Sanders.
Reminiscences of Captain Storr. Trans. Ivan Sanders. New York: Vintage, 1989.
A masterpiece by a talented writer with a thorough grasp of fine psychological details.

Gaspar, Lorand, *Word at Hand*. Trans. Roger Little Dublin: Daedalus, 1995.
A fine, sensitive poet.

Jókai, Mór, *Tales from Jókai*. Trans. R. Nisbet Bain New York: Books for Libraries, 1971.
One of the most popular Hungarian authors of the nineteenth century.

József, Attila, *Selected Poems and Texts*. Trans. John Bakti Cheadle: Carcanet, 1973.
Winter Night: Selected Poems. Trans. John Bakti Oberlin: Oberlin College Press, 1997.
Perched on Nothing's Branch. Trans. Peter Hargitai. Buffalo: White Pine Press, 1999.
The Iron-Blue Vault. Trans. ZsuzsannaOzsvath and Frederick Turner. Newcastle: Bloodaxe, 2000.
Arthur Koestler compared Attila József to the medieval robber-poet François Villon, and described his life and work as oscillating between the opposing forces of Marx and Freud.

Karinthy, Ferenc, *Spring comes to Budapest*. Budapest: Trans. István Farkas and D.M. Garman Corvina, 1964.

Karinthy, Frigyes, *Grave and Gay*. István Kerékgyárto, Ed. Budapest: Corvina, 1980.
A popular writer with a virtuoso pen.

Kertesz, Imre,. *Kaddish for a Child Not Born. Trans.* Christopher C. Wilson and Katharina M. Wilson Evanston: Hydra, 1997.

Kertesz, Imre, *Fateless*. Trans. Christopher C. Wilson and Katharina M. Wilson.Evanston: Hydra, 1996.
The winner of the 2002 Nobel Prize for Literature was for many years hardly read, even in Hungary. He finds the words for the unspeakable, writing about life in Nazi concentration camps.

Konrad, György, *The Case Worker*. Trans. Paul Aston, London: Hutchinson, 1975.
The Loser. Trans. Ivan Sanders. New York: Harcourt Brace Jovanovich, 1982.
A Feast in the Garden. Trans. Imre Goldstein New York: Harcourt Brace Jovanovich, 1992.
The City Builder. Trans. Ivan Sanders. New York: Penguin USA, 1987.
One of Hungary's foremost intellectuals.

Kosztolanyi, Dezso, *Anna Édes*. Trans. George Szirtes. New York: New Directions, 1993.
Skylark. Trans. Richard Aczel. New York: Central European University Press, 1996.
One of the most enduringly popular Hungarian authors, he found fame at 22 with his first novel. His writing is acid, incisive, and illuminating.

Krasnahorkai, Laszlo, *The Melancholy of Resistance*. Trans. George Szirtes.New York: New Directions, 2002.

Krúdy, Gyula, *Sunfllowe*. Trans. John Bakti. Budapest: Corvina, 1997.
Krudy's Chronicles. Trans. John Bakti. New York: Central European University Press, 2001.
An extravagant private life led this prolific author to write ever more to sponge his mounting debts. He is perhaps the most emblematic of all Hungarian authors.

Magris, Claudio, *Danube*., Trans. Patrick Creagh. London: Harvill, 1989.
An enthralling, unmissable book that pays homage to this mighty river.

Makkai, Adam, Ed. *In Quest of the Miracle Stag: The Poetry of Hungary*. Chicago: University of Illinois Press, 1996.

Márai, Sándor, *Memoir of Hungary*, 1944-1948. Trans. Albert Tezla, Budapest: Corvina, 1996.
Embers. Trans. Carol Brown Janeway, New York: Vintage, 2002.
A brilliant journalist and linguist who was a great friend of the highly influential psychoanalyst Ferenczi Márai. He lived through the dramas of the early twentieth century in Europe before emigrating to the United States, where he finally took his own life in 1989. He was one of the great masters of prose style.

Moricz, Zsigmond, *Be Faithful Unto Death*, Trans. Stephen Vizinczey. New York: Central European University Press, 1996.
A prolific writer from the early part of the twentieth century, who wrote realistic and sympathetic studies of the relationship between peasants and landowners in the Hungarian countryside.

Nádas, Péter, *A book of Memories: A Novel*. Trans. Ivan Sanders and Imre Goldstein, New York: Farrar, Straus & Giroux, 1997.
The End of a Family Story. Trans. Imre Goldstein. New York: Penguin USA, 2000.
A Lovely Tale of Photography. Trans. Imre Goldstein. Prague: Twisted Spoon, 1999.
Love: a Novel. Trans. Imre Goldstein.*New York*: Farrar, Straus & Giroux, 2000.
Nádas' work is characterized by the exploration of both personal and national memories.

Nemeskürty, István, *A History of Hungarian Literature*. Budapest: Corvina, 1982.

Örkény, István, *The Flower Show and the Toth family*. Trans.. Michael Henry Heim and Clara Gyorgyey. New York: New Directions, 1982.
One Minute Stories. Trans. Judith Sollosy. Rose Bay, NSW: Brandl and Schlesinger, 1994.
One of the great European figures of the Absurd.

Pilinszky János, *Metropolitan Icons: Selected Poems in Hungarian and in English*. Trans. Emery George. New York: Edwin Mellen Press, 1995.
Conversations with Sheryl Sutton: the Novel of a Dialogue. Trans. Peter Jay and Eva Major Riverdale: Sheep Meadow, 1992.
A dazzlingly talented contemporary poet.

Szerb, Antal, *The Traveler*. Trans. Peter Hargitai. New York: Corvin, 1994.

Szerb, Antal, *Journey by Moonlight.* Trans. Len Rix. London: Pushkin, 2001.
This literary critic and historian was one of the most feted authors of the period between the two world wars. He was murdered in 1945 by the Fascists.

Szirtes, George. *The Adventures of Sindbad*. New York: Central European University Press, 1998.
Selected Poems 1976-1996. Oxford: Oxford University Press, 1996.
The Budapest File. Newcastle upon Tyne: Bloodaxe, 2001.
Ed. *The Colonnade of Teeth: Modern Hungarian Poetry.* Newcastle upon Tyne: Bloodaxe, 1997.
Portrait of my Father in an English Landscape. Oxford: Oxford University Press, 1998.

Vörösmarty, Mihaly. Ed. Géza Bodoly. *Collected Works*. Budapest: Akademiai Kiado, 2000.
One of the greatest of Hungarian Romantics, who also played an active role in Hungarian political life. His work is characterized by epics, ethereal plays, and, towards the end of his life, visionary poems imprinted with a sense of absolute despair.

Zilahy, Lajos, *The Dukays*. North Pomfret: Trafalgar Square, 2001.
Century in Scarlet. New York: McGraw Hill, 1965.
Two Prisoners. Trans. John Pauker. London: Prion, 1999.
The three-volume novel *The Dukays* is a sweeping panorama of one family's lives in the declining years of the Austro-Hungarian empire.

GASTRONOMY

Alkonyi, Laszlo. *Tokaj: The Wine of Freedom*. San Francisco: Wine Appreciation Guild, 2003.

Bennett, Paula Pogany. *The Art of Hungarian Cooking*. New York: Hippocrene, 1997.

Halasz, Zoltan, *The Book of Hungarian Wines*. Trans. Zsuzsa Béres.Budapest: Corvina, 1981.

Liddell, Alex. *Wines of Hungary*. London: Mitchell Beazley, 2003.

INDEX

ACKNOWLEDGMENTS

This book could never have been written without the unstinting help and friendship of Alain Fleischer and Danielle Schirman, who both share my passion for Hungary, a country that I first discovered ten years ago and that I never tire of exploring. I also wish to express my deepest thanks to my wife, Marie-Christine Labourdette, who has seen this book through with me to the end, and who has been a constant support.

I would also like to express heartfelt thanks to Mr. Péter Medgyessy, prime minister of Hungary, for kindly accepting to write the preface for the present book. Warmest thanks also to his assistant Karoly Toll.

Thanks must also go to Silvia Benedetti, whose precious aid and ever-ready willingness to discuss the project with me have helped me shape the book, day by day.

On our journeys, we have received help above and beyond the call of duty from the Hungarian Tourist Office, Magyar Turizmus Rt., both in Budapest and in the provinces, and particularly from the successive directors, László Arva and Gábor Galla, and their cheerful, welcoming staff: Ágnes Kelecsényi, Nadin Kenderesy, Béata Payer, Melinda Stein, Ágnes Újvári, and Anita Vigh. Orsolya Horváth's seamless efficiency smoothed the path in the early days of the project. We also must thank Zsofia Szabó, with the assistance of Péter Palotai, for their untiring and unceasing efforts to organize meetings and help us in any way they could. Thanks also to Mélanie Rosselet in Rome, and Gyula Harbula, director of Accor-Pannonia Hotels Rt., for all their time and willingness to answer our questions.

I would also like to extend my warmest thanks to all the public institutions and their unfailingly courteous staff and to the private individuals—many of them now personal friends—who helped me in so many different ways, opening their doors to me: first of all, Anikó Rákossy and Ádám Farkas, always ready to lend a helping hand, and also; János Árvay, Joël Aubert, Michel and Nadir van den Avont, András Bacsó, Marián Bán, Leonóra Becker, Vajk Cserményi, Comtesse Marie von Degenfeld, Mária Eckhart, Antal Englert, Patrick Faucheur, László Fehér, Carmen Buján Freire, Vince Gergely, Katalin Hampel, Attila Hotyek, György Kéves, Tamás Kieselbach, Károly Kincses, Sarolta Kodály, Tamás Konok, Judit and György Konrád, Tibor Kovács, János Krajcsovics, Jean-Louis Laborde, Kader Lejri, Tamás Leotszky, Thomas Lindner, Orsolya and Pierre-Emmanuel Maire, László Meszaros, Véra and István Nádler, Zoltán Polgár, Judit and László Rajk, Rita Rubovszky, Anna and József Román, Véronique and Patrick Soulé, Ágnes and Miklós Szabó, Hajnalka Szabó, István Szepsy, Miklós Szüts, Gergely Téglásy, András Tözök, Katalin and Tamás Trombitás, Julia and András Varadi, Márta Vágvölgyi, László Vass, Ferenc Vesztergombi, Ágnes Vincze, Péter Vladimir, and Ferenc Zweiber.

Finally, I would like to thank Ghislaine Bavoillot at Flammarion for her boundless confidence in this project and for guiding me past the pitfalls. Thanks also to Karen Bowen, Sylvie Ramaut, and Nathalie Demoulin for their help at every stage.

Editor
Ghislaine Bavoillot
Design
Karen Bowen
Maps
Edigraphie, Rouen
Translated from the French by
Lisa Davidson and Sally Laruelle
Copyediting
Susan Kennedy
Typesetting
Octavo
Proofreading
Slade Smith and Lisa Barnett
Color Separation
Edit-Press
Printed in Italy by Canale

Simultaneously published in French as
L'Art de Vivre en Hongrie

© Éditions Flammarion, 2003.

English-language edition

© Éditions Flammarion, 2003

26, rue Racine
75006 Paris

All rights reserved. No part of this publication may be reproduced in any form or by any means, electronic, photocopy, information retreival system, or otherwise, without written permission from Éditions Flammarion.

03 04 05 4 3 2 1

FC0418-03-XI
ISBN: 2-0801-1143-4
Dépôt légal: 11/2003